COMING FULL CIRCLE

*Redefining God
in the Age of Reason*

PARTH ATREY

This book is intended as a reference volume only. It is sold with the understanding that the publisher and author are not engaged in rendering any professional services.

Published by River Grove Books
Austin, TX
www.rivergrovebooks.com

Copyright ©2016 Mukul Sharma

All rights reserved.

No part of this book may be reproduced, stored in a retrieval system, or transmitted by any means, electronic, mechanical, photocopying, recording, or otherwise, without written permission from the copyright holder.

Distributed by River Grove Books

Design and composition by Greenleaf Book Group
Cover design by Greenleaf Book Group
Cover image © Jurik Peter, 2016. Used under license from Shutterstock.com

Cataloging-in-Publication data is available.

Print ISBN: 978-1-63299-150-8

eBook ISBN: 978-1-63299-151-5

First Edition

To my parents, wife, and children.
May our accumulated wisdom belong to the coming generations.

Contents

ACKNOWLEDGMENTS vii

PREFACE: Redefining God ix

   CHAPTER 1: A Traditional Definition of God 1

   CHAPTER 2: Our Oldest Traditions:
                   The Aryan Conception of God 15

   CHAPTER 3: The Ancient Egyptian, Chinese,
                   and Greek Conceptions of God 53

   CHAPTER 4: The Age of Belief:
                   Judaism, Christianity, and Islam 87

   CHAPTER 5: The Age of Reason:
                   Development of the Scientific Method 141

   CHAPTER 6: God According to Scientists and Philosophers 182

   CHAPTER 7: A Journey through Time:
                   Coming Full Historical Circle 202

   CHAPTER 8: It's All in the Mind:
                   Rational versus Emotional Definitions of God 228

   CHAPTER 9: Satisfying Our Rational and Emotional Needs:
                   Coming Full Circle Again 250

   CHAPTER 10: What Does It All Mean for Me? 274

NOTES 303

Acknowledgments

This book would not have been possible without the love, support, and inspiration of my parents, my wife, my kids, and my friends. I am forever grateful to:

- My parents, for bringing me up in a home that encouraged me to think, question, read, and explore.
- My wife, for providing her unconditional love and support during our thirty plus years of marriage and for tolerating me for the past ten-odd years while I was obsessed with reading and writing this book during my time off.
- My kids, for being the inspiration for this book. It was their insightful questions and fresh outlook on everything that led me to write it.
- All my friends who encouraged me to express in black and white what I would often express to them.

PREFACE

Redefining God

Many people—in my generation and my children's generation, products of the scientific age—face questions about faith, God, and religion that are not easily brushed aside and not adequately addressed by the clergy. Over the past two decades, I have spoken to a large number of friends and acquaintances about their views on God. Most of them attend church, synagogues, or temples on a fairly regular basis. When pressed about their belief in an omnipotent God, their perspective lay somewhere between atheism and agnosticism. Relatively few of my children's friends actually believe in a God as we have historically defined him: a being who performs miracles and fulfills the wishes of the faithful. This situation is true in just about all developed countries of the world. In most countries in Europe, well below twenty percent of the population attends church on a regular basis, and this number has been falling for the past fifty years.[1]

In many ways, this book is a very personal journey of exploration for me. Growing up Hindu, in a family where science was on the menu in every discussion, I sometimes had a hard time reconciling the religious traditions that I adhered to with the scientific principles I was so deeply influenced by. Why did we have to follow the rituals of the daily prayer? So what if these rituals have been around for thousands of years? My dad, who studied and taught physics in college, encouraged this inquisitive and skeptical attitude toward faith and organized religion. Clergy or scientists I have spoken with were either very knowledgeable about the scriptures but not about the social and physical sciences, or the other way around.

This book is an attempt to reconcile some of our religious beliefs and rituals with our modern-day scientific understanding of the universe and nature. I'll approach this topic from a historical perspective, and we will discuss the basic conceptions of God in religious traditions dating back to the Indo-Europeans and Egyptians. We'll follow this development through the Abrahamic religions and the Renaissance, all the way to the scientific age. This historical journey will allow us to integrate the incredible wisdom of the ages and bring it to bear on these age-old questions.

I have found, in traversing the last five millennia, that our ideas about God have come full circle—from marveling at God's creations in an age of wonder, through the age of belief and an era of rationality—and have returned back to a time of wonder about the laws of nature. This is not to say that we are back where we started—not in the least. We are in what can best be described as an age of enlightened wonder, where the advancements in science have allowed us to view God and his creation in a whole new light. In essence, we can redefine God in terms of our most ancient conceptions of God but with a much clearer rational understanding of the universe.

I am neither a religious scholar nor a member of the clergy, but I have been a university professor for thirty plus years. I have written a great deal in my professional career, although it has been almost exclusively technical papers on specific topics of relevance and importance in my field. This has made me appreciate the importance of knowing the details before arriving at a big-picture understanding of any subject. Through teaching very bright young undergraduate and PhD students, I have learned to simplify and integrate complex themes and present them in a coherent, logical sequence. This is what I have attempted to do in this book. In the process, the book has helped me bridge the gap between my faith and the world of science that I have been a part of for the past four decades. It is my hope that this book will also serve as a similar bridge for others.

Why Is This Important?

Today, as people of different religious beliefs interact in a world made smaller by travel, instant communication, and the Internet, questions about religious faith and belief take on even more urgency and importance.

Religion is such an important part of our social fabric that it is impossible to overlook. Everything we do has a religious dimension. Churches, temples, mosques, and synagogues are not only religious institutions, but also social and political ones. It is, therefore, imperative that we reconcile the significant differences among different religious groups.

Some Christians believe that anyone who does not devote their life to Christ will suffer eternal damnation. This is their interpretation of the Bible. Some Muslims may believe that all nonbelievers—non-Muslims—should accept their faith or be put to the sword. That is one interpretation of the Koran. Although these points of view appear extreme, there are a surprisingly large number of people who believe that these interpretations of their religious texts are not only right, but also beyond debate.

Should we continue to cling to such medieval religious beliefs? If we do, it will inevitably lead to serious geopolitical consequences: social conflict, war, illiteracy, and superstition, as it has in the past. For evidence of the dangers of inflexible religious belief, look no further than the suicide bombers in the Middle East, who commit unthinkable acts of terror in the name of religion. In our modern global community, we all need to offer each other sufficient religious wiggle room if we want to avoid such disastrous consequences.

Over the past 200 years, developments in science and technology have revolutionized the way we live and the way we view the world around us. There is very little doubt that improving mankind's understanding of the universe through observation and reason has had a profound effect on the way we view the world. Today, we would be unable to function as an organized society without the relatively modern concepts of personal liberty and individual rights. These concepts, coupled with the fruits of technology and science, have led to unprecedented prosperity throughout the world. Is it somehow possible to use these ideas that have so profoundly changed our everyday existence to modify our religious belief systems? Can religious beliefs become more consistent with modern-day scientific principles?

Religious scriptures, such as the Old and New Testament, the Koran, and the *Bhagavad Gita*, have a profound impact on the beliefs of well over two-thirds of the world's population. Clearly, these religious texts were penned by wise men, whose essential message of love and compassion for our fellow human beings should remain intact. Many of these teachings address questions about the human condition that transcend time. However, many of the parables, rituals, and traditions are clearly reflective of the time and place they were originally written and, therefore, should be interpreted in a way to make them relevant to modern society. Doing this does not dilute the message, but strengthens it. The interpretation of religious scripture through a rational lens may lead to a stronger connection between the physical world we live in and the world of religious belief. This path leads away from fundamentalism and violence toward a more compassionate and peaceful world.

There are three very important reasons we must modernize any religion while preserving its essence.

- Modernizing and creating a rational review of our religious belief system offers us a chance to better understand other belief systems and a way to appreciate alternative viewpoints. This has direct social and political consequences—less propensity for conflict, for one.
- Rational interpretations of religious scripture produce a population that is well equipped to reject medieval notions of superstition, wizardry, and witchcraft. Less gullible and more educated people make better citizens in a democratic world.
- Finally, the most obvious benefit of modernizing is to satisfy the intellectual curiosity that drives us to find meaning in our lives.

In this book, we'll take a journey through time, exploring religious beliefs and—more particularly—ideas about God as they have evolved over the past five millennia. As we make this journey, you'll realize that many of the belief systems put forth by prophets and sages have much more in common than we would think judging from modern-day rhetoric. We'll also see that blending religion, philosophy, and science is a natural evolution of the process of discovering the hidden secrets of the universe.

Perhaps most surprising, this fascinating journey, in many ways, takes us back to our earliest philosophical roots.

A Traditional Definition of God

Perhaps what makes us human more than anything else is our ability to ask the same questions that mankind has asked since the dawn of civilization: Where did this universe come from? Is there a Creator? Why are we here? Is there a purpose for our existence, a grand design?

There are no clear, definitive, and universally accepted answers to these questions. However, since they are central to our existence, to our very being, we must try to provide some semblance of an answer, however incomplete it may be. Without answers to these questions, we are, on some level, unable to direct our lives and find meaning in our existence. As human beings, we have not only the ability to ask these questions, but also the propensity to remain profoundly dissatisfied until we find plausible answers to them.

In just about every culture, answers to these questions have been inextricably linked to the existence and nature of God. Lacking logical explanations, the only way forward has been for humans to invoke an entity so powerful and pervasive that it can provide an answer to any question.

God has been defined in so many different ways—by different denominations of religions, by agnostics, philosophers, scientists, and atheists—that it is difficult to clearly spell out one unambiguous definition of God. It is, therefore, important to define up front what we mean when we invoke the word *God*.

The Big Guy in the Sky

If you asked a million people how they define God, you will likely get just about as many definitions. Within Christianity, there are well over 3,000 denominations, all of which interpret God and God's will slightly differently. Hindus are said to have thirty-three million manifestations of the one Supreme Being. Are these manifestations of God, or should the one Supreme Being be defined as God? Then there are definitions of God put forth by philosophers and scientists that vary from the material universe to nature to a figment of our imagination.

The concept of God that most religions espouse in practice is one of a divine, generally benevolent, but sometimes vindictive being who not only created the universe, but is also responsible for order in it. Praying to this entity can lead to the fulfillment of hopes, aspirations, and wishes. Ignoring or disrespecting him can incur his wrath. This being can be merciful to the good and merciless to the bad.

Indeed, there are some common attributes that such a God has been commonly ascribed. This God—

- Can do anything
- Can see everything
- Exists everywhere
- Can be appealed to for intervention
- Is difficult to completely comprehend
- Must be worshipped to get on his good side
- May have offspring or avatars that descend to earth who are, in turn, to be worshipped

For brevity and convenience, I refer to this definition of God as the *Big Guy in the Sky* (BGITS).

This common belief in a supernatural and all-powerful being who acts as a caretaker for this universe is aptly captured in a few verses in the hilarious, satirical poem "In Westminster Abbey" by the British poet and humorist John Betjeman. The poem was written in 1940, during the most trying times of the Second World War.

Gracious Lord, oh bomb the Germans.
Spare their women for Thy Sake,
And if that is not too easy

We will pardon Thy Mistake.
But, gracious Lord, whate'er shall be,
Don't let anyone bomb me.
    [. . .]
Although dear Lord I am a sinner,
I have done no major crime;
Now I'll come to Evening Service
Whensoever I have the time.
So, Lord, reserve for me a crown.
And do not let my shares go down.

This is perhaps the best definition of a BGITS God anyone can muster: a benign fatherlike figure who protects the good and smites the evil and, above all, listens to the prayers of true believers.

What Do We Believe?

A national poll of 900 registered voters conducted in the United States in 2003 for Fox News showed that over 90 percent of those polled believed in God.[1] The survey results also showed that "about a third of Americans believe in ghosts (34 percent) and an equal number in UFOs (34 percent), and about a quarter accept things like astrology (29 percent), reincarnation (25 percent), and witches (24 percent)." The survey had a margin of error of three percentage points. Those of us who are surprised by these results may question the validity of the survey. However, similar surveys conducted by other organizations have come up with broadly similar results.

The number of Americans who say they have no religious affiliation has doubled since 1990 and now stands at over 16 percent of the population. However, only 4 percent of the population identifies itself as atheist or agnostic. These numbers are by no means universally accepted. In fact, an article in the *Washington Post* claimed, "Surveys designed to overcome the understandable reluctance to admit atheism found that as many as sixty million Americans—a fifth of our population—are nonbelievers."[2] Significant differences in the percentages of people believing in God do arise, depending on how the question is asked, because people define God in so many different ways that it is virtually impossible to decouple the question of belief in God from a definition of God.

There is very little reliable data on the percentage of people who believe in God in other countries. A recent article in the *Wall Street Journal* presented data on the percentage of people in Europe who attend church at least once a week.[3] The numbers are low, with Denmark reporting less than 10 percent of its citizens attending church regularly.

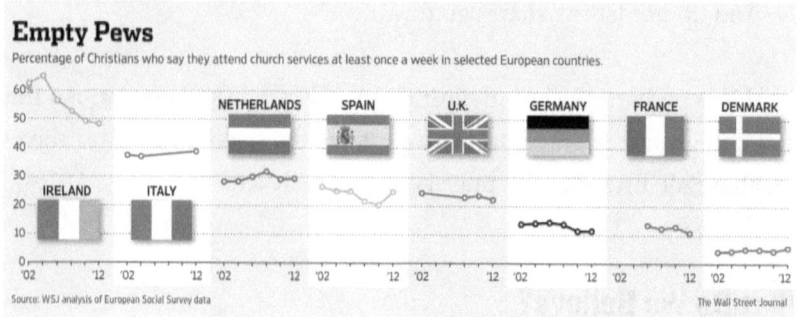

The same article reports that the percentage unaffiliated with any religion varies from a high of 52 percent in China to 42 percent in Netherlands, 28 percent in France, 25 percent in Germany, 21 percent in the United Kingdom, and 16 percent in the United States. By contrast, the numbers for less-developed countries, such as Brazil (8 percent) and Nigeria (0.4 percent), are much lower. From this data, it also appears that the percentage of religious people is higher in developing countries than in developed countries.

Although these numbers don't tell us directly about people's opinions about God, one thing is clear: A large percentage of people on our planet, particularly in the developing world, believe in a BGITS God. The overwhelming evidence of people's fervent belief in divine intervention is all around us. We need only observe the large number of people flocking to churches, temples, mosques, and synagogues to ask him for favors or seek his forgiveness.

Paradoxes and Questions Arising from This Common Definition of God

If we stick with the BGITS definition of God—an omnipresent, omniscient, omnipotent creator of the universe—then we have at least a consistent and common definition. Let's see how we can reason for or against the existence of such a God.

Many arguments have been put forward to support the existence of a BGITS God. For a believer, nothing could be more self-evident than the existence of an omnipotent creator. For an agnostic who is open to questioning this belief, the matter is wide open.

I do want to emphasize that my approach here is one of reason, not of belief. I cannot and do not intend to address anyone for whom belief is sufficient, and logical reasoning unnecessary. I have tried to present the arguments most commonly made for the existence of God and the questions and paradoxes that can arise as we reason our way through this eternal question.

The Creationist Paradox

The most common argument for the existence of God is the creationist view. This point of view, in short, states that this wonderful, intricate universe of ours must have been created by intelligent design. A deliberate and purposeful creator must surely be responsible for its existence. How else could we have such a marvelous and wonderfully complex creation? The creator, in all his wisdom, surely must have a grand design, a purpose, and a master plan for his creation. Why else would he create it?

The fallacy in this argument is obvious. The argument presupposes that everything must have a creator. If this is assumed to be true, God must also have a creator. Alternatively, if we are willing to admit that not all things have a creator (for example, God does not have a creator), it might well be that the universe has no creator.

Bertrand Russell, one of the most influential philosophers of the twentieth century, describes his discovery of the fallacy of this *first cause* argument in his autobiography[4]:

At the age of eighteen, however, shortly before I went to Cambridge, I read Mill's *Autobiography*, where I found a sentence to the effect that his father taught him the question "Who made me?" cannot be answered, since it immediately suggests the further question "Who made God?" This led me to abandon the "First Cause" argument, and to become an atheist.

The point is humorously illustrated by a famous story retold by Stephen Hawking in his book *A Brief History of Time* and ascribed to Bertrand Russell: A well-known scientist was giving a lecture on astronomy. After the lecture, an elderly lady came up to the scientist and told him that he had it all wrong.

"The world is really a flat plate supported on the back of a giant tortoise," she claimed.

Not knowing how to respond, the incredulous scientist asked, "And what is the turtle standing on?"

The lady triumphantly replied, "You're very clever, young man, but it's no use. It's turtles all the way down."

Arguing that the universe must have been created by God because everything needs a creator-God is a circular argument. It leads to the unavoidable question, *If everything must be created, who created God?* And if God has simply always existed, there is nothing that prevents me from claiming that the universe has also always existed. The first cause argument is not logically sustainable.

Does the Existence of Life on Earth Require a Creator?

Until recently, the existence of life on earth was proof enough for the existence of a creator. Since man is unable to create life in any form or shape, the argument goes, the existence of the wide variety of life-forms on this planet is clearly proof that a creator must be responsible for this incredibly wonderful creation so abundant in diverse life-forms.

Scientists are just beginning to understand how life on earth began spontaneously from nonliving building blocks 3.5 billion years ago. In the 1950s, Stanley Miller and Harold Urey, at the University of Chicago, showed that amino acids, the building blocks of proteins, could be formed quite readily under the right conditions from the basic elements present on early earth. Going from amino acids to proteins and enzymes turned out to be a lot more challenging. This process was thought to be fundamental in the creation and self-replication of DNA, the basic building block of all known life-forms.

In a recent article in *Scientific American*, Alonso Ricardo and Jack Szostak pointed out the basic paradox that scientists have struggled with for many years: It takes preexisting proteins and information stored in the DNA's double helix to make specific proteins. How, then, did the first organisms convert amino acids into specific proteins and enzymes? One possible solution to this paradox is that the first organisms may not have required specific proteins at all. Perhaps the RNA and DNA for these first organisms formed spontaneously, without the genetic code of an existing DNA helix. It is well known that molecules called lipids that contain hydrophilic (water-loving) and hydrophobic (water-hating) properties can self-organize into membranelike structures. These lipid bilayers constitute the basic building blocks of most cell walls. Within these self-organized cell walls, molecules similar to RNA and DNA could self-organize.

When modern cells make proteins, they first copy genes from DNA into RNA and then use the RNA as a template to make proteins. The last stage could have existed independently at first. Later on, DNA could have appeared as a more permanent form of storage, thanks to its superior chemical stability.[5]

Scientists have created simple life-forms such as viruses and bacteria in the lab as far back as 2002 using other precursor molecules or organisms. More recently, they are attempting to synthesize such building blocks of life from chemicals available in a laboratory.[6] The story of the making of synthetic life-forms (without the use of any existing life-forms) still has a ways to go, but most scientists today agree that simple and complex life-forms will be synthesized by humans in the laboratory from basic elements and compounds.

One thing is now crystal clear. We do not need to invoke a supernatural creator to explain the existence of the different life-forms on earth.

Biology and chemistry have provided us adequate explanations for how simple precursor biological molecules were created and how this led to the creation of the first simple life-forms. Subsequently, much more complex life-forms evolved from these simple life-forms. The incredible diversity of life-forms on earth is a product of our evolutionary past. Simple life-forms leading to ever more complex life-forms. The empirical evidence for such evolutionary pathways is overwhelming.

The Purpose of Existence Paradox

Another line of reasoning leads to what I call the *purpose of existence* paradox. According to this argument, God put us on earth for a reason. Each of us has a purpose; otherwise, we would not be here. This line of thinking is clearly motivated by a desire to provide a purpose to our existence and can be quite inspirational.

Everything around us appears to have a purpose. Most of us can quickly identify the useful purpose most inanimate objects serve. But when it comes to explaining our own purpose, it is a difficult, if not impossible, task. In most religions, our purpose is linked to God's purpose for us. There are many passages in scripture that clearly state that we are here to serve God's will. This begs two important questions: What or who is God and what is his will?

The answer, of course, depends on whom you ask. Christians, Jews, Hindus, and Islamists point you in the direction of their holy books to look for answers, and you will find many different interpretations within each faith. The acceptance of such revealed truths about the purpose of our existence requires a giant leap of faith (for example, we must accept the writings as divine revelation), and they each have their own view of our purpose in life. Does this imply that people of different religions have different purposes in this world? Is one holy book better than the others? Is our purpose in life simply a matter of unquestioning faith and belief in a book written a few millennia ago? No rational person can reason their way to this conclusion.

There is very little doubt that there is a deep-rooted emotional and psychological need in each of us to discover a purpose for our existence. This is, of course, very different from saying that there is a logical requirement for it. Although we may believe in the Big Guy in the Sky (BGITS) conception of God or in a holy book (that we can choose or that is chosen for us on the basis of our upbringing) to provide a purpose to our lives, there is no logical basis for this.

Whatever the purpose of our existence—assuming there is one—it must transcend religious scripture or belief. An example of such a purpose that would apply to all humanity would be to make the world a better place. This human-defined purpose is independent of religious scripture and does not require postulating the existence of God.

Bad Things Happen to Good People

Steven Gideon (not his real name) was an honest hardworking father of two who had led, by all accounts, an exemplary life. A family man and an honest factory worker who attended church every Sunday, Gideon was a volunteer firefighter and had gone on missions to poor parts of South America to build medical facilities for the less fortunate. He was a deeply pious and generous man. Steve was diagnosed with an incurable form of cancer that took his life in a matter of six months at the young age of forty-five. He left behind his beautiful wife and two adoring children. Why?

One of the apparent paradoxes that arises when we invoke the existence of a kind and benign God is the lack of a reasonable explanation for why terrible things happen to the most wonderful and God-fearing people. If God is all-powerful and merciful, why does he allow these kinds of injustices to happen? Does he not see the good being slaughtered by the evil? Does he not care when an innocent child dies of starvation?

As you might imagine, there has been a great deal written about this topic, starting as far back as the Book of Job in the Bible. Among the many religious discourses and treatises written on reconciling this paradox, I recommend two popular contemporary books with remarkably similar titles: Harold S. Kushner's *When Bad Things Happen to Good People* (Anchor Books, 2004) and Melvin Tinker's *Why Do Bad Things Happen to Good People?* (Christian Focus, 2006). Judging from the popularity of these books, a lot of people have been bothered by this question and have thought about it a great deal.

Kushner, a conservative rabbi, presents a particularly poignant account of how he lost his young son. As you might imagine, this question developed a personal significance for him. He presents one of the most compelling cases for the need to reconcile our belief in an omnipotent God who will let no harm come to his flock with the reality of the incredible callousness, indifference, and outright brutality we see in the world around us. His own reconciliation of this dilemma comes from a firm personal belief in a power that is clearly beyond human rationality but provides emotional solace that no other conception can provide. His justification goes beyond the rational and into the emotionally soothing realm of faith.

Those who are not blessed with the gift of faith don't find this to be a comforting thought or a satisfactory explanation. If God is indeed the caretaker of this world and is kind and benevolent, why does he not come to the rescue of the needy and the disconsolate? If he does not intervene and help the faithful, what good does it do them to pray to him? Why do we spend such large portions of our resources and time building churches, mosques, and temples—places of worship of a God who does not particularly care about the condition of his devotees? These questions go the core of our beliefs. Surely our prayers and level of devotion are influenced in large part by how we view him and our relationship to him.

One way to resolve this dilemma is with the *watchmaker* conception of God. God does not micromanage the world. He lays down the rules by which the world works and then lets the chips fall where they may. He went through the intricate process of creating the universe, wound it up, and let it go. As the clock of eternity ticks away, the laws of nature apply like clockwork, equally to good people and bad. A moral, honest man is just as likely to get run over by a truck if he jumps in front of it as is an evil murderer. The laws of nature don't know our sense of morality or our code of ethics. It is these dispassionate laws of nature that govern this world; man's value judgments do not affect them one bit.

Whether these laws were laid down by a watchmaker God is a matter of belief. No rational arguments can be made to prove the existence of such a God. You might claim that the laws of nature are God's laws, as only he could have laid them down. Or you might argue that these laws of nature just *are* and do not require a creator. This takes us back to the need for a creator discussed earlier. Some people have even been bold enough to say that these laws of nature define God.

The Catch-22 of Achieving a Level of Understanding

One argument that particularly defies logic is that you don't understand God's will because you have not read the scriptures in enough detail to allow you to appreciate it. This is a perfect example of a catch-22 dilemma.

According to this line of reasoning, only if you agree with a particular point of view (based on belief) are you sufficiently well versed in the scriptures. Developing an understanding of subjects that involve intricate concepts certainly requires a depth of knowledge in the field that may require years of study to acquire. To really grasp the conceptual framework of string theory and how it relates to the origin of the universe requires a broad understanding of the principles of modern physics, with perhaps a good understanding of differential equations and other mathematical subjects, such as topology. You could easily make the case that a person would need a fifteen-year (or longer) program of study before Roger Penrose's lectures on string theory would make any sense at all.

Can a similar case be made for our understanding of the scriptures? The answer is an unqualified no. There is no question that a detailed analysis of any classical work of philosophy or religion can require many years of study and contemplation. Theological seminaries and madrasas around the world bear testimony to the fact that people will spend many years—sometimes a lifetime—studying religious texts. The commentaries and essays on various interpretations of the word of God could surely occupy many good-sized libraries. Can we make the case that those who do not subscribe to a particular belief system are simply too poorly read to understand it? If they were to spend enough time reading and studying the texts and the commentaries, would they eventually get it?

There is one very important distinction between the two examples given above: The complex concepts of science (quantum mechanics, string theory, and the like) require many years of intense study to understand; however, they make predictions that are relatively easy to verify and comprehend. Every scientific theory or idea must be verified by empirical observations. This verification forms the backbone of scientific inquiry. Experts and non-experts examine the facts, make relevant observations, and compare them with every proposed theory. They conduct deliberate experiments to test the theory and its predictions. If these observations are consistent with the predictions of the theory, the theory is accepted. Many theories may be widely accepted—until observations are made that refute the theory; then we have no choice but to abandon it and develop a better one that is consistent with the observations.

A good example are Newton's laws of motion. As they were proposed several hundred years ago, they satisfactorily explained every observation. The motion of bodies on earth and the other planets all seemed to consistently follow Newton's laws, without exception. Had there been a single observation that contradicted the theory, it would have been rejected as being incorrect, or at least inadequate. And in fact, this happened in the twentieth century, when Einstein clearly showed the limitations of Newton's laws and the conditions under which they would and would not apply. Einstein's replacement theory was itself contested and debated by the scientific community until there was compelling observational evidence that its predictions were consistent with cosmological observations.

Religious and theological theories and contentions must also be subjected to observational tests. Only if the theories and contentions hold up under scrutiny should they be accepted as valid. Unfortunately, such verification is rarely applied to religious ideas. When one does apply direct observational tests to religious claims, many of them are clearly invalid and inconsistent. Arriving at this outcome does not require us to spend decades researching and studying religious texts. The hypothesis that a BGITS God exists and is the caretaker of this universe is clearly in conflict with so many observations in our everyday lives that we are justified in rejecting it without having to spend many decades in religious study. The conflicts with observational evidence are reason enough. For example, there is no empirical evidence of any cause-and-effect relationship between prayer and divine intervention by a BGITS God to ease human suffering. There is no empirical evidence that the world was created 6,000 years ago as suggested in scripture. Many other examples of inconsistencies arise when we postulate the existence of a BGITS God.

We can choose to rely on a belief system and simply set logic aside. Anything that is a matter of belief is beyond the realm of reason and logic and, therefore, cannot be open to debate. However, discussion requires the exchange of ideas and reasoning. We are, ultimately, rational creatures who must limit our debates to the confines of logic. Simply saying that the other side does not understand is not enough. It is dismissive and, ultimately, an ineffective means of argument.

There Is No Rational Basis for a BGITS God

On the basis of empirical evidence, we cannot rationally establish the existence of a Big Guy in the Sky concept of God. With the incredible changes that science and technology have brought to our current knowledge of the universe and our current way of thinking, we can say with more certainty than ever that many of the justifications our ancestors may have had for the existence of an omnipotent creator are no longer valid.

Some believers may argue that this question is beyond rational thought. I reject this notion. If we open ourselves to ideas that are beyond rationality, we have started down a very slippery slope. We open ourselves to wizardry and witchcraft, alchemy and superstition, with no basis for rejecting the claims of the supernatural. We would walk away from the triumphs of centuries of science and technological development. We have come a long way from the Dark Ages to a firm base in a rational thought process that we cannot and should not abandon in our quest for understanding the nature of God. Matters of faith can and should be addressed with the incredible tools of human rationality at our disposal.

How, then, do we logically define God and his relationship to us?

Coming Full Circle: Historically and Rationally

In the chapters that follow, we begin this journey with a historical exploration of humanity's quest for God. We'll trace the definition of God from the earliest human writings to our modern concepts of God and through this historical journey show how we have come full circle: Our current conception of God, based on the accumulated wisdom of humanity, is entirely consistent with the teachings of some of the most ancient prehistoric cultures. We may have made many detours along the way, but we have arrived where we started—albeit with a much clearer and better understanding of why we are here.

While we have concluded that there is no logical proof of the existence of God, an overwhelming majority of humanity does believe in a BGITS God. We will explore the reasons for this and in doing so recognize the importance of satisfying not only our rationality, but also our deep-rooted emotional needs and desires. Faith and belief are essential tools to satisfy these emotional needs. We will go through a process of redefining God that satisfies both our rational and our emotional needs. This allows us to reconcile rationality with faith and brings us full circle again. Finally, we will come to the incredible realization that this redefinition of God based on rational faith is consistent with one of our most ancient definition of God.

2

Our Oldest Traditions: The Aryan Conception of God

Every human civilization, almost without exception, established a pantheon and placed great emphasis on the worship of these gods and goddesses. It was believed that appeasement of the gods ensured the worshippers' own well-being. This almost universal approach of invoking a BGITS God and taking refuge in some conception of an all-pervading, omnipotent being is central to the traditions of many historically and geographically diverse cultures. God was ascribed the attributes of creator, protector, benign and benevolent father or mother figure, and—above all—of someone who dispensed justice through appropriate rewards for good and punishments for evil.

Despite this apparently universal and unifying theme, the ideas and images of gods that emerged in different cultures are diverse, and there are stark differences in the approaches taken to define God and his message. The Greek gods would be unrecognizable to the ancient Inca or the Chinese, for example.

Let's begin our exploration of this most compelling and complex of human intellectual adventures by studying the different paths that various cultures have taken. The consequences of these vastly different intellectual explorations of the metaphysical are profound and have shaped the course of human history.

Our Most Ancient Musings about God and Creation

There is no better place to begin this discussion than with a translation of a set of *shlokas* or hymns taken from one of the most ancient texts known to man, the Rig Veda. The verses duplicated here are taken from a segment of the Rig Veda referred to as the *Nasadiya Sukta* (Rig Veda 10.129).[1] It is a short hymn of seven verses that some have declared to be the most sublime philosophical song in human writing. Judge for yourself; the composers of these verses would have it no other way:

1. There was neither non-existence nor existence then; there was neither the realm of space nor the sky which is beyond. What stirred? Where? In whose protection? Was there water, bottomlessly deep?
2. There was neither death nor immortality then. There was no distinguishing sign of night nor of day. That one breathed, windless, by its own impulse. Other than that there was nothing beyond.
3. Darkness was hidden by darkness in the beginning; with no distinguishing sign, all this was water. The life force that was covered with emptiness, that one arose through the power of heat.
4. Desire came upon that one in the beginning; that was the first seed of mind. Poets seeking in their heart with wisdom found the bond of existence in non-existence.
5. Their cord was extended across. Was there below? Was there above? There were seed-placers; there were powers. There was impulse beneath; there was giving-forth above.
6. Who really knows? Who will here proclaim it? Whence was it produced? Whence is this creation? The gods came afterward, with the creation of this universe. Who then knows whence it has arisen?
7. Whence this creation has arisen—perhaps it formed itself, or perhaps it did not—the one who looks down on it, in the highest heaven, only he knows—or perhaps he does not know.

These musings of ancient man marveling at the absolute wonder of creation clearly show how age-old the question of the existence of God really is. Through the next 5,000 years, we have grappled with the same question. Through religions and theologies, science and metaphysics, voodoo and magic, faith and agnosticism, we have asked and answered this question—perhaps to the satisfaction of some but certainly not all.

In this chapter, I will introduce you to our ancestors, authors of this incredible poetry. Clearly, these ancient people had completely open minds about creation and the creator. Theirs was not a prescriptive religion that provided definitive answers to the ultimate questions. Their writings, instead, exude a burning curiosity guided by the wisdom of humility that allowed them the courage to say that they were on a journey of discovery. Nothing was set in stone; there could be many possible answers to their questions. They were open to the possibility that humans—and even God himself—may be unable to fathom the ultimate nature of reality. Their sense of wonder and inquisitiveness leaves one in awe. Who were these people, and how did they reconcile these core questions?

The Aryans

The word *Aryan* is derived from the Sanskrit word *arya*, which means "noble." In today's parlance, the word has many connotations, and is often associated with its use by the Nazi regime. This is certainly not the usage intended here. In fact, the Aryans represent an ancient people that were the forebearers of the Indo-European people.

A great deal has been written about these prehistoric Indo-Europeans, or Aryans, as we shall refer to them here. The evidence of their existence and traditions (which persist today all across Asia and Europe) is overwhelming, even though there remain many doubts about their origins, their migrations, and their way of life.

The Aryans, as best we can tell, first settled in the steppes of central Asia and perhaps in the northwestern parts of the Indian subcontinent. They built agricultural settlements of modest size and herded cattle. They were by and large a peaceful people that were held together by a common language and culture. Although no massive monuments have been excavated, archaeological evidence of many highly developed settlements have been unearthed that indicate that these prehistoric people thrived for many centuries about 5000 years ago. These early Aryans migrated into central India, the Middle East, the Mediterranean states, and all the way to Western Europe and Scandinavia.

We do not know whether the Aryans were contemporaries of or preceded the great civilizations of Mohenjo-daro and Harappa (c. 3000 BCE), which flourished on the banks of the Indus River and are collectively referred to as the Indus Valley Civilization. For our discussion, this aspect of their history is not crucial. We will focus instead on their beliefs, which we know quite a bit about because they were well preserved by a remarkable oral tradition.

We refer to these ancient Aryan people as *Indo-European* because they occupied and migrated to a good part of Europe and central and south Asia. The most direct and compelling evidence for the common origin of the Indo-European peoples comes from ancient and modern social customs that are common across a great part of Eurasia and from their languages, which have a common origin. Many of the words from these languages are clearly related, and there is ample evidence for a common root language that must have been the mother of Sanskrit and Latin and all their daughter languages. A few examples of some of these commonly used words are listed in table 1. A more complete list that clearly illustrates the common root language is available in Gundev (2014). The similarity is evident and is clearly not a coincidence. Linguists and ethnographers agree that the link between these languages is unmistakable. Indeed, it is now well established that there is a common protolanguage for Indo-European languages. The languages of the Aryans were an early form of Sanskrit and its close cousin Avestan.

Table 1. Examples of English Words with Sanskrit Roots.[2]

Root Sanskrit Word	*Median Word*	*Derived English Word*
a- (prefix meaning "not")	a- (prefix meaning "not")[a,b]	a- (prefix meaning "not"; ex: theist-atheist)
agni (meaning fire)	ignis[a]	ignite
an (prefix meaning "not")	un[a,b] (meaning "not")	un (prefix meaning "not" ex: undo)

Root Sanskrit Word	Median Word	Derived English Word
ashta (meaning eight)	octo[a]	eight
bhrathr (meaning brother)	phrater[b]	brother
chandra (meaning moon)	candela[a] (meaning "light")	candle
danta (meaning teeth)	dentis[a]	dental
dasha (meaning ten)	deca[b]	deca
devas (meaning god)	devos[b]	god, divine
dhama (meaning house)	domus[a]	domicile
dwar (meaning door)	doru	door
gau (meaning cow)	bous[b]	cow
hrt (meaning heart)	herto[c]	heart
kaal (meaning time)	kalendae[a]	calendar
kri (meaning to do)	creatus[a]	create
loka (meaning place)	locus[a]	locale
ma (meaning me/my)	me[a]	me
madhyam (meaning medium)	medium[a]	medium
maha (meaning great)	magnus[a]	mega
mala (meaning dirt/bad)	malus[a]	mal as in malicious, malnutrition…
man (meaning mind)	mens[a]	mind
matr (meaning mother)	mater[a]	mother
mithya (meaning not real)	mythos[b]	myth
mrta (meaning dead)	mortis[a]	murder
mush (meaning mouse)	mus[a]	mouse
na (meaning no)	ne	no
naama (means name)	nomen[a]	name
naas (means nose)	nasus[a]	nose
nakta (meaning night)	nocturnalis[a]	nocturnal
nara (meaning nerve)	nervus[a]	nerve, nervous
nava (meaning new)	novus[a]	nova – new
navagatha (meaning navigation)	navigationem[a]	navigation
paad (meaning foot)	pedis[a]	ped as in pedestrian, pedal, etc.
pancha (meaning five)	pente[b]	penta, five
patha (meaning path)	pathes[b]	path
pithr (meaning father)	pater[a]	father
raja/raya (meaning king)	regalis[a]	royal

Continued

Root Sanskrit Word	Median Word	Derived English Word
sama (meaning similar)	similis[a]	similar
sapta (meaning seven)	septum[a]	seven
sarpa (meaning snake)	serpentem[a]	serpent
thri (meaning three)	treis[b]	three
vastr (meaning cloth)	vestire[a]	vest
yauvana (meaning youth)	juvenilis[a]	juvenile

[a]Latin. [b]Greek. [c]Proto-Germanic.

One example is the word used for *god*. The word in Sanskrit is *devas*. In Latin, this becomes *deivos* or *deus* (origin of the English *deity*); in Proto-Celtic, *devos*; and, in Lithuanian, *devas*. As Bloomfield pointed out,[3] this noun is connected in its origin to the sanskrit verb *div* or *dyu*, which means "to shine." The early Aryans appear to have derived their divine inspiration from the sun, which provided them with light and cleared away the darkness. Similarly, the Sanskrit word *bhaga* is the root word for *bhagwan* (God) in Hindi, *bhaga* in Avestan, *bogu* in Slavic, and *baga* in Old Persian.

These and other related words for more complex concepts, such as faith, clearly point to a common language and common ancestral roots for many of these Indo-European people. By following the languages, we can gather a picture of the migration of these people south and east further into India to establish the Vedic traditions of India or toward Persia and Europe to establish the traditions of Zoroastrianism. Their beliefs traveled with them: The philosophies and ideas expressed by Zoroaster in his writings are clearly related to the writings in the Rig Veda, the most ancient compilation of writings of the early Hindus.

Friedrich Max Müller,[4] Maurice Bloomfield,[5] and David Anthony[6] each point to evidence that leaves very little doubt that there is a common ancestral heritage to the Aryan people that now inhabit countries all the way from Europe to India. Cuneiform tablets, dated to 1600 BCE, containing letters from King Dushratta of Syria to the Egyptian pharaohs, mention the names of his brother Artashuvara and his grandfather Artatama. Other well-known names of Aryan rulers of Persia are Artaxerses and Artaphernes.[6,7] The stem *arta*, which is commonly used in these names, has the same root as *asha* in the Avestan and *Rtá* in the Vedas. As we will see later, these words all mean "the order of the universe" and are central to the religion of the early Vedas.

What do we know about the thoughts and musings of these ancient people? Very little is preserved in writing that is properly dated and whose authorship is traceable. However, because of a remarkable oral tradition among the Aryan peoples (and one that survives in India to this day), the accumulated wisdom of the ages has been passed down through many hundreds of generations in the form of recited and memorized *shlokas*. It is through this oral tradition that many of these ancient legends, rituals, and beliefs are still available to us, and they provide just a glimpse of the literature and religion of the time. In later Aryan periods (c. 1500–1000 BCE), many of these hymns were written down. The oldest of these compilations is the Rig Veda.

The Rig Veda: The Early Vedic Period

The Rig Veda is the oldest of the four major Vedas, hymns compiled over several hundred years: the Rig Veda, the Yajur Veda, the Sama Veda, and the Atharva Veda. The word *Veda* literally means "sacred knowledge" and is derived from the Sanskrit word *Vid* ("to know"). The tradition of the Vedas was an integral part of the religious and social traditions of the ancient Indo-European people and, remarkably, still remains the dominant philosophical tradition in India.

The Rig Veda consists of 1,028 hymns, each containing ten verses. Estimates of the precise date and origin of the verses vary greatly. Hymns were passed down orally from generation to generation by recitation and rote, which leaves questions about authorship and precise dates of origin extremely difficult to nail down. What we do know is that they were composed by a nomadic people about 5,000 years ago (and some compositions may be much older than this). At some point, a group of scholars, or *rishis*, of the time, compiled and codified them into texts of sometimes coherent and sometimes disparate ideas and verses. The texts have been dated by historians to somewhere between 2500 and 1500 BCE.

Scholars such as Bal Gangadhar Tilak claim that the wording and the description of nature in the Vedas suggest that they were originally authored by peoples living closer to the Arctic Circle, sometime around the last ice age.[8] Descriptions of the seasons in the verses suggest that the sun rose and remained in the heavens for many months and that when it set, there was darkness for many months. If this hypothesis is correct, it would place the origin of these verses 13,000 to 14,000 years ago. During the last ice age, as temperatures dropped and ice covered large parts of Europe and northern Asia, these people would have migrated to more temperate climates—either to the steppes of central Asia or to what is now northern India, where they would have been protected by the Himalayas. Verses in the Rig Veda contain elaborate descriptions of sunrises, sunsets, and the night sky. They bear testament to the wonder and amazement that these people must have felt at the world around them. These ancient people were awestruck by the magnificence of nature and its incredible beauty and power.

There is little archaeological evidence to support this hypothesis; the precise date of the Rig Veda is not central to our discussion here. It is sufficient to say that they are among the oldest recorded thoughts of mankind.

The verses were documented in Sanskrit, which is fortunate, because Sanskrit is perhaps the only language that has largely preserved its script, grammar, and vocabulary for the past 5,000 years. Modern-day Hindi still uses the same writing system (the Devanagiri script) and grammar (Panini's grammar) that were used in the Rig Veda. This means that the texts can still be easily read, a tremendous advantage for those trying to ascertain the meaning—both written and implied—in these ancient writings. What remains uncertain is the interpretation of specific words and their contextual symbolism. This means that two English translations of the same Sanskrit text can differ in some important respects, depending on how certain words have been interpreted. In many instances, the words may have lost their context or changed meaning over time, but in most cases, the basic message of the Rig Veda comes through loud and clear.

Unlike many religious texts, which purport to supply answers, the Rig Veda is a book that asks questions; it is, in fact, riddled with riddles. Its style is one of innocent questioning and wonderment at the beauty of natural phenomena and the paradoxes that appear to be unresolvable. It makes no apologies for not answering the questions it poses and, in fact, wears it as a badge of honor. It remains open-minded to other points of view and challenges others to come forth and express their own interpretations of the world. This approach stands in stark contrast to more modern religious texts, which often claim to be the word of God—and, in most instances, the only true word of God.

The Early Vedic Pantheon

The early Aryans, like many ancient civilizations, deified the incredible forces of nature into gods. There was Surya, the sun god; Vayu, the wind god; Agni, the fire god; and many others. Each god had his or her characteristics, imagery, and stories. Sacrifices had to be performed to please them, and elaborate rituals needed to be followed to ensure that the gods were properly placated. These rituals and traditions exist in all ancient religious traditions. The Egyptians, the Romans, the Aztecs, the Incas, and the Phoenicians each had their own pantheon of nature-based gods and sets of strict rituals, usually guided by a priest.

The gods occupied a practical and personal part of the cultures that believed in them. Ensuring that they were happy was not just a philosophical construct but a very real and immediate imperative. Sacrifices and rituals were not to be taken lightly; if not performed properly, they could threaten the very existence of a family or village. If the gods were displeased, it might not rain, and the community could starve to death. In most ancient civilizations, these matters dominated societal interaction. Large portions of religious texts are devoted to rituals and the precise procedures that must be followed to appease the gods. The Sama Veda, the Yajur Veda, and the Atharva Veda, for example, describe in excruciating detail the ritual protocols of the early Aryans.

Early Aryan texts place a great deal of emphasis on animal sacrifices. The famous horse sacrifice, or Rajasuya Yajna, took place when a king let a white steed roam free in his kingdom. If anyone dared to try and capture the horse, it was seen as a challenge to the authority of the king and the challenge was settled in a battle to the death. If no one dared to try and capture the horse, the animal was sacrificed in a great feast meant to establish the supremacy of the king over his subjects and to offer a sacrifice to the gods.

As the Aryans settled down in northern India, their emphasis on ritual sacrifices decreased. The physical acts of sacrifice were replaced with symbolic representations, and along with them, an increased reflection on the meaning of the sacrifice rather than the sacrifice itself.

In the Rig Veda, the most powerful of the gods was Varuna, the keeper of universal order, the Rtá. He has a special place in the pantheon of Vedic gods because he ensured that all the other gods respected and followed the Rtá, and he stands alone above them.

In terms of the sheer number of verses devoted to one god, Indra occupies a central place. He is a feisty fellow who rides in a golden chariot driven by white steeds, who partakes liberally of *soma rasa* (the extract of a plant supposed to make the gods immortal) before vanquishing his enemies. Indra is ascribed human qualities, not all of which are positive. He can be lusty, greedy, and downright warlike. He wields a club and slays dragons, demons, and all manner of evil beings. Although he appears to be a god who is more human than cosmic, his powers to regulate the rain and the seasons set him apart.[9] The following verses indicate a typical description of Indra, the dragon slayer.[10]

> Let me know the aerobic deeds of Indra, which he that wields the club performed of yore. He slew the dragon, broke the way for the waters; he cleft the belly of the mountains.
> He slew the dragon layup on the mountain. Gordon forged for him to his heavenly club. Like roaring cattle down came the waters, flowing swiftly to the sea.
> Lusty as a bull, Indra demanded Soma; from three vats he drank of the pressed drink. His missile bolt he took in hand, the generous God, and slew the firstborn of the dragons.

Despite his obvious importance, the primary role of Indra is to guide us to the path of Rtá.

O Indra, lead us on the path of Rtá, on the right path over all evils. (Rig Veda, 10.83.6)[11]

Next in order of importance sits Agni, the god of fire, personified in the ritual flame that forms the core of all Vedic rituals. The word *agni*, meaning "fire," later evolved into Latin *ignis*, Lithuanian *ugnis*, and Slavic *ogni*. Although the gods of fire take on a female personification in the Greek and Roman traditions, the Vedic Agni is portrayed as a robust male figure. He is referred to as the "son of strength," presumably because it takes some doing to produce fire by rubbing two sticks together. The son of the union between the two sticks then consumes its parents (the sticks). Agni dispels darkness and the demons associated with it.

The god of fire plays an important role in the rituals associated with prayers to all the other gods. Agni represents the infinite divinity (the Rtá) in sacrificial offerings. Fire represents the embodiment of everything that is pure, because it has the power to purify. Even today, all *havans* performed by Hindus in the Vedic tradition involve making offerings of *ghee* (clarified butter) and *samagri* (sanctified wood chips and filings) to a ritual fire surrounded by the participants. The shlokas recited during this ritual date back to the Rig Veda and to the other more recent Vedas.

Usha, the goddess of the dawn or first light, is another nature deity who receives a great deal of attention in the Rig Veda. Agni is her son and he is prominent in morning offerings to the gods. Some of the most beautiful poetry in the Rig Veda is reserved for the goddess of dawn. The coming of the dawn clearly held great significance for the early Aryans. A few examples of the hymns to the goddess of dawn show the reverence and importance the Aryans had for this personalized goddess.

> We have crossed to the farther bank of this darkness;
> Radiant Dawn spreads her webs.
> Smiling like a lover who wishes to win his way,
> she shines forth and with her lovely face awakens us to happiness.
> (Rig Veda 1.92.6.)[12]

Legends and myths abound about Usha and her relationship to the other gods in the Rig Veda: Surya, the sun god; Vayu, the wind god; and Prajapati, the god of creation.

Despite the rich and impressive pantheon of nature-based and anthropomorphic gods and the incredibly complex legends and elaborate rituals, the Rig Veda makes it very clear that they are all ultimately governed by and at the service of the Rtá.

The Vedic Concept of Rtá

The ancient Aryans were unique for their time because they took one giant step beyond nature-based gods. Although they recognized the power of the forces of nature and ascribed divine authority to them, they also were quick to add that every one of these gods was subject to a higher order. This higher order they termed Rtá. The concept of Rtá is the most profound religious conception in the Rig Veda and occupies a central place in this philosophical tradition. It is best described in Maurice Bloomfield's commentary on the Rig Veda:

> As the basis of cosmic order the *ṛta* rules the world and nature. The established facts of the visible word, but especially the events of nature that recur periodically, are fixed or regulated by *ṛta*. Those daughters of heaven, the Maidens Dawn, shine upon the morning sky in harmony with *ṛta*, or when they wake up in the morning they rise from the seat of *ṛta*. The sun is placed upon the sky in obedience to the *ṛta*. He is called the wheel of *ṛta* with twelve spokes. This means that he courses across the sky as the year of twelve months. Even the shallow mystery that the red, raw cow yields white, cooked milk is "the *ṛta* of the cow guided by the *ṛta*." The gods themselves are born of the *ṛta* or in the *ṛta* (*ṛtajāta*); they show by their acts that they know the *ṛta*, observe the *ṛta* and love the *ṛta*.[13]

The word *Rtá* is derived from the root *ri*, which means "to move"; it doesn't define a static universe; it defines the rules and laws that govern the dynamics of that universe. The changes in the seasons, the movement of the stars, the ebb and flow of water, the birth and death of people and animals are all examples of the constantly changing universe in which we live. The ancient Aryans marveled at the order in this complexity and realized that these patterns were far from random and, indeed, must be governed by a universal set of laws, which they called the Rtá.

It is important to note that according to these early Aryans, the order in the universe is not governed by the will of God but by some universal, unchanging, eternal, and immutable set of laws that bring harmony and order to both the physical and moral realms. There was no shortage of gods in their religion—dozens of nature gods played an important role in their everyday lives. However, the Aryans were unique in their recognition that the gods themselves must obey some set of laws beyond themselves.

The gods did not create the Rtá; it is viewed as unborn and eternal. In fact, the gods existed only because they respected, loved, and conformed to the Rtá. Should they deviate from this path, they would join the forces of darkness and evil.

> It is even said that gods owe their existence to Rtá, as they are born of Rtá. The Gods are described as governors who uphold *gopa rtasya*, practice *rtayu*, and oversee the physical order and also the moral order of the universe—Rtá. The Gods reward the virtuous and punish those who infringe on Rtá. Even the Gods are subject to its laws, and they have to abide by it.
>
> The concept of Rtá asserts that the order in nature is self-regulated and operates by its own laws (*svabhava*) and not necessarily by the will of Gods.[14]

The concept of the Rtá is complex and inclusive. It not only represents the order in the universe but defines the relationships between man and nature, between man and god, and between human beings and all living things. Human concepts of morality and virtue, as well as our relationships with the multitude of Aryan gods, are defined by this universal order. Filled with wonder at the majesty of creation, the Aryans worshipped not only powerful nature gods, but also the all-powerful guardian of the gods—the Rtá, which established order in every aspect of nature.

Dharma: The Moral, Ethical, Aesthetic, and Religious Dimensions of Rtá

To appease the gods, man's deeds must be in accordance with the Rtá. Therefore, ethical behavior was defined simply as actions in conformity with the Rtá. Unethical activity was referred to as *anrtá*, going against the Rtá. How can a lay person comprehend and apply such a grand concept in everyday life? For a common person, the universal laws reduce to a set of social, moral, ethical, and religious laws, or *dharma*. Accordingly, in the later Vedas, such as the Atharva Veda, the term Rtá is sometimes replaced with dharma. Varuna is now the guardian of the dharma, not the Rtá. Sin, according to the Rig Veda, arises from failures of human character; true evil lies in the hearts and minds of men. Such evil emanates from a lack of understanding of the Rtá or a lack of respect for it.

This definition of morality in terms of going against the laws of nature is important and substantially different in the way ethical behavior is defined in later organized religions. Morality, for the Aryans, was not defined by a holy scripture or the revealed word of a supernatural being but by order of the universe. Human actions done in accordance with the Rtá are good for humanity as a whole. Moral action does not require a heaven as reward or hell as punishment, much less a deity to hand out either. It requires a person to recognize the greater good and to act accordingly. It defines a person's dharma, their duty or obligations. This is Rtá made personal in every aspect of man's everyday actions. Truth, honesty, and respect for the environment and for all living creatures emerge as natural extensions if we are guided by these laws.

All people, including kings and priests, are by their nature good and virtuous (not sinners that need to be redeemed). But we commit sins (*paapa*) and stray into the path of anrtá because of the inherent weaknesses in our nature, our ignorance, our lack of will, bad company, and the temptations of the world (*maya*). The Rig Veda provides many examples of anrtá, or actions that must be avoided: murder, stealing, lust, anger, thoughtlessness (RV 7.86.6).[15] A person's sins are, in a sense, a debt to society that can be repaid through good deeds and honest repentance. A person who has disturbed the harmony and order of the universe must work to restore this harmony through virtuous words and actions. In so doing, he returns order to the universe and ourselves to the path of the Rtá. This concept of good deeds, or *karma*, being able to make up for past bad deeds is the foundation for later karmic philosophies in the Upanishads.

We also see a clear appreciation of the close connection between human activity and our environment. In fact, many verses in the Rig Veda speak of the unity of all life on earth, how nature is connected to the different living beings, and how the Rtá regulates the relationships between all creatures and their environment. By eliminating chaos and bringing order to everything around us, the Rtá provides us with a universe full of beauty and elegance.

These ancient Aryans were clearly fascinated not only by the glory and power of the natural elements, but also by the inherent order in the world around them—the laws that guided the universe. The orderly movement of the heavenly bodies, the coming and going of seasons, the rising and setting of the sun, and the unbridled power of thunder, lightning, and rain are all seen through the lens of the Rtá.

From Varuna to Ahura Mazda and Indra

As the Aryans in the Central Asian steppes and the Indian subcontinent developed into a great civilization 5,000 years ago, they domesticated the horse and invented the chariot. With their newfound mobility, they ventured far from their traditional grazing grounds. One group, the Angirasas, ventured east, deeper into India, while another group, the Bhrigus, led by Zoroaster (or Zarathustra, as Friedrich Nietzsche would later refer to him[16]) ventured west, toward Persia, and became the Zoroastrians. Along the way, their preferences for the gods evolved. Indra's name is mentioned in the Zend Avesta (Andra), the holy book of the Zoroastrians, where he is depicted as a demon. This clear difference between the Vedas and the Avesta (as well as other evidence) points to the fact that the early Aryans split into two groups that did not get along very well with each other.[17] It is likely that Zoroaster migrated westward from the original home of the Aryans after being persecuted by the followers of Indra, who were becoming increasingly warlike. Serious religious and philosophical disagreements arose between the Bhrigus and the Angirasas. One group's gods (Indra) became the other's demons. Zoroastrianism remained the dominant religion in Persia and much of the Middle East for several centuries.

The Brighus

The Bhrigus favored the worship of the formless (*nirakara*) and supreme god Varuna and preached strict adherence to the path of the Rtá. They disallowed idol worship and insisted on a strict form of monotheism that recognized the divinity of only Varuna, who was to be prayed to through the purifying flame of Agni in elaborate *yajnas*. Their rituals and religious doctrine were initially codified in the Atharva Veda. They did not accept the divinity of the younger gods, such as Indra, who for them were too warlike and aggressive and did not follow the righteous path of the Rtá.

Some Indian scholars have claimed that the Atharva Veda, sometimes referred to as the Brighu Samhita, was at some point formally split into two versions, the Angirasa Veda and the Bhargava Veda (the Veda of the Bhrigus). The former is what the Hindus in India today recognize as the Atharva Veda; the latter was adopted by the Bhrigus and formed the basis for the Zend Avesta, the holy book of the Zoroastrians. Whether this is true is debatable. What is beyond doubt is that the Zend Avesta is very closely related to the Rig Veda and the Atharva Veda. The Zend (derived from the Sanskrit *chhanda*, meaning "meter") Avesta (derived from *apistaka*, meaning "book") literally means "the book of hymns" and comprises four books: Yasna (the book of hymns), Yashta (the book of prayers), Visparatau (the book of Rtá, or right conduct), and Vidaevadata (the book of laws).

The first book, the Yasna, is relatively small (seventeen songs, or *gathas*, composed of 238 verses) but is by far the most important. These hymns glorify the great god Ahura Mazda as one who follows the righteous path, the way of the Rtá—although the term *Rtá* is replaced by *Asha*. Asha is the set of eternal and immutable laws of the universe, which everyone—including Ahura Mazda, the high god—must obey. Asha is the path of righteousness, the greatest good, and the underlying principle that brought the universe into existence and that sustains it. As is the case with Rtá, Asha is also the moral and aesthetic path we must follow. As Rtá is in the Rig Veda, Asha is the central and defining concept of the Zend Avesta.

The Atharvans, or Bhrigus, led by Zoroaster, who was an extraordinary thinker and leader of his time, established themselves as the dominant religious group in Persia for many centuries. Very little is known about Zoroaster's life beyond what he said about himself in the Gathas. He is described as having descended from a long line of *raja rishis* (sage kings) of the Brighu clan who claimed to be descendants of the great Vedic rishi, Vashistha. He describes himself as an *atharvan* (fire priest), a *zoatar* (*hotar* in Sanskrit, meaning "a priest who performs a yajna"), and a reciter of mantras (*mantrono dutim*, YS, 32.13).[18]

The concept of God in Zoroastrianism was similar in many ways to the one in the Rig Veda. In the Zoroastrian system, Ahura Mazda was the primary god, who regulated order in the world. His name is derived from the Sanskrit words *asura* ("the formless god") and *mahat* ("the great one") and was a well-known alternate name for Varuna. Ahura Mazda is described as the creator of the universe, the most wise and benevolent, the upholder of the Asha (Rtá), all-powerful, and protector of the righteous. He was the divine father and the ultimate authority that all other beings must follow.

Zoroaster preached that there was only one God. He was formless beyond any human description and the only one worthy of worship. Zoroaster's uncompromising monotheism was inherited directly from the Rig Veda. He regarded meditation and unfettered devotion to the supreme lord as the only path to discovering the ultimate truth and gaining the favor of Ahura Mazda.

The westward migration of the Aryans into Persia and all the way to the Mediterranean Sea led to the spread of Zoroastrianism throughout a large portion of the Middle East. This ancient religion dominated life in Asia and perhaps parts of Eastern Europe for many centuries until the coming of Judaism, Christianity, and finally Islam. Their ancestors still live in India today, primarily in Mumbai, and form a prosperous and close-knit community, the Parsis.

Inscriptions from the Rig Veda have been found as far as northern Syria and date to about 1500 BC. The Mittani dynasty ruled over Syria during this period. Their local language was Hurrian, the native language of the Anatolian uplands and closely related to the Caucasian languages. As David Anthony pointed out in his book *The Horse, the Wheel, and Language*—

> All the Mittani kings, first to last, took Old Indic throne names, even if they had Hurrian names before being crowned. Tus'ratta I was Old Indic *Tvasa-ratha* 'having an attacking chariot," Artatama I was *Rtá-dhaaman* "having the abode of r'ta" [Rtá], Artas's'sumara was Rtá-smara "remembering r'ta," and S'attuara I was Satvar "warrior." The name of the Mittani capital city Waššukanni, was Old Indic vasu-khani, literally "wealth-mine." The Mittani were famous as charioteers, and, in the oldest surviving horse-training manual in the world, a Mittani horse trainer named Kikkuli (a Hurrian name) used many Old Indic terms for technical details, including horse colors and numbers of laps. The Mittani military aristocracy was composed of chariot warriors called maryanna, probably from an Old Indic term marya meaning "young man," employed in the *Rig Veda* to refer to the heavenly war-band assembled around Indra. Several Royal Mittani names contained the Old Indic term r'ta, which meant "cosmic order and truth," the central moral concept of the *Rig Veda*. The Mittani king Kurtiwaza explicitly named four Old Indic gods (Indra, Varuna, Mithra, and the Nāsatyas), among many native Hurrian deities, to witnesses treaty with the Hittite monarch around 1380 BCE. And these were not just any Old Indic gods. Three of them—Indra, Varuna, and the Nāsatyas or Devine Twins—were the three most important deities in the *Rig Veda*. So the Mittani texts prove not only that the Old Indic language existed by 1500 BCE, but also that the central religious

pantheon and moral beliefs enshrined in the *Rig Veda* existed equally early.

Why did Hurrian-speaking kings in Syria use Old Indic names, words, and religious terms in these ways? A good guess is that the Mittani kingdom was founded by Old Indic–speaking mercenaries, perhaps charioteers, who regularly recited the kinds of hymns and prayers were collected at about the same time far to the east by the compilers of the *Rig Veda*. Hired by the Hurrian king about 1500 BCE, they usurped his throne and founded a dynasty, a very common pattern in Near Eastern and Iranian dynastic histories. The dynasty quickly became Hurrrian in almost every sense but clung to a tradition of using Old Indic royal names, some Vedic deity names, and Old Indic technical terms related to chariotry long after its founders faded into history. This is, of course, a guess, but something like it seems almost necessary to explain the distribution and usage of old Indic by the Mittani.[19]

We do not know how far the influence of the ancient Aryans spread during this prehistoric time. What is clear is that the Aryans who migrated westward had a significant influence on the peoples of present-day Iran, Iraq, Syria, Egypt, Israel, and the entire Middle East—and probably beyond. This is remarkable given the fact that the wheel and chariots driven by horses had just been invented.

The Angirasas

The Angirasas are described as the "sons of the flame." They were more adventurous and less respectful of the ancient gods and traditions. They migrated south of the Indus River Valley, with conquest and adventure on their minds. They no longer worshipped Varuna the righteous, but Indra the conqueror, whose dreaded thunderbolt struck fear in the hearts of his opponents. Indra occupies a central place among later Vedic gods and was the Aryans' Big Guy in the Sky, a demigod representing nature as a battle between good and evil, but he didn't guide their daily life as much as

Varuna had. His role was to ensure that the other nature gods were not hijacked by evil and to guide humans to the path of Rtá, away from evil.[20]

The temporary ascendance of Indra was clearly driven by the Angirasas's lust for conquest. The soma-drinking, thunderbolt-wielding Indra was a far more popular and attractive god for people that were on the move, with their newly tamed horses hitched to their war chariots. The idea of the Rtá would come back to dominate later Vedic thought and philosophy in the form of Brahman, in the Upanishads.

The Decline of Varuna and Rtá

Over the course of time, Varuna became an omnipotent and omniscient god, and he intervened in the daily lives of people. In hymns in the seventh mandala of the Rig Veda, referred to as the Varuna Suktha, his role in the rules of human conduct is laid out in no uncertain terms: Varuna is the keeper of the Rtá, and he demands that we all avoid evil thoughts, anger, lust, avarice, gambling, and cheating, because they are all against the universal order. The impetus to follow these basic laws then came not from a believer's desire to maintain balance in the universe but from fear. As an enforcer, Varuna would punish the evil and protect the good.

By the later Vedic period, the importance of Varuna and Rtá diminished, and other more strident gods like Indra and Prajapati took power. The later Vedic hymns deplore the lack of importance of the Rtá. The poet Kutsa lamented, "We ask of Varuna, the knower of the path, I utter this from my heart; let the Rtá be born anew." In the Yajur Veda, Varuna became the god of life-giving water and the herbs and plants that it nourishes. Through this association, he is also a revered deity in Ayurveda, Vedic herbal medicine. His stature is diminished, and his role is more pragmatic and practical in that it deals with the issues the Aryans faced in their everyday lives. Gone are the fanciful flights of philosophy and the sense of wonder and awe that had inspired the grand vision of the Rtá and its keeper, Varuna.

Is it surprising that a BGITS version of God emerged from the philosophical pinnacle of the Rtá? Perhaps not. The simpler logic of a BGITS God is far easier to accept and comprehend than the rather complex logic of deriving ethical precepts from an abstract conception of a transcendental god needed to maintain order in the universe. The human mind is, in many ways, inclined to accept the BGITS conception of God in favor of any other more abstract conception. So it is no wonder that popular belief laid the grand conception of the Rtá aside and marched forward with more accessible gods, first Indra and later Brahma, Vishnu, and Shiva or Mahesh.

What is unique about the Vedic, or Aryan, belief system is that, despite the many hundreds of gods and goddesses, the concept of an underlying set of universal principles or laws never went away. To a Vedantist, or to most present-day Hindus, personal gods, or *Ishvara*, are essential and, indeed, most important in everyday life. However, it was and still is philosophically self-evident that they (the personal gods) are not really in charge, that they simply personify an underlying consciousness. Our personal gods are simply manifestations of the laws of the universe, and all reality—including the gods—must abide by them.

The concept of the Rtá was pushed to the background, to be discussed by philosophers and rishis while the common man developed his own pantheon of personal BGITS gods to satisfy his emotional needs. The concept of the Rtá all but disappeared from later Aryan writings until the end of the Vedic period, when in a resurgence of philosophical discourse the concept was revived, refined, and renamed *Brahman*. Even though the term *Brahman* appears in the Rig Veda, its meaning and connotation are different from its meaning in the Upanishads (written at the end of the Vedic period).

The Upanishads: Late Vedic Conceptions of God

Vedic thought and philosophy evolved considerably over the next thousand years—after the compilation of the original verses in the Rig Veda. It is impossible to develop a precise chronology of the philosophical developments in the Vedas; the ideas came fast and furious during this incredible period. To quote Bloomfield,

> In the transition from the nature gods, the legends, the ritual, and the folklore practices, to the settled theosophy of later times, many

conceptions flit like phantoms across the vision of these speculators or seers, sometimes not to be heard of a second time. The air is charged with experimental, electric thought. No religious or philosophical literature of ancient times has buried so many "lost children" as the Hindu in the storm and stress period that ends with the Upanishads. No people of thinkers have started to rear so many edifices of thought to be abandoned without regret or scruple when found wanting in the end. They have left behind them many a ruin which they might well enough have finished, and within which the religious thinkers of any another nation, less exacting, would have cheerfully settled upon as permanent and congenial habitations.[21]

Over the course of the Rig Vedic writings, the later mandals, or volumes—particularly the ninth and tenth—begin to take on more philosophical questions about the nature of the many early gods. There was a great deal of dialogue among the Brahmin priests, the masters of Vedic scripture and ritual, and between the priests and kings, who clearly held the priests in high regard but questioned them incessantly, not about matters of state, but about the higher philosophical questions of the time. The dialogue often took the form of a poetic, philosophical question and answer session called a *brahmodya* or "speculation about the Brahman."

The riddles and questions are described in texts all the way from the Rig Veda to the much later Kena Upanishad. These riddles varied in subject matter from the mundane to the cosmic. Sometimes, answers were provided; sometimes, the poet left the questions unanswered and reveled in the unknown. The poets were clearly grappling with questions of natural phenomena and cosmic riddles that perplexed them, and which they were impossibly handicapped to answer. They were, as Albert Einstein would say three thousand years later, "trying to read the mind of God."

This open dialogue, based on a mind open to new ideas, led to the development of at least six major schools of philosophy.

The Six Orthodox Indian Schools of Philosophy

From the sixth century BCE to the fourth century CE, many philosophers, scholars, sages, and rishis developed their own philosophical schools and documented their existence in texts available to us now. Many of their ideas were not new but had been debated for millennia. They were, however, systematized and organized for the first time into a cohesive whole. The term *orthodox* refers to the fact that these schools all accepted the authority of the Vedas and the central ideas inherent in them. We will discuss each of them very briefly and continue our focus on what they said about the nature of God.

Sankhya

Sankhya is one of the oldest philosophies in the Indian pantheon. It distinguishes our true eternal self, or *purusha*, from the material world of objects, thoughts, and desires, or *prakriti*. This is clearly a dualistic philosophy, although the dualism is not between the mind and body, as in the West. Instead, it is between the perceived reality of matter, our mind and its associated thoughts and the "self" that lies beyond the mind and body, the "observer" that dispassionately observes the coming and going of everything that is transitory and impermanent. We achieve liberation, *nirvana*, or *moksha* when we can clearly separate purusha from prakriti and when we realize that our true eternal nature is purusha, not prakriti.

Yoga

If Sankhya is the philosophy, yoga is the how-to manual. *Yoga* means "to yoke or tie together the mind and the body." It is no coincidence that the words *yoga* and *yoke* are similar; they both originate from Indo-European. The legendary Patanjali compiled the *Yoga Sutras* some time in the second or third century BCE. This document is remarkable in its brevity and its density of ideas.

Patanjali lays out eight steps to achieving moksha: Moral discipline comes first, followed by the disciplining of the body and the calming of the mind. This is where the exercises, poses, and practices associated with modern yoga and meditation would best fit in. These have been described in various other texts associated with the practice of hatha yoga. This is followed by a systematic method of controlling the senses through controlled breathing (*pranayama*) and mental concentration on a single object. The final stages of yogic achievement involve intense concentration and objectless focus or complete absorption. In this state of complete equanimity and calm, a person is capable of realizing the true nature of the self, *purusha*.

Nyaya

Nyaya is the Indian school of logic. A group of philosophers associated with this school believed that the only way to achieve salvation and rid ourselves of worldly suffering was to acquire and analyze knowledge about the world around us.

According to the *Nyaya Sutras*, compiled around the second century BCE, there are only four ways in which knowledge can be acquired: direct perception, inference, analogy, and reliable testimony. The *Nyaya Sutras* lay out very clear criteria for distinguishing between valid and invalid inference, limits to perception, and what should be considered valid and verifiable knowledge.

Nyaya philosophers attempted to establish a methodology that clearly would distinguish between fact and fiction. This system of logic was widely used and accepted by all the other Indian schools, in much the same way that Aristotelian logic had such a profound influence on Western philosophy. Within the Nyaya system of philosophy, scholars argued about the existence of God both ways: Some provided detailed logical arguments for the existence of God, while others denied the existence of a supernatural creator.

Vaisheshika

Founders of the Vaisheshika school are sometimes referred to as the *atomists*. This school was started sometime in the sixth century BCE and taught that all matter could be divided into smaller and smaller entities until we reached an indivisible unit, which they referred to as *anu*, or the atom.

For these early rationalists, knowledge could only be acquired through direct observation and inference. The universe consisted of atoms, each infused with its own unique consciousness, properties, and purpose through the Brahman. This made the Brahman the driving force behind the universe. The goal of humanity was, therefore, to understand the nature of the Brahman and how and why it infused the atoms with consciousness. Given their limited ability to empirically observe matter on a small scale, these early ideas may seem primitive. However, they were remarkable in their claim that the world around us could be explained on an empirical and rational basis without the need for a supernatural, interventionist God.

Mimamsa

Teachers from the Mimamsa school of philosophy firmly believed that the path to salvation lay in strict adherence to Vedic rituals and sacrifices. The performance of ritual prayer or the chanting of mantras in precisely the correct intonation would ultimately lead to the unification of what we know as Atman with the Brahman. The emphasis here was on ritual and purity of thought in prayer, not unlike the Confucian ideals and emphasis on the Li (see chapter 3).

Vedanta

The last and by far the most influential of these philosophical schools was the Vedanta school. *Vedanta* simply means "the end or culmination of the Vedas." This philosophical school, therefore, combines the teachings of the ancient Vedic texts with later philosophical developments. The Vedanta lays the foundation for what is now regarded as classical Hinduism.

Toward the end of the Vedic period, the essential elements of Vedic philosophy were distilled into the Upanishads, which contain the philosophical basis and the higher religion of the early Vedas and represent the culmination of the Vedic intellectual tradition. There are 108 Upanishads, with about eighteen being considered the most important. It was a remarkable time of intellectual and religious turmoil in India that set into motion the philosophical traditions that have remained essentially unchanged for over 2,000 years.

The idea of a single supreme being is codified in the Vedanta as the Brahman, the one true reality from which all else flows. The Brahman represents permanent, all-pervading, unchanging reality; all else is transitory and superficial. It is not personified as a godlike entity. Great pains are taken in the Vedanta to distinguish it from the sort of god that can be imagined in human form. Gods are mere manifestations and personifications of the Brahman.

Paradoxically, the Upanishads say that the Brahman is impossible to describe and comprehend. In two famous shlokas of the *Bhagavad Gita*, the Brahman is described as one that weapons do not cleave, fire does not burn, water does not wet, and wind does not dry. In another passage in the Upanishads, the Brahman is described in terms of what it is *not*. *Neti neti*, meaning "not this, not this," is the Upanishads' way of making the important point that the ultimate reality transcends all that is material and impermanent. Since the Brahman is limitless, it cannot be defined in limiting terms.

This abstract concept of a supreme being that defies comprehension is consistent with the older Rig Vedic idea of the Rtá and, indeed, follows directly from it. Varuna, who played such an important role in the Rig Veda, now takes a backseat and becomes just one of the many gods in the pantheon of the Rig Veda.

The human being is perceived as more than body and mind. The Atman originally equated with *prana*, or breath, came to signify the true nature of the self. Equating the Atman with the different pranas that pervade the body must have been a natural offshoot of the idea that there is something essential that leaves the body when it dies, when the last breath causes a person to go from a living being to a lifeless body. It is this last breath that was the original conception of the Atman. In the later Vedas, the Atman signifies more; it comes to mean the true self. It is the observer, or seer, that guides the mind and body and, as such, is distinct from both.

The Vedas make another startling claim: We—all of us and, indeed, all of creation—are intrinsically one with the Brahman. The essence of each individual is indistinguishable from the universal self—the Brahman. The spark of ultimate reality resides within us and is our true nature. This fusing of the Atman (the essential breath and being in all of us) with the Brahman (the universal consciousness), a purely philosophical and mental conception, provides a great monistic convergence that completes one of mankind's great philosophical traditions: Advaita Vedanta.

The true nature of the inner self, Atman, is that it is one with the universal self, the Brahman. This is stated in no uncertain terms in the following two terse sentences in the Upanishads: *Aham Brahamasmi*, which translates to "I am Brahman," and *Tat tvam asi*, which translates to "Thou are That" (again, meaning the Brahman).

The claim that our true self is one with the Brahman is such a departure from all previous and subsequent religious beliefs that it takes some getting used to. According to the Upanishads, the Supreme Being is the universal consciousness that pervades us all. Understanding the nature of the Brahman is the ultimate goal of us all. If and when this goal is accomplished, the soul is liberated and the person achieves moksha, nirvana, or salvation. The world around us is viewed as being full of imperfections, full of petty desires and material distractions that lead to sorrow and frustration. The material world must, therefore, be a poor reflection of the ultimate reality that we should all seek.

A key concept in later Hindu theosophy is that of karma and rebirth. Since the Atman transcends the perishable body and mind, it lives on after death in another body. As the *Bhagavad Gita* puts it,

> Just as a person casts off his worn-out clothes
> and puts on new ones,
> So also does the true self (Atman) cast off an old body
> and enter a new one.[22]

Many commentaries have been written about the philosophical traditions of the Upanishads. Perhaps the most complete are the commentaries by Shankaracharya (or Adi Shankara), one of the greatest exponents of Advaita Vedanta. He lived in the eighth century CE and had a lasting impact on reviving Vedic traditions in Hinduism at a time when a pall of ritual and superstition had been cast over the philosophical gems of the Upanishads. A more recent authoritative and accessible translation and commentary on the principal Upanishads is provided by S. Radhakrishnan, the second president of India (1962–1967). Perhaps even more accessible are the commentaries on the *Bhagavad Gita*, which is a part of the epic *Mahabharata* and is a synopsis or the essence of the Upanishads. Many excellent commentaries on the *Bhagavad Gita* are available in English (Chinmayananda, 1996[23]; Nikhilananda, 1949[24]; Mehta, 1970[25]; Parthasarthy, 2008[26]).

Yoga: The Different Paths to God

Since it is so difficult to know the nature of the Brahman, how can we move toward the ultimate goal of knowing it? The traditional methods of yoga prescribed by Patanjali required the tutelage of a guru, renunciation, nonviolence, pranayama, and deep contemplation. This was impractical for most people who had to work diligently for a living, farmers who tilled the land, or kings and warriors (the *kshatriyas*) who defended their empires. How could they carry on with the duties thrust upon them by the world while pursuing a quest for ultimate truth? Could they also seek *mukti*, or salvation, from the constant cycle of birth and rebirth?

The solution to this conundrum is summarized in the *Bhagavad Gita*, where Krishna himself (an avatar of the god Vishnu) explains to the greatest of the Pandava warriors, Arjuna, how this apparent paradox can be resolved.

The setting for this divine education is the battlefield of Kurukshetra. The two largest armies ever assembled are arrayed before each other, pitting cousin against cousin, teacher against pupil, friends against family. Arjuna, great warrior and yogi that he is, asks his charioteer, Krishna, to drive his chariot between the two armies. As he reviews the battle lines on either side of him, Arjun is filled with dread and doubt. How can he fight and kill his cousins and his teachers? Would that not be against his dharma?

"I do not want kingdom or glory, riches or wealth, palaces or territory if it means that I have to kill my own kin to achieve these ephemeral material things. I would rather walk away from this bloodshed than kill my own brothers. Why should thousands of people lose their lives to satisfy my ambition and ego." Saying this, Arjuna lays down Gandiva, his celestial bow, and tells Krishna that he will not fight because he feels it goes against everything he has been taught.

This is a classic dilemma for all philosopher kings throughout history.

Overcoming evil sometimes requires abandoning the cherished principles of *ahimsa,* or nonviolence. How, then, can evil be vanquished to ensure that peace and order are maintained in this world? Krishna's response to Arjuna's dilemma lays out in exquisite fashion the essence of the Vedanta philosophy. He preaches that it is possible to attain *moksha* in many different ways.

The Upanishads and the *Bhagavad Gita* teach that each person is intrinsically different in their intellectual and psychological makeup and, in their role in this world. We must choose our own path in this most essential of all human missions—the discovery of the nature of the Brahman and, therefore, of the self. The *Gita* broadly categorizes these different paths into four main groups:

- The path of knowledge, or jnana yoga
- The path of action, or karma yoga
- The path of devotion, or bhakti yoga
- The path of physical or bodily perfection, or hatha yoga

These paths are not mutually exclusive, nor are they meant to be hard and fast separators of such human endeavors. They are meant to be guideposts that direct us along paths that best suit our own personalities and play to our inner strengths. I will discuss each of these very briefly, since they offer a glimpse of the incredible philosophical heights the Upanishads attained in defining the relationship between man and God.

Jnana Yoga: The Path of Knowledge

Jnana yoga, or the path of knowledge, is the path that rationalists, thinkers, scientists, and philosophers are inclined to take. It is, the Upanishads and *Gita* claim, the most intellectually demanding path to understanding God. With this path, an individual must, through sheer intellect and mental reasoning, be able to penetrate the impenetrable mysteries surrounding God and creation. Individuals must travel this path alone and discover for themselves the true nature of God. The exploration of nature, the many eastern and western philosophical traditions, and the path of scientific discovery are very much in the spirit of jnana yoga.

Karma Yoga

For most of us who live a life full of daily activities, karma yoga offers us the path to God. Is conducting our daily lives in a righteous manner sufficient to improve our understanding of God, or do we need to do more? Since we must all act to live our lives, are we all karma yogis?

In the Vedic tradition, the answer is no, we are not all karma yogis. Here too, the Vedanta offers a profound and unique perspective and one that I have found to be of utmost importance in the way I conduct my life. In living life, we must perform activities directed at improving ourselves and the world around us, fulfill responsibilities both personal and toward society, and follow a path of righteous action. However, to truly live the life of a karma yogi, the actions must be performed in a specific way.

To be a true karma yogi, a person must not only perform actions to the best of their ability, but the act must be divorced from the desired outcome. This desireless action, or *nishkama karma*, represents the ideal way we should perform all our duties and actions in the world. The elimination of desire is a profound and central aspect of the teachings of the *Bhagavad Gita*. We have the right and duty to perform action, but are not entitled to the fruits of our actions. We should not consider ourselves the cause of the results; neither should we ever be accused of not doing our duty. As we shall see later, teachings of the Buddha and the Tao are strongly influenced by this central idea.

Divorcing the desire for a certain result from our actions may seem completely counterintuitive at first. However, on further reflection, it becomes clear that this is the most effective and efficient way to accomplish our goals and to remain focused and happy along the journey. Including desire in our actions leads to greed, avarice, jealousy, sorrow, and other negative emotions that can be minimized if desire is delinked from the action.

On a personal note, the example I have often given my children is a game of tennis, which my family enjoys immensely. A player who is too focused on the end of the game, or the set, or even the point in play is more likely to lose the point. The winner will focus on hitting the ball well with every stroke and will not worry about the end result. This works every time. Concentrating on the end result is a distraction that takes the focus away from excelling at the immediate task at hand.

I have discovered one other important reason to follow this philosophy: It recognizes the fact that the result is determined only partly by our actions. In almost all instances, the final result of anything we do is determined at least as much by the actions of the people and things around us—over which we have little or no control—as by our own actions.

In physics, this would be called a *many-body* problem. Imagine many balls on a billiard or pool table. The motion of any ball is not controlled by its motion alone but by the motion of the other balls. If we, as individuals, do our best and expect to obtain a reward that meets our high expectations, we will often be disappointed. This is precisely because, although we may be doing our best, our environment (over which we have very little control) may be sometimes more and sometimes less cooperative. This is not deliberate or planned any more than the complex trajectories of all the balls on the billiard table conspire to bounce against each other. Each element in this complex dance follows the laws of physics. The result of this complex interaction among the thousands of elements that make up our environment is impossible to predict and cannot be the product of the actions of one element (me) in this environment. Each element is simply and loyally following the Rtá, the unseen but ever-present laws that govern our universe.

All that an individual can be expected to do, therefore, is his or her best. This does not guarantee a good result, since all the other elements, over which we have no control, must align to ensure a good result. Not expecting the best result in return for our best efforts allows us to reach a state of mental composure and helps us avoid emotional highs and lows.

The ability of a person to maintain a state of equanimity in good times and bad defines a true karma yogi. This equanimity is attained by decoupling the desire of the fruits of our labor with the task at hand. I have personally found this philosophically immensely rewarding, and it has had a profound effect on my life and the way I live it.

Bhakti Yoga

Bhakti yoga directs us to revel in the beauty of God and nature so we can comprehend them better. *Love* and *devotion* are the key words here.

Perhaps no one has expressed this better than Bloomfield in this discussion of a quote from the famous Bengali ascetic Ramakrishna Paramhans:

> By knowledge they discover the Supreme Intelligence and perceive its essence; by devotion (bhakti) they feel the sweetness of the Supreme Being and reciprocate its loving intent. So the *Bhagavad Gita*, the "Song of the Celestial" can finally make the Supreme Being say of the pious man: "Through love he recognizes me in truth, in greatness and my essence. He that loves me is not lost." It comes to this finally, that knowledge of the Supreme Being is but a preparation for what we call love of God. In the words of the modern Bengali saint and ascetic Ramakrishna: "Patience and knowledge of God may be likened to a man while the love of God is like a woman. Knowledge has entry only up to the outer rooms of God but no one can enter into the inner mysteries of God save a lover, a woman has access even to the privacy of the Almighty." And finally the same thinker arrives at the last possible conclusion: "knowledge and love of God are ultimately one and the same. There is no difference between pure knowledge and pure love." You might have predicted the same result. To a religion which strives with all its might to know the truth, truth's sister, love, does not long remain a stranger.[27]

Hatha Yoga

The last of the yogas, hatha yoga, is perhaps the most familiar to most Westerners as simply yoga. Here a person achieves oneness with Brahman through mindfulness, meditation, and physical exercises designed to create a healthy body and a calm, focused mind. In practice this is achieved through the practice of certain poses (asanas), breathing (pranayama), and meditation. For the serious hatha yogi, the ultimate goal is to attain "Samadhi," a state of pure bliss and happiness, completely detached from the cravings and demands of the physical world. Many texts and schools of hatha yoga have emerged over hundreds of years. We can say without exaggeration that the practice of hatha yoga has helped tens of millions of people live happier, healthier lives.

Gautama Buddha: The Enlightened One

Buddha's disciple: What is the nature of God, the Supreme Being, and the ultimate reality?
The Buddha: These questions are not relevant and so do not deserve our attention.
Buddha's disciple: But surely, O Enlightened One, you can tell us what you think is the nature of God.
The Buddha: Let me tell you a story. A person was once shot by an arrow. When his rescuers arrived, he asked them to immediately attend to healing his wound. He did not ask what the name of the archer was, who shot him or which village he came from, what direction the arrow came from, or who made the bow and arrow. If he had wanted answers to all these questions, he would surely have died before he had all the answers. Questions such as these are irrelevant to one who has more urgent and important needs and concerns. Similarly, my friend, our concern in this world is only to see how we can put an end to human suffering, not when and how this suffering came to be and who is at the source of it all. Because if we go down this fruitless path, we will surely be long dead before we can reach any answers.

This legendary tale, often told in Buddhist texts, reflects the agnostic position taken by one of the great philosophical traditions of our time. Buddhism is based on the quest for the true self, as a way to overcome the pain, suffering, and dissatisfaction inherent in the human experience. This path requires careful regulation of the diet, the practice of yoga to train the body, regulated and conscious breathing, and mental contemplation to eliminate the ego and any material desires.

The Buddha was born Siddhartha Gautama, in Kapilavastu (present-day Nepal) around the fourth century CE. His father was the elected chief of the Sakka region, and Gautama was expected to succeed him in this role. It is said that Gautama was a particularly handsome young man, tall, broad-shouldered, and imposing. There are many stories indicating that Gautama was a particularly sensitive, compassionate, and caring individual. He felt a deep empathy for the beggars on the streets and the suffering and pain he saw around him convinced him that the material world, or *samsara*, was full of pain, suffering, and dissatisfaction, or *dukkha*.

This outlook was consistent with the prevailing philosophy of the day. The great Samkhya philosophers had reached a similar conclusion. They had argued that the only way out of *dukkha* was to discover your true self. This process of self-discovery was long and arduous. A person could achieve moksha by systematically severing links to everything material and recognizing that the world we perceive is only a shadow of true reality. Renunciation would have to be followed by a systematic training of the body and mind so that they could be prepared for long periods of meditation and contemplation. This meant careful regulation of the diet; the practice of yoga, physical postures, and exercises to train the body; regulated and conscious breathing (*pranayama*); and mental contemplation (*dyana*) to eliminate the ego and any material desires. It was an extremely demanding regimen that might have been suitable for an ascetic or renouncer but was clearly impractical for a common man.

As he matured into his late twenties, Gautama felt compelled to find a way to end the cycle of human suffering. One day, he left his wife and child as they slept and entered the life of a wandering ascetic. His family must have been shocked and disappointed in his leaving the comfort and safety of the princely existence he had lived since birth to adopt the modest clothes and lifestyle of an ascetic. But he was determined to find a way forward that would lead him to a place beyond the material pleasures and *dukkha* of this world.

As he set out to pursue his dream, he had no grand idea or even a concept of what path he would follow, so he decided to explore the many spiritual paths laid out by the Samkhya sages, yogis, and gurus before him. Remember, this period was one of great spiritual awakening in India, and many influential philosophers and sages debated and preached their own ideologies. He subjected himself to fasting and severe penance, and deprived himself of every conceivable material pleasure, as prescribed by some of the best-known yogis and ascetics of the day. As a devoted student, he followed the way of the Samkhya teachers and before long was a star pupil capable of mastering the art of meditation and exploring the deeper reaches of his subconscious. Despite these achievements, he was still dissatisfied and felt that the mental states that transformed him into states of higher consciousness were ephemeral. He returned to his imperfect existence and the pressures of the material world all too soon. He then subjected himself to extreme physical penance but was equally disappointed.

His experiments and dissatisfaction with the well-established philosophical and religious traditions of the day convinced Gautama that he had to explore his own path to self-realization, or nirvana. He realized that he had been fighting basic human nature that drives us toward things that give us pleasure and physical and mental satisfaction. It may be possible, he argued, to achieve self-realization while maintaining the activities we enjoy with the people we hold dear and participating fully in the world around us. His journey of self-discovery left an indelible impression on his teachings. He would later say, "Never accept the teaching of sages and gurus without questioning it first and ensuring that it appeals to you personally." Constant questioning, regardless of its source, is central to Buddhist teachings. He often said that his disciples should not even accept his own word until they convinced themselves that he was right. His was not the revealed word of God but, rather, the words of an uncompromising individual searching for the truth. He freely admitted that different people may reach different conclusions and different paths to nirvana based on their own investigations.

Gautama meditated to discover for himself the path that human beings should follow to overcome the superficial, transitory *maya*, or temptations, that surround us. How could an individual be free of *dukkha* and liberated from the slavery of everyday material strife? After forty-nine days of deep meditation, while sitting under a pipal, or Bodhi, tree in Bodh Gaya (now in the state of Bihar, India), Gautama attained enlightenment and would henceforth be known as the Buddha, the enlightened one. His teachings were summarized by his pupils and followers based on his many sermons and dialogues.

The Buddha laid out Four Noble Truths:

- The world we live in is full of *dukkha*.
- *Dukkha* arises because of our endless desires and cravings.
- The key to the cessation of *dukkha* is the elimination of desire, lust, and craving.
- The middle path, or the eightfold path, is the way to overcome *dukkha*.

In rejecting the extreme measures adopted by the ascetics and yogis, the Buddha established a middle path. He taught that it was not necessary to go to either extreme—a life of complete renunciation or a life of excessive desires and consumption. In fact, we should live a life of moderation and eliminate the connection between our actions and our desires. To achieve this, he recommended an eightfold path, which consists of Right View, Right Intention, Right Speech, Right Action, Right Livelihood, Right Effort, Right Mindfulness, and Right Concentration.

Through the practice and implementation of this eightfold path, we can achieve the ideal of desire-free action, which ultimately leads to the elimination of *dukkha*. The Buddha was able to eliminate *dukkha* from his life, and even though he was subject to the same physical effects of disease and death as everyone else, the practice of constant mindfulness helped him achieve nirvana—the state of being where he was no longer saddled with the baggage of unfulfilled desires and ambitions. He had soared above the mundane material existence and found inner peace and self-realization by cutting off all connections to those desires and ambitions. The term *nirvana* (or *nibbana* in Pali, the language of the Buddha) simply means "extinguished, cooled off, or put to rest." What the Buddha probably meant by this term was that he had successfully extinguished all desires and cravings, the root cause of *dukkha*.

The similarity between the Buddha's insistence on the elimination of desire from all action and the conception of *nishkama karma* (action with no craving for the rewards of the action) that is preached in the *Bhagavad*

Gita is unmistakable. The Buddha was quite specific about how to achieve such desireless action. By being mindful of every thought that crosses our mind and every action that we perform, no matter how mundane, we can achieve this path to self-realization. It is through this mindfulness that a person can shed the false facades of the ego, realize his true self, and develop compassion and kindness toward all creatures.

It is important to note the absence of any supernatural being in this theology. There is no need to invoke god or any such metaphysical entity. This is a radical departure from all other religions. For most religions, the concept of the Supreme Being is at the very center of all theological and moral discussions. Buddhism remains deliberately silent about the existence of god.

Buddha's ethics and morality were derived from his eightfold path; it did not require the postulation of a higher authority. He clearly denied the existence of a BGITS God who could intervene in human affairs. There was no heaven or hell, no necessary god or devil, no rewards or punishment for good and bad actions. In fact, the Buddha was probably one of very few religious teachers who remained completely agnostic to the existence of God.

Summary

The religion of the Veda provides a grand conception of God, not as a capricious, all-powerful being that intervenes directly in human affairs but as the very laws that govern the universe. The essence of man is, in fact, the essence of the universe. There is one eternal truth of which we ourselves are part. The unity of the self, Atman, with the universal being, Brahman, is the central and overarching idea in the Upanishads and the Vedas. The concept of the Brahman flows directly from the idea of the Rtá.

Later, Samkhya, Vedanta, and Buddhist philosophies would look deeply into the self, not only to examine the subconscious mind and its potential, but also to explore different means of self-discovery. It would seem that such diverse philosophical traditions would have very little in common, but when we compare them, we find a great deal of similarity and a deep-rooted common thread that runs through them all:

- They freely acknowledged that theirs was not the only path to God, to salvation, or to self-realization. They were tolerant faiths that coexisted for thousands of years with no historical evidence of major religious conflict. Samkhya philosophers lived side by side with Vedic and Buddhist philosophers and openly debated and discussed their disagreements.
- None of these religious traditions was based entirely on the revealed word of God as documented in religious scripture. Every one of them was based on the religious and philosophical teachings of sages and men of learning who perhaps had a better concept of the supernatural and of the inner workings of the human mind and spirit.
- None of the founders of these faiths claimed to be God, godlike, or even a messenger of God. Although later clergy may have, in some instances, ascribed godlike attributes to the founders of some of these religious traditions, this was certainly not part of the original teachings.
- No one group claimed to have the complete answer, but—as should be the case—they provided a menu of answers and questions for us to explore and choose from. Many of these faiths encouraged their followers to question tradition and to find their own path, guided by the light of the teachings of wise men and women who preceded them. These are questions, after all, that may not have a single answer that satisfies us all.

This was indeed an age of wonder, when our ancient ancestors truly sought to resolve some of the most difficult questions we face as human beings with very little science to guide them. It was an age of discovery and genius, in a time of primitive scientific understanding, that led to some of the most profound speculations about the workings of the human mind, the soul, the nature of God, his creation, and our role in it all.

3

The Ancient Egyptian, Chinese, and Greek Conceptions of God

As the Aryan peoples were exploring the eternal questions and reaching the philosophical pinnacle of their achievements in the Vedanta, different interpretations of religion and God were being explored in Egypt, China, and Greece. During the years between about 600 and the birth of Christ, we see a remarkable number of great teachers all over the world, such as the Buddha, Confucius, Lao-Tzu, and many Greek philosophers. They taught and preached radical new ideas on morality, religion, and God, charting unexplored philosophical frontiers.

Our discussion in this chapter covers a large swath of history in diverse places with vastly different traditions. It is important to briefly delve into the history and culture of these peoples to fully appreciate the reasons they developed different conceptions of God. We will focus primarily on these conceptions of God along with morality and religion, and will place these central themes in the context of the social and political ethos of the day.

The Gods of Ancient Egypt

There is more archaeological data available about Egypt than about any other ancient civilization. This makes it possible to document in reliable detail the evolution of many aspects of Egyptian civilization over 3,000 years. As in most ancient civilizations, the gods in ancient Egypt were primarily nature gods. They were, in every sense of the term, BGITS gods. People prayed to them to seek favors and for blessings in this life and the afterlife. The gods were all-powerful entities, each with their own sphere of influence. There were gods of the sun, the moon, the rain, the wind, love, war, harvests, sexuality, rivers, and even perfumes. A partial list of some of these gods is provided below.

- Aah, the moon god
- Amun, the air god
- Atum, sun god and creator
- Baal, the war god
- Hathor, the cow goddess
- Ishtar, goddess of war and sexuality
- Isis, goddess of love
- Meskhenet, goddess of good fortune
- Nefertum, god of perfume
- Neith, goddess of war
- Neper, god of the harvest
- Nut, goddess of the sky
- Osiris, god of death
- Ra, the supreme solar god
- Seshat, goddess of writing
- Shu, god of the wind

Within this extensive pantheon, some were more important than others at different periods in Egyptian history. New gods were added as the Egyptian empire expanded, and older ones were sometimes forgotten or discarded. Some gods from conquered peoples, such as Baal, a god of the people of Canaan, were incorporated into the pantheon. The pharaoh was anointed at his coronation as the Son of God. With this divine authority came the dynastic tradition.

Amun-Ra, the Highest God of the Pharaohs

One of the most ancient and powerful gods in the Egyptian pantheon was Amun. In hieroglyphs from the fifth dynasty, Amun is represented as the god of air, perhaps to signify his universal presence and invisible nature. His name means "the hidden one." Unlike every other Egyptian god, Amun had no physical form. He was an invisible force that transcended the physical world. He represented all that is good and holy and therefore sat alone above the pantheon of other nature gods. Temples were built throughout Egypt to celebrate the glory of Amun, including the Luxor Temple and the great temple at Karnak. During the Opet Festival, dedicated to Amun, his statue was taken by boat from the temple at Karnak to

Luxor, where his marriage to Mut was celebrated. At this festival, Amun was celebrated as the creator. The three deities—Amun, Mut, and their son, Khonsu, the moon god, who make up the Thebes Triad—were worshipped and celebrated.

Through many centuries, Amun was associated with different animals. In the early dynastic period, he was mostly associated with a goose or a ram, as a symbol of fertility. In later hieroglyphs, he is represented in anthropomorphic terms, as a man with a crocodile or ram's head. These depictions are not meant to demystify his transcendental nature but are used as a matter of convenience for representing him in physical terms.

Since Amun was so difficult to comprehend and describe in physical terms, he was frequently associated with and worshipped together with other physically revealed gods. The most famous among these is Ra, the sun god. Amun-Ra is the best known and most powerful god in the Egyptian pantheon, who represents the union between the source of power behind the gods (Amun) and the sun god (Ra), creator of the universe. This was a clever pairing of the nonphysical properties of a god, such as goodness, holiness, justice, and the ability to create, with a physically recognizable and vitally important symbol—the sun. Amun was also associated with other gods to convey the idea that these gods were imbued with the same holiness as Amun.

The religion of Amun-Ra was so pervasive and deeply entrenched that Egyptians believed that Egypt was blessed and ruled by Amun-Ra and that the pharaoh was simply his instrument. Amun-Ra took the form of the king when he impregnated the queen to provide a successor to the throne. The word of Amun-Ra was conveyed to the king through oracles and priests, who became increasingly powerful as time passed. In some instances, this religious fervor posed a significant challenge to the power of the pharaoh. For instance, during the reign of Akhenaten, in the twenty-first dynasty, the pharaoh made a valiant attempt to revise people's worship of Amun-Ra and was almost overthrown for it. This pattern would be repeated many times in history, when the clash between clergy and royalty would dominate the politics of the state and the lives of its citizenry.

Maat: The Source of Order in the Universe

Early Egyptians were well aware of the recurring patterns in nature. The order and predictability of these natural cycles indicated that there was some underlying force that established and maintained this order. The Egyptians observed this order in nature and ascribed it to Maat.

Maat controlled the physical and moral order in the world. She was the daughter of Ra and wife of Thoth and bore eight children. The most important of these was Amun; the rest were the primary gods of the temples at Hermopolis and were the creators and caretakers of the universe.

Maat is often depicted as a woman wearing an ostrich feather in her hair and holding a scepter in one hand. Many of the Egyptian kings are depicted with ostrich feathers to represent their devotion to her. She is also represented as the mound where Ra stood to create the world and where he set in motion the principles of Maat that govern the world.

The ostrich feather had another important significance in Egyptian society and religion. The Egyptians believed that the heart of a dead person was weighed against the ostrich feather by Anubis. In later Egyptian tradition, Anubis was replaced by Osiris as the gatekeeper of Aaru. The scales used in the weighing symbolized Maat. If the heart was heavier than the feather, it implied that it was burdened by evil and sin, and the dead person's soul would be consumed by Ammut, the lioness, and he would be condemned to live forever in the Duat (the underworld). If, however, the heart was lighter than the feather, he would be granted eternal life in Aaru (the Egyptian version of eternal heaven). This explains why the heart was left in Egyptian mummies while all other internal organs were removed.

Maat literally means "truth" in Egyptian, and she signified everything that was pure, just, and orderly in the universe. Even though she is portrayed as an actual goddess in hieroglyphs and in writing, her true significance lies in the fact that she stands for the fundamental concept of goodness in Egyptian religion. The rulers of Egypt, each and every one of them, periodically expressed their loyalty to and love for her. Many of them incorporated Maat into their royal titles. To do so was to signify their commitment to order and justice in the kingdom. The Egyptian justice system in place from 2500 BCE was based on the recognition that societal ethics and laws must be based on principles laid out by Maat. Because of this, the minister of justice and the judges themselves wore emblems that contained depictions of Maat. It was the duty of every Egyptian citizen to live their life in accordance with Maat and help preserve her order.

Maintaining this order required harmony among all humans and nature, which was achievable through proper rituals and sacrifices to Maat. Social norms and ethics were based on commonsense laws that ensured the preservation of harmony but which had to be blessed by Maat. The Egyptians understood very well that if Maat didn't exist, Nun, the god of chaos, would reclaim the world.

This may sound familiar; it is very similar to the Aryan concept of Rtá. It is remarkable that two great ancient civilizations developed such similar fundamental religious beliefs. There is no evidence of one civilization borrowing or being influenced by the other. There is certainly no mention of Maat in the Vedic texts or of Rtá in Egyptian hieroglyphs or papyrus writings.

There are also important differences. Maat existed as both the principles that govern the universe and a goddess. She was on the same plane as the gods, who were all imbued with the principles of Maat. The goddess was prayed to with elaborate rituals. The priests, oracles, and the king could communicate with her and convey directives from her to the people. Maat the goddess embodied justice and the rule of law, as laid out by the gods. You'll notice this is different from Rtá, which transcended humanity, nature, and even the gods, who also had to abide by it.

Despite their differences, the concepts of both Rtá and Maat underscore the importance that these ancient civilizations placed on the order and organization they observed in the natural world around them. The natural cycles of nature, the rise and fall of the tides, the waxing and waning of the moon, and the movement of the stars must have fascinated them. The grand notions of Rtá and Maat were their recognition of these ordered natural phenomena. While they were clearly inadequately prepared to provide any explanations for them, they did recognize that an explanation must exist. Rtá and Maat were representations of this universal, eternal set of laws—whatever they might be.

The Gods of Ancient China

Early China: The Sons of God

Some of the earliest archaeological finds trace Chinese culture to the Shang dynasty in the Yellow River Valley between 1600 and about 1000 BCE. The Shang believed in an all-powerful god whom they named Di. He was omnipotent, omniscient, and almost completely controlled the world in which the Shang lived. The success of the harvest, the flooding of rivers, and battlefield outcomes were all controlled by the will of Di. If the Yellow River flooded, as it very often did then surely Di was displeased. If the rains failed and hunger and famine afflicted the people, Di had to be appeased. In short, this high god had all the characteristics of a BGITS God. The kings of the Shang dynasty believed that they were the sons of Di. In the words of Karen Armstrong,

> It was said that Di, a supremely powerful deity who usually had no contact with human beings, had sent a dark bird down to the great plain of China. The bird had laid an egg, which was eaten by a lady. In the course of time, she had given birth to the first ancestor of the Shang monarchs. Because of his unique relationship with Di, the king was the only person in the world who was allowed to approach the High God directly. He alone could win security for its people by offering sacrifices to Di. With the help of his diviners, he would consult Di about the advisability of undertaking a military expedition or founding a new settlement. He could ask Di whether or not the harvest would be successful. The king derived his legitimacy from his power as a seer and intermediary with the divine world, but on a more mundane level he also relied on his superior bronze weaponry.[1]

After a king died, he was believed to live with Di in heaven. This belief imparted divine status not only to Di but to all the royal ancestors, who were worshipped as gods in their own right. This concept of ancestral worship ultimately percolated down to the masses and had such a large impact on Chinese culture that it is practiced in many parts of rural China even today. When a king or nobleman died, he was buried with great ceremony.

Lavish wealth and ornaments were buried with the deceased, along with sacrificed animals and soldiers that he would need in the afterlife. Tombs of kings excavated from this period show the remains of sacrificed soldiers placed all around the king's coffin, along with the few remaining valuable artifacts that survived the ravages of time and looting.

The worship of ancestors was an integral part of all ceremonies meant to appease Di. Elaborate rituals were developed to appease the spirits of the deceased. At these ceremonies, Di no longer remained an abstract high god; instead, his material creations and manifestations on earth were appeased. The earth, the sun, the wind, and the rain were part of the pantheon of nature gods, but they were ultimately controlled by Di. Prayers to Di or the ancestors were usually inscribed on cattle bones or turtle shells, thousands of which have been excavated.

Di could be an unreliable god. Despite the king's best efforts to communicate with him, floods, famine, death, and disease persistently plagued the region to such a degree that people began to question the power of Di and his influence on the forces of nature. Over time, his importance diminished, and the prayers were primarily directed toward ancestors and the nature gods.

The end of the Shang dynasty came quickly around 1000 BCE, when the king's army was defeated by noblemen from the Zhou peoples. But Zhou nobility had a problem explaining their victory: Since kings were anointed by the gods, the Zhou seemed to have defied them by triumphing over the Shang kings. How could they prove their own divine mandate? Their explanation was simple. Di had looked down on the Shang rulers and concluded that they had been cruel and unjust. He had decided to strip the Shang of their heavenly mandate and, instead, bestowed that trust and mandate on the Zhou rulers. The people's cries for justice and mercy had been heard.

The introduction of the idea that the gods would only support a king if he were just and compassionate was entirely new and had a lasting influence on Chinese thought and politics for centuries to come. For the first time, a king could only maintain his God-given right to rule if he was ethical and had the best interests of his people at heart. Sacrifices and rituals alone were no longer sufficient to placate the gods.

Although this overarching philosophy might suggest that the Zhou would somehow change the political and social status quo, they did not. Instead, ancestral worship and the worship of the nature gods and the divine right of the kings continued as it had for the past eight hundred years. Religion and politics were indistinguishable. The king was the political as well as the religious head of his empire. He was the *tianzi*, the son of heaven, and as such, his word was God's word. Although the concept of a god who transcended this world remained, it had no practical meaning, since he spoke and acted through the king.

The king was divine and all-powerful, but he was also responsible for behaving in accordance with the *Tao*—"the way." In principle, this meant that his social policies and military campaigns were determined by a higher authority. In practice, it allowed the king to be an absolute monarch, as long as he followed the Tao by ascribing his decisions to Di and performing the requisite ritual duties precisely. This, the Zhou kings did with great pomp and splendor.

Rituals and sacrifices—known as the *Li*—became ever more elaborate and the rules and procedures more carefully defined. They were used to preserve political and social order, so that society would operate smoothly in accordance with the Tao, the way heaven intended it. Over time, these rituals became more public, and large numbers of people participated in them. Many of the ancient Chinese classics describe these rituals in excruciating detail. During the annual spring planting festival, the king and queen auspiciously began the season by plowing their own land. Large numbers of inhabitants of the capital city and surrounding areas gathered to celebrate the coming season. Sacrifices were made to all the elements of nature, in particular to the earth god. The importance of conducting each detailed element of the ceremony perfectly became increasingly important. The Chinese believed this pleased the ancestors and the gods and, for a few brief moments, allowed the living to experience the heavenly abode of their ancestors.

Heaven and earth were closely linked and formed a part of one continuous whole. Human endeavors were considered to be a part of the divine process. When the farmer tilled his land or the soldier vanquished his enemies, they did so in accordance with the Tao, as part of the divine plan to maintain order in the universe. The Chinese were still an agrarian, feudal society that had not turned inward to reflect on the significance, meaning, or efficacy of these rituals. For them, the cause-and-effect relationship between their rituals, honed to perfection, and the favorable attention of the high gods was reason enough to continue the age-old tradition.

Quoting Karen Armstrong again,

> The *Record of Rights*, a text that was only completed after the Axial Age, remarked that the Shang had put the spirits in first place, and the rites second, but the Zhou put the rites first and the spirits second. The Shang had wanted to use the rituals to control and exploit the gods, but the Zhou had intuitively realized that the rites themselves contained a much stronger transformative power.[2]

Confucianism: God in Ritual

By about 500 BCE, the Zhou dynasty declined, and provincial noblemen became increasingly rich and powerful. With no central authority, they openly flaunted the rules and etiquette so carefully laid out by the Zhou. A man named Kong Qui came into prominence during this politically turbulent time; in the West, we know him as Confucius. Kong was born and raised in a family of modest means. His aim as a young man was to gain political office and serve in one of the royal courts. He was remarkably unsuccessful in this pursuit. His real passion, however, was the study and practice of the Li, which he firmly believed could bring China back to the glory days of the early Zhou rulers.

Many of the practitioners of the traditional rites had lost their positions of influence and had become disillusioned with the new political order. The principalities ruled by noblemen were constantly at war. The political order and peace derived from a strong central presence had been shattered. All of China yearned for peace, stability, and order. Confucius was convinced that to restore that order, the people must return to the Tao. He recognized that as a commoner, he could not define the Tao, but he could educate the people and the noblemen about it. Confucius recognized the old rites and rituals as the only way to the rightful path of the Tao. It was obvious to him that the root cause of the social evils pervading society was the greed and egotism that had taken over the mind-set of the nobility. To restore order, one must return to the path of the Tao by careful observation of the Li.

Confucius was careful to point out that he was not preaching anything new but was reintroducing concepts that had long been established in the Li.

In fact, Confucius's approach was different from the traditional approach. For ritualists during the Zhou dynasty, the Li focused on rituals and detailed ceremonies to honor the gods and the ancestors. To Confucius, the gods in heaven mattered little. He was much more concerned about more practical and mundane matters related to how kings, noblemen, and commoners should live their lives. When asked about God and heaven, Confucius was careful to avoid speculation about such metaphysical matters. He always deflected such questions by saying it was more important to serve humanity than to speculate about matters humans knew so little about and that we must first serve humanity before we can serve the gods. This sage advice rang true for most Chinese during these trying and uncertain times, when their primary concern was survival—not speculation about the mysteries of the universe.

Confucius traveled extensively, preaching his love of the Li. He took on many disciples—from commoners to noblemen. His only requirement was that they be open-minded and enthusiastic about learning. He was a man of the world who enjoyed the company of whoever cared to listen and debate matters of import to society. He was clearly a compelling personality and a well-loved teacher. Many stories tell of him tirelessly debating matters with students, only to ultimately admit he had been wrong and accept the point of view of his younger colleagues. He was, in fact, as much a student as his pupils were. His refreshing, down-to-earth attitude was clearly appealing; crowds thronged to listen to this unassuming preacher. His was not the word of God but a bold restatement of the ancient wisdom of the Chinese people. His was not a metaphysical discourse on the mysteries of the universe but a pragmatic approach to living a good, happy, and fulfilling life.

Through the understanding and practice of the Li, we can achieve proper balance in life and ensure that all human beings respect each other and work together in harmony. The perfect gentleman, a *junzi*, was not a person born to such privilege or a person who could impose his rights by force, but a person who followed the way of the Tao. Incessant wars and the heavy price paid by ordinary peasants and farm workers were a direct result of the nobility straying from the Tao. The early Zhou kings had focused on ceremonies in ancestral temples with prayers and sacrifices purportedly to please their god. But almost invariably, the ceremonies were a flattery of whoever had commissioned them. A person's status in society was determined in large part by how elaborate his rites had been.

Confucius spoke out vehemently against this interpretation of the Li, citing the ego and human vanity as the primary causes of society's evils. The practice of the Li applied not only to physical acts but, more importantly, to the conducting of these rites in the correct spirit. A person must first replace his personal ego with a sense of humility and self-effacement, service to society, and respect for others. These feelings of empathy and service to our family and, ultimately, to our fellow human beings are the true hallmarks of a *junzi*.

The rites must be performed in the spirit consistent with what he called *Ren*. The word is difficult to translate. What it represents is the quality in a human being that allows him or her to relate in a humane way with others. A person following the way of the Ren would be kind and understanding, generous and gracious, and have perfect mastery of the Li. He would act without egotistical baggage and for the good of others. If everyone, including kings and nobles, behaved in this manner, there would be no wars and no political struggles for power. Note how similar these teachings are to those of the Buddha. This may explain why Buddhism was so widely accepted in China later.

This interpretation of Li was a subtle but important departure from the traditional attitudes that had pervaded Chinese society for millennia. Confucius transformed the Li from a purely ritual practice to an ethical framework. If society could follow such ideal, ethical, and moral directives, there would be no need for God or heaven. This movement away from debates and discussions about God and his intentions was in many ways unique to the Chinese philosophers. Nowhere else in the world were philosophers so pragmatic and focused on societal issues as in China. For them, ritual and ceremony became a vehicle on which society's entire ethical edifice could be delivered and thrive. Confucius cleverly used the ritual tools that the Chinese had revered for centuries while giving them a new twist of pragmatic ideals that had a lasting impact on Chinese society for centuries to come.

The Concept of Qi: Looking Inward

For a century after the death of Confucius in 479 BCE, the warring Chinese states were consolidated into three major empires. Trade and industry grew, and a new level of prosperity developed in the central plain of China. Large cities developed in the provinces. By about 300 BCE, the city of Linzi established an academy to promote the study of the Li. The academy's thinkers and philosophers were generously supported by the king and, in this period of relative calm, developed their own ideas about God and the self.

It was during this time that the Chinese began to look inward. Many Chinese philosophers of this time thought that to truly become a *junzi*, a person must look inward and discover their true self. Although the Confucians had focused on societal interactions with the outside world, these thinkers redirected a person's focus and attention inward. An enlightened person should meditate in quiet contemplation, emptying his mind of desires and passions, and focusing on the true nature of his being. The term *qi* can be best translated as the essence of all forms of matter—what gives it form, shape, and its unique qualities. When something dies or is transformed into something different, its qi remains. Everything around us, including ourselves, is pervaded by qi.

In looking inward and meditating, we can discover the true essence of our inner self. To achieve this, we must free the mind of all desires, feelings, and emotions and contemplate the qi. In this way, a person will experience an inner calm and peace that truly was the way of the Ren.

If these ideas seem similar to the inward-looking philosophies of India, it is perhaps no coincidence. In this period, trade and travel between China and India was increasing. Ideas and philosophies were for the first time being exchanged between China and its neighbors. There is extensive historical documentation to show that Buddhist influences in China came about as a result of extensive cultural and social exchanges with India.

Taoism: The Tao Te Ching

At about the time of the later Upanishads and about 200 years after the death of the Buddha (between 500 and 300 BCE), the *Tao Te Ching* was written by Lao-Tzu, the founder of Taoism, the second most important philosophical or religious movement in China.

Lao-Tzu's life is shrouded in mystery; the only records we have are those maintained by the imperial court of the Chou dynasty. In fact, Lao-Tzu was a keeper of the imperial archives until he retired into seclusion as an old man. The date of the *Tao Te Ching* is uncertain, but estimates vary between 500 and 300 BCE. It is estimated that Lao-Tzu was about twenty years older than Confucius, who had great admiration and respect for the older master. Conversations between the two are documented in several ancient texts such as the Li Chi Confucian texts.

The *Tao Te Ching* does not represent the thoughts of a single individual but the collective wisdom of many generations of Chinese. It is the compiled knowledge of a great many masters and ordinary people and represents the spirit and intellectual traditions of the time. It is not a religious text and does not refer to any of the ideas as being revealed by a divine source. It is very much a practical commentary on how a ruler should rule, how a man should live his life, and what his relationship should be with the world around him. In the process Lao-Tzu invokes some of the most elegant poetry and imagery seen in ancient texts.

WHAT IS THE TAO?

The *Tao Te Ching* emphasizes the importance of living a life that is in tune and in harmony with the Tao. But what *is* the Tao, exactly? I have selected some verses from one of the better translations of the *Tao Te Ching* that elucidate the nature of the Tao. The very first verse expounds on the nature of the Tao.

> The Tao is both named and nameless.
> As nameless it is the origin of all things
> as named it is the Mother of 10,000 things.
> Ever desireless, one can see the mystery;
> ever desiring, one sees only the manifestations.
> And the mystery itself is the doorway to
> all understanding.[3]

> Tao is always nameless.
> Small as it is in its Primal Simplicity,
> It is inferior to nothing in the world.
> If only a ruler could cling to it,
> Everything will render homage to him.
> Heaven and Earth will be harmonized
> And send down sweet dew.
> Peace and order will reign among the people
> Without any command from above.[4]

It is hard to miss the similarity in this description of the Tao with the essence of the universe as defined by the Rtá. Both represent a single universal truth that is difficult to comprehend yet remains at the center of everything in the universe. All creatures must abide by the Tao. This nameless entity is not given form or substance or embodied in any godlike figure. In fact, the thoughts expressed in these verses could very well have been written by the creators of the Rig Veda many centuries earlier.

KARMA YOGA AND THE TAO

Many of the verses in the *Tao Te Ching* offer advice on how to live a noble and happy life. Quite remarkably, the similarities between the Tao concepts in these verses and Buddha's Four Noble Truths and the karma yoga ideas of *nishkama karma* (the act of working without desire for a certain outcome) are stated in simple and elegant terms. Clearly, the way of the karma yogi is in complete conformance with the Tao.

> Tao never makes any ado,
> And yet it does everything.[5]

The Tao also teaches us the importance and wisdom of doing without the desire to accumulate wealth and satisfy the ego.

> Learning consists in daily accumulating;
> The practice of Tao consists in daily diminishing.
> Keep on diminishing and diminishing,
> Until you reach the state of Non-Ado.[6]

The non-doer is not a person of inaction but, as in the Vedantic and Buddhist teachings, a person who clearly dissociates his own ego and desires from the action. Anyone who craved material things was not an enlightened soul and was not following the Tao. This is the way of the karma yogi in the Aryan traditions as well.

The rules for governance are also prescribed by the Tao much the way the Tao governs the way humans live their lives: A ruler should strive to govern in accordance with the Tao. Only then will he be loved by his subjects and admired by his peers.

One striking aspect of the *Tao Te Ching* is that it scarcely mentions a supernatural being, much less a BGITS God. Tao's conception is not one of an entity to which one must pray for favors but a code of ethics and conduct that leads to a fulfilling life. It is a recipe for social harmony through personal introspection and behavior modification, where no claims of divine revelation or intervention are made or implied. Indeed, the Tao, while it is mysterious and difficult to define, remains well within the rational realm, with no need to invoke the supernatural to embrace it.

The Spread of Buddhism in China

We have already spoken about two of the important philosophical traditions of China, Confucianism and Taoism. The third and most recent philosophical and religious movement in China was Buddhism. By about 220 CE, the collapse of the Han Dynasty led to a period of uncertainty and turmoil. Traders from the West had established the Silk Route over the Himalayas, and were continuously exchanging goods, services, and ideas with other Asian civilizations such as those of India, which extended at the time all the way to present-day Afghanistan.

We know about the history and the spread of Buddhism from the writings of several well-known Chinese scholars who traveled to India and studied at Buddhist monasteries and universities, such as the famous university at Nalanda, which flourished from 400 to 1200 CE, when it was sacked and burned to the ground by marauding Turkish invaders. The most famous among these scholars was Xuanzang, who studied in Nalanda for a period of sixteen years. He returned to China with over seven hundred volumes of Vedic and Buddhist writings in Sanskrit and Pali. The emperor, who had been informed of Xuanzang's incredible journey and his scholarship, established a seminary for him and commissioned him to translate seventy texts into Chinese. These translations, which were clearly influenced by the Taoist upbringing of many of the translators, led to the many schools of Chinese Buddhism. Vedic concepts such as dharma and nirvana found new Chinese interpretations

It is surprising that Buddhism was able to establish a foothold in China considering it was foreign to a land that already had well-established homegrown philosophical traditions. Buddhist texts had to be translated into Chinese, and their ideas and traditions did not include traditional Chinese customs such as ancestor worship. Perhaps it was a combination of clarity of thought in the Buddhist texts, royal patronage, or the similarity to local pragmatic traditions that led to the widespread adoption of Buddhist practices. Whatever the reasons for Buddhism's success, by about the sixth century CE there were over 30,000 Buddhist monasteries and over two million practicing Buddhists in China. A multitude of Chinese Buddhist schools emerged from the amalgamation of Buddhism with Taoism.

Chan Buddhism ultimately made its way to Japan via Korea in the form of Zen Buddhism. Buddhism was married to the indigenous Shinto traditions to provide a uniquely Japanese version of Buddhism.

Early Greek Civilizations: The Minoans and Mycenaeans

The oldest known Greek civilization, the Minoans, were a peace-loving people that flourished in the Greek islands and Cyprus from about 2200 BCE to 1300 BCE. Excavations of ancient Minoan sites show very little evidence of war or weapons. They built impressive, elaborate palaces and, as best we can tell, prayed to nature gods. As with every other culture of this age, they had a tradition of animal sacrifices to placate the gods. The kings ruled with the authority of the gods, many of whom would form the core of the Greek pantheon.

In about 1650 BCE, the Minoans were overthrown by the Mycenaean Greeks, who had built themselves powerful war chariots and an impressive army, likely based on their interaction with the Hittites. Archaeological digs of the Royal Shaft Graves at Mycenae have been dated to that time, which coincides with the rise of the Hittite Empire in Anatolia. Both of these empires declined at the same time in about 1150 BCE, probably ravaged by the sea peoples who plundered the coastal cities of the Mediterranean. As we have noted earlier, the Hittites, the Mittanis (who ruled northern Syria), and the Mycenaeans were Indo-European people with traditions dating back to the early Aryans, as evidenced by the fact that all the Mittani kings took on Indic names such as *Rtá-Dhaaman* (having the abode of Rtá) and *Rtá-Smara* (remembering Rtá) derived from the traditions originating in the Rig Veda.

The Mycenaeans worshipped the sky and the thunder through the king of the gods, Zeus. Poseidon ruled the oceans. Many other nature gods were worshipped in temples throughout Greece. Much of what we know about them is through the writing of later Greek classics that lionized the Mycenaean warriors and kings. Well-known characters in *The Iliad* and *The Odyssey*, which were written over 1,000 years later, were derived from stories and legends passed down orally from generation to generation. These writings represent only a small portion of the pantheon of poetry and prose that the Mycenaeans created over their 500-year empire in Greece. The Trojan War and the stories of Achilles and Agamemnon are well known to the modern western world. These characters and their military exploits tell a tale that rings true, even today. They are men of character and honor caught in circumstances quite beyond their control. Others, such as Odysseus, tell of a fantastic journey into unknown and uncharted waters that fascinated these early seafaring Mycenaeans. Later Greek civilizations would revere this period of heroism and accomplishment and would be inspired by its characters and legends.

The Early Greek Gods: An Unruly Bunch

The Mycenaean civilization disappeared just as suddenly as it appeared. We are not sure what caused the sudden demise, but for a period of about 500 years, Greece and the area around the Mediterranean went through what are called the Greek Dark Ages. There was no dominant kingdom or empire to rule over the many archipelagoes that dotted the Mediterranean and Aegean seas. Local chieftains fought for control over their local territories. It was a world of uncertainty and strife, with a constant struggle for military superiority and incessant fighting between rival cities and local tribes.

It is no wonder, then, that from this social and political milieu emerged a pantheon truly different from any others highlighted in this book. Traditional gods in most cultures would be benevolent to the good and downright ruthless toward those who did not believe in them. The Greek gods were different. Greek mythology tells the story of the creation of a race of gods that was full of incest, lust, and violence. This story must reflect the Greek ethos at the time. At first, there were two primordial gods, Chaos and Gaia (the earth god), each of whom had children of their own. Gaia first gave birth to the heavens (Uranus) and the sky, followed by the oceans, the mountains, and rivers. Gaia then slept with her son Uranus and gave birth to the first race of gods, the Titans. Uranus hated his children and forced them back into Gaia's womb. Desperate to give birth to her twelve Titan children, Gaia asked her unborn children for help. In response, the youngest boy, Cronus, cut off Uranus's penis the next time he penetrated Gaia. Cronos then became the leader of the Titans, who then mated among themselves and gave birth to the next generation of Titan gods, some of whom we are familiar with today, such as Prometheus and Atlas.

The story of the children of the other primordial god, Chaos, is even more involved and confusing. We will not get into that story here. It suffices to say that Greek mythology of this era seems to be preoccupied with patricide, incest, and violence. There is an overpowering sense of tragedy and pessimism overshadowing all else. It was almost as if the Greeks had made up their mind that the gods were cruel and that any good news was only temporary and would be followed by calamity. This mind-set would not change substantially, even during the development of later Hellenistic traditions that remain one of the most influential cultural and philosophical traditions that the world has ever seen.

The Beginning of the Greek Philosophical Tradition

By the eighth century BCE, the Greeks had established small city-states and were trading actively with coastal towns all along the Mediterranean. With trade came prosperity and a period of peace and stability. From this point forward, the Greeks would develop a sophisticated array of philosophical traditions that has influenced Western civilization to this day. However, their religious doctrines, practices, and gods remained tied to the pantheon of the ancient Mycenaeans. With no move toward monotheism, the Greeks reorganized and reestablished ancient mythological tales and with them elaborate rationales justifying their existence.

While on one hand, the Greeks made a great deal of effort to reconnect to their ancient past in their religious and mythological traditions, they were moving rapidly forward as a society and establishing new social orders and political structures. City-states (or *poleis*) were established throughout Greece. As these city-states grew in size and sophistication, battles for control erupted frequently. Each polis was forced to arm and equip all its citizens, regardless of social status, in time of war. This was the beginning of the hoplite army. All able-bodied men were obliged to defend the polis.

As they trained and fought together, a new sense of equality among all citizens emerged. Every citizen of a polis had the same rights and responsibilities. Matters of social and religious import were openly discussed and debated. Truly egalitarian laws were formulated and implemented for the first time. There was no clear demarcation between farmers and warriors as had been the case in most ancient agrarian societies. The nobility and princes were no longer isolated from the common man. There was no god-given right for a particular class of people to rule their subjects. Depending on the will of the people, the heads of state could be removed from power and replaced with a more acceptable and competent ruler. These ideas were revolutionary for the time. Indeed, Greece was unique in the implementation of such egalitarian ideas. While the rest of the world would continue its feudal and agrarian ways, the Greeks would go in a different direction.

They had laid the foundations of a truly democratic system of government that would form the basis of later western democracies. This had a profound effect not only on Greek society, but also on the philosophical traditions that would emerge from such an open and free society. This does not mean that Greece did not have its own share of kings, emperors, despots, and tyrants over the course of its history. These, it would appear, came about despite democratic ideals. Their reigns were, however, shorter-lived and less tyrannical than those of other less-democratic societies.

Gods in Pre-Socratic Greece

The formation of hoplite armies and the continuous threat of war had one other important consequence. It led to more logical and pragmatic discussions in society, rather than any soul-searching philosophical discussions about the nature of God. There was no time for conjecture when faced with daily life-or-death situations. This meant that logic—*Logos*—carried the day in both physical and metaphysical matters. Whether it was a lack of rainfall, the failure of a harvest, or the building of a chariot, logical explanations lay within reach of human cognition, and the solutions lay well within human ingenuity. The gods might be pleased or displeased, but humans must do their part to ensure that the physical world around us was molded to our needs and desires.

The gods played an important but complementary role relative to a mortal human hero in most Greek ceremonies. Because the gods lived up in the high heavens and were immortal, they were not as concerned about human affairs as the gods in the Indian or Chinese traditions. They were neither compassionate nor cruel, but rather indifferent to the human drama that every Greek hero endured. Indeed, in *The Iliad* and *The Odyssey*, Homer portrays his human heroes with much more gusto and vigor than he does any of the gods. The gods watched an entire saga but were largely spectators when the true hero—a human—took center stage. As a result, the gods did not evolve much during this incredible period of social change. There was no introspection or soul searching as happened in India and China, no flights of philosophical fancy speculating about the nature of the Supreme Being. The Greeks remained rooted to their traditional gods.

Homer's writings were so influential that his version of the pantheon of Greek gods became widely accepted. This considerably simplified the pantheon and made it much more logical and understandable. The gods were considered part of the human experience, not some otherworldly beings that controlled the activities of nature or mankind. The Greek mind did not usually look for supernatural explanations to worldly events. Even though the gods might involve themselves in human affairs, they did so with indifference, detached amusement, or curiosity. An Olympian who excelled at sport was blessed by Pelop; if a warrior achieved fame on the battlefield, he was imbued with the spirit of Ares, the god of war. There was no metaphysical mystery to be resolved; everything that happened in this world happened for a reason and in accordance with Logos. For the Greeks, the supernatural was, in many ways, subject to the same rules that the physical world was.

The Milesean School: The Origins of the Scientific Method

The ancient Greek city of Miletus is of special significance because it is there that we find the first evidence of a group of philosophers discovering natural laws and using them to explain the workings of the world around them. Miletus is located on the western coast of Anatolia and was probably founded at the time of the Minoans. It was occupied during various phases of its history by the Babylonians, the Persians, and the Hittites, from whom the Greeks took it in about 400 BCE.

The founder and most prominent citizen of Miletus was a philosopher named Thales, born in about 620 BCE, who was later quoted and referred to by Aristotle and Plato. Although we know very little about him, Aristotle wrote that Thales was able to predict complex natural phenomena, such as solar eclipses, by using a postulated set of natural laws. The writings of Thales indicate an acceptance of the idea—at least among the intelligentsia—that natural phenomena could be explained on the basis of simple natural laws and without the need for theology. This was a radical departure from the past, and it would prove to be a controversial idea for the next 2000 years.

Pre-Socratic philosophers such as Pythagoras and Thales laid the foundations of the scientific age by using simple rules of geometry to estimate the height of pyramids and the distance to incoming ships. These rather practical uses of geometry were seen as useful and important, and they allowed Thales to become a person of some importance both politically and in business. He believed that earthquakes occurred because the earth floated on a sea of water and disturbances in this sea resulted in movements in the earth. He also postulated that all natural materials were derived from water and that "Everything is water and the world is full of Gods."[7]

Thales's great contribution was not the proper scientific explanation of complex natural phenomena but his proposition of the radical idea that natural phenomena could be thought of in terms of natural laws, deductive reasoning, and rational thought. This was unthinkable for most people at a time when divine intervention and gods' will were the only explanation that anyone could conceive of.

Today, with the benefit of 2,500 years of scientific development, we expect to be able to precisely predict and observe not only solar eclipses, but also supernovae and other cosmic events unknown to the ancients. Today, if a person were to suggest that a volcanic eruption or a drought was the result of the wrath of God, most of us would dismiss him or her as rather uneducated and uninformed. There are well-established models built on scientific principles that provide an explanation of such natural phenomena and perhaps, more important, what—if anything—can be done to prevent or prepare for them. No human or animal sacrifices are necessary to appease the gods. Something a lot more fruitful can be done to ensure people's well-being: This is the power of the scientific method and of viewing God in the proper perspective. Thales got this scientific ball rolling by thinking about natural phenomena in an entirely new way, using nothing more than his favorite tool: Logos.

Socrates and Plato

About 400 BCE a short, pudgy young man was wandering the streets of Athens passionately discussing anything and everything that anyone wanted to talk about. Socrates came from a humble stonecutter's family, and even though he had no philosophical training or education, he became a master of logic and reasoning. He applied these tools not to the metaphysical questions of God or creation but to the more pragmatic questions of how we should live our lives and make the world a better place. In this sense, he was like the Buddha or the Chinese sages.

To achieve these ideals, he said, a person must understand what it means to be ethical. Only through this knowledge and the examination of our own preconceived notions can a person strive to be good. This examination of our minds and souls is essential to understanding our inner being, or *psyche*. Here, for the first time, is a Greek philosopher deeply examining the nature of the self, a topic that was the focus of the Indian sages. For Socrates, the purpose of human life was the proper understanding and cultivation of the psyche. This ultimately led a person to consistently perform correct actions and to be successful in the world.

Socrates is probably best known for the method he used to help people with this process of self-examination. He would begin a discussion on a topic of his pupil's choice, usually one that the pupil thought he knew a lot about, and through a series of relentless questions, Socrates would prove to the hapless student that he actually knew very little about the subject, and that the answers that emerged were often very different from what the student had initially believed. This dialectic form of education is now known as the Socratic method. It involves a persistent inquiry into a subject until the discussion has revealed the core elements of the topic and the answers to some of the fundamental questions are laid bare.

Socrates was not trying to impose his views or ideas on anyone. On the contrary, his method was two-sided, and neither side knew the answer to begin with nor even knew which way the discussion would ultimately lead. This was and is the true appeal of the Socratic method: There was no established dogma and no predetermined answers. Every individual could discover the truth for himself.

The people of Athens were hooked. Young and old alike flocked to dialogues Socrates organized. Through dialogue and the power of Logos, he resolved some of the deepest mysteries and paradoxes brought to him. A Socratic dialogue was not just a logical exercise, but also an emotional experience. The purity of the intent and the laser focus of the practitioners no doubt resulted in unexpected twists and turns and revelations. This was not the Logos of the Sophists, who argued for argument's sake without reaching conclusions of any practical import. Ultimately, the participants emerged from the dialogues with Socrates's intended result: They resolved matters they had been unable to resolve in any other way, and thereby headed off to lead a better and happier life.

Quite often, the conclusions went against well-established norms and traditions. This meant that the socially and religiously conservative members of society were offended by Socrates and his method, which they claimed was blasphemous and would lead to divine punishment. Letting go of the crutch of established dogma was too hard to digest, so when things began to go wrong in the Peloponnesian War, and Athens's star was on the decline, people began to look for a scapegoat.

By this time, Socrates was seventy years old and had lived a full life and made his share of friends and enemies. He was a model citizen. He had fought in the Peloponnesian War, abided by most Orthodox Greek customs and traditions, and other than his penchant for discussion and debate and the resulting controversy, he had done nothing to displease the ruling elite. It was, however, a dark and pessimistic time for Athens. The famous plays of Euripides, with their bleak characters and unforgiving endings, were playing more to the Athenian psyche than anything Socrates could provide.

He was put on trial for corrupting the youth, disrespecting the gods, and introducing unauthorized and unacceptable new gods. Socrates defended himself by asserting that he had always worked for the betterment of Athens and its people. He had never had any goal in his life other than to ensure that people could better their lot and improve their lives through honest self-examination. The judges at his trial were unconvinced, and he was sentenced to death. His friends and pupils encouraged him to go into exile, an option that he refused. Socrates believed in Athenian justice, and even though he felt he had been wrongly sentenced, he preferred to face his sentence as a good man would.

His most famous pupil, Plato, attended his execution and was deeply disturbed by the proceedings. Socrates bathed himself and, surrounded by friends, quietly and calmly drank hemlock, the prescribed poison. His contemplation of the world around him had clearly bestowed on him the ability to follow his own teachings of never seeking retribution for an act of violence. His legacy would continue on through his many friends and pupils who so greatly admired his teachings.

Plato was thirty years old when Socrates was put to death. Unlike Socrates, he came from an aristocratic family and was very much a man of the world. Under other circumstances, he would have entered the world of politics and, like his ancestors, sought a position of political authority in Athens. Instead, disillusioned by the political establishment, he dreamed of philosopher kings who would bring order and justice to the polis. He travelled to the other Greek islands and established ties with Socrates's other pupils and like-minded philosophers.

His response to the political instability around him was to found the Academy, a school of philosophy and mathematics on the outskirts of Athens. Here, Plato and his colleagues and students met and discussed, in a Socratic manner, far-ranging issues from politics to mathematics. Arriving at the truth at the core of any of these issues required an extensive exploration of the facts, empirical observations, and the application of systematic and methodical logic.

This method was not an exposition of well-thought-out conclusions passed from a teacher to a pupil, but an open-ended discussion that led inexorably to some logical conclusion, not unlike the Brahmodyas of the ancient Aryans in India. The sequence of dialogues was by no means meant to constitute a logical progression of thoughts. Instead, it is clear from the many written texts that Plato moved from one dialogue to another rather whimsically, sometimes applying the logic and conclusions of one to another entirely different and unrelated set of issues. What emerged from what we would now call "brainstorming sessions" was a coherent philosophy that laid the foundation for later western intellectual traditions.

Plato recognized the impermanence of the material world around him. Objects decayed and were constantly changing with time. Plato argued that there must be something that transcends this ever-changing landscape of the material world. This transcendent reality, which represents the essence of all reality, must be unchanging, perennial, and permanent. He termed this underlying reality the *forms* or *modes* of reality. His *theory of forms* thus claims that it is possible to discover through proper intellectual training a level of reality that goes beyond the physically perceived objects around us. Every object in the material world, whether it be animate or inanimate, has an underlying, unchanging form associated with it that defines its essence.

Therefore, a table or chair has its obvious attributes, which are perceivable with our senses, such as the quality of its wood, the size of its legs, the color and smoothness of its surface, and so on. However, beyond these obvious physical attributes, which will change over time, the table also possesses some underlying forms that define its essence. These forms could include the laws of geometry that control its construction or the form or shape that defines the concept of a table in our mind. These forms are permanent, regardless of the physical changes of the table. Any philosopher or mathematician must, therefore, seek to look beyond the obvious physical attributes of the world around us and instead focus on discovering the world of forms that underlie and form the essence of the physical world.

To explain the doctrine of the forms to the people around him Plato turned to one of the most famous allegories in Western thought, the parable of the cave. In his most famous book, *The Republic*, Plato attributes to Socrates the story of a group of men who have been tied to chains in a cave so that their faces are turned away from the sun. All they can see are the shadows of the external world on the cave walls. What would reality look like for this group of men? The flickering shadows on the cave walls would be their reality. They would be completely unaware of the beauty, complexity, and true nature of reality outside their cave. Similarly, the physical attributes of the objects around us are but shadows of the true nature of these objects—their forms—which so permanently and completely describe their essence.

Plato recognized that few people in society would have the ability, courage, patience, or desire to recognize and understand the deeper essence of the universe, and in fact those who did would probably not be readily accepted by society. Socrates was well aware of this problem, too. Indeed, if some of the men chained in the cave freed themselves and saw reality in all its glory, it would not be easy for them to convince the others that such a reality even existed. This change of perception must come gradually; otherwise, the unchained people who have been exposed to the true nature of reality would be branded as liars, traitors, or madmen. However, it would be their duty to return to the cave and ensure that the others are slowly but surely made aware of the true nature of reality. This is their God-given duty and responsibility to society.

The Influence of Hellenic Rationalism on the Concept of God

Plato was by no means unique in looking for permanence in an apparently transient material world. As we saw in the previous chapter, Confucius found his permanence in the Li, the ceremony and ritual of his ancestors. For Lao-Tzu, the Tao was the underlying essence of all reality. For the ancient Aryans, the Rtá and the Brahman underlay all reality. Each of these philosophical pioneers was looking for something beyond the transitory, material world. The one big difference that separates Plato from the others is that he saw this transcendent reality as being accessible to all human beings through rational thought. He firmly believed that the application of logic would reveal the true nature of reality to any human being who made the effort. There was nothing supernatural or incomprehensible, from the human perspective, about the true nature, or *forms*, of reality. This firm belief in the ability of mankind to look beyond the obvious physical characteristics of objects and delve into the underlying forms that comprise their essence and their nature was to have a transformative effect and drive humanity from the mystical to the rational.

The goal of all men now became the logical understanding and conquest not of the world of objects but of the world of forms that lay hidden and immutable underneath the physical world of objects. So while human existence on the surface may be full of chaos and misery, this was not the real world but a pale shadow of the ultimate reality that every human being has the ability to grasp through logical reasoning—without resorting to divine intervention. This was the path to immortality and the land of the gods.

For the Greeks, the place for gods still remained in the heavens. They had crafted this earth and the stars above, but it was not within their power to control mankind's destiny. That lay within a comprehensive logical framework defined by the forms. Even the gods played within this framework of forms and Logos. The concept of a divine being concerned about the everyday events in a human being's life and intervening in human affairs would have been preposterous to Plato. The existence of a BGITS God would be inconsistent with his doctrine of the forms. The universe was governed solely by a logical set of rules, and its true nature was revealed in the forms that underlay every physical object.

Plato realized that this rather abstract conception of the underlying nature of reality was not going to mean very much to the less philosophically inclined. For them, the idea of not offering prayers and sacrifices to Zeus, Athena, and Poseidon in return for favors seemed completely counterintuitive. After all, these Olympians guarded over Hellenic interests for many millennia, and their temples and priests adorned every polis and every home. The Greeks could not abandon these age-old traditions, or, in Socratic terms, move the shadow-watching cave dwellers to see the light of day, in a short period. Plato, therefore, accepted the role of these gods, but reduced their status. The gods could not be placated and changes to the human condition could not be achieved by prayer, ritual, or sacrifice to the gods. Instead, the festivals, rituals, temples, prayers, celebrations, and sacrifices that were so common to everyday Greek life were a means to an end. They helped put us in the right frame of mind to guide us to the path of Logos. They helped guide people to lead moral and ethical lives, bring inner psychological peace, and avoid social conflict. It is clear, however, in Plato's writings that these activities are subservient and inferior to the pursuit of philosophical and logical arguments and conclusions that lead to a clearer understanding of the forms. Logos was the path to the one true, ultimate, permanent reality.

The Republic outlines the ideal republic as one ruled by a philosopher king rather than a democracy. Everyone in the republic must conform and accept the supremacy of the forms and the method of logical reasoning. For Plato, any opposition to this viewpoint should result in capital punishment. There was no room for dispute or disagreement. The uneducated must be properly educated and trained so that they all accepted his ideal societal view. If they refused to accept this orthodox philosophy of logic, they would be executed. Poets would be restricted in what they could write. Tragedies such as the ones made so famous by Euripides would be banned, since they detracted from the primary goal of understanding the nature of the forms of reality. Any activities, writings, or speech that elicited negative emotional responses would be not only discouraged but banned. Plato's Utopia would certainly not comport with the utopian ideals of the more tolerant sages in the East. It was a totalitarian theocracy that afforded no compassion or mercy for the nonbeliever. It was left to his brilliant student and successor, Aristotle, to review and revise this rather stark viewpoint and make it more humane and democratic.

Aristotle: The Founder of Modern Rationalism

Aristotle, perhaps more than any of the Greek philosophers, stands out as a giant among his peers and predecessors. This is perhaps because he was standing on the shoulders of giants. He assimilated and integrated the best of the Hellenic thought that had come before him, organized it, and presented it in a logical framework as had never been done before. His contributions extend from biology to metaphysics, from philosophy to politics.

Aristotle was born in 384 BCE in the Greek colony of Macedonia. His father was a physician for the king, and Aristotle grew up playing in the royal household with the king's son Philip. His father afforded him every luxury and ample opportunity for an intellectually stimulating atmosphere. Aristotle arrived at Plato's Academy when he was eighteen years old and spent the next twenty years as a loyal but rebellious student of Plato. He mastered the Socratic method and, true to its spirit, debated and questioned his teacher's teachings.

Aristotle established a reputation for himself and when his friend Philip became king, he asked Aristotle to return to Macedonia and tutor his son Alexander, who was then a rather wild thirteen-year-old ball of fiery energy. For two years, Aristotle tutored the young Alexander and established a close relationship with him, doing his best to influence his worldview. However, Alexander had world domination on his mind, and before his teenage years were over, he embarked on expeditions that would ultimately lead him to conquer all the known lands between Greece and India—an empire more vast than the world had ever seen.

Aristotle retuned to Athens and established his own school, the Lyceum.

Being the tutor of Alexander the Great, he had enough resources and recognition to build a cadre of eminent assistants and scribes. Very soon, he was attracting many more students than he could accommodate, and he was forced to restrict entry into his school to the very best and brightest. As it turned out, this allowed Aristotle to be prolific in his writing and his ability to gather and analyze data. It is likely that some of his students compiled his notes and materials into compendia that took the form of books. Aristotle wrote several hundred books in a relatively short life span, including a series of books related to logic and the method of logical deduction.

ARISTOTLE THE PHILOSOPHER

As he better understood Plato's theory of forms, Aristotle began to question it and became increasingly convinced that the separation of an object's physical attributes from its form was artificial. Indeed, he was convinced that it may not be useful to separate and study the forms for their own sake. Certain abstract ideas and philosophical constructs are beyond the physical attributes of the objects. Many of these abstractions are beyond human understanding and therefore of very little value to humans. Instead, he focused his attention on studying the physical attributes of the objects themselves. He found enough mystery and interest in these objects to occupy him for the rest of his life.

One of the key differences between Aristotle and Plato is that Aristotle was not too concerned by the temporary or transitory nature of reality. In fact, he found this impermanence particularly interesting. This meant that he did not seek an underlying reality that was unchanging, immutable, and permanent. For Aristotle, change was good; permanence was death. For him, the process of material transformation and evolution was more important than studying any underlying permanent structure that may or may not exist. He focused on a much more pragmatic approach, a study of the material world.

ARISTOTLE THE LOGICIAN

More than any other ancient Greek philosopher, Aristotle should be credited with establishing the methods and rules of logical reasoning. By carefully defining every aspect of logical reasoning, he took this once loose and poorly defined art and converted it into a well-defined science.

Man is the only rational animal capable of reasoning and logical thinking, he noted. We must therefore apply this rationality to understand the ultimate nature of reality. Aristotle established specific logical rules that laid the foundations of philosophical reasoning. He understood the structure of a logical argument, and by starting with axioms and applying acceptable logical rules until the full argument could be put in place, he arrived at an incontrovertible conclusion. For him, human well-being depended on the application of such logical methods to questions and problems of everyday life. Unlike emotions, which could be subjective and variable, the complete objectivity of logical argument allowed humans to unravel universal truths.

ARISTOTLE THE SCIENTIST

The Greeks had established quite a track record of philosopher scientists, such as Thales, who had developed some basic ideas about astronomy, and Democritus, who postulated that all matter was made up of atoms. Aristotle took these hypotheses and imbued the ideas with the rigor of logic.

The tool that Aristotle used to study the changes that occurred in matter and in nature was a rational thought process, which he had learned so well from his teacher and which he perfected. His passion from an early age was biology. He gathered data on plants and animals and studied their characteristics in more detail than had ever been done before. He was fascinated by how an egg slowly converted into a chicken and how a seed could grow into a tree. He wrote books on physics, astronomy, and science in general. He postulated theories about the movement of the planets and the nature of objects in motion. His insights were not dramatically different from those of other scientists of his day, and he was frequently wrong, but the breadth of his writings is truly astounding. He single-handedly created a compendium of the scientific knowledge known to man at that time. Perhaps most important, he showed that it was possible for humans to rationally explain the world around us without invoking supernatural beings and divine intervention.

In addition to being a committed logician, Aristotle was an empiricist.

He was fascinated with changes that occurred in nature, such as the growth of plants, trees, and animals. He carefully measured, gathered data, and charted the growth of plants and investigated the organs of animals by dissecting them. By combining his measurements with logical reasoning, he found that he was able to unlock these mysteries. Here was the beginning of the scientific approach to understanding nature.

ARISTOTLE'S CONCEPTION OF GOD

Aristotle noted that every change was caused by something he called *the mover*. As he reasoned his way to the ultimate cause of the universe, he postulated that there must be an "unmoved mover," an "uncaused cause," which he defined as God. This inevitable starting point for any logical argument about the origin of the universe was the Supreme Being, or form, that existed apart from the material world. Aristotle's unmoved mover was very different from the Olympian gods, in that he had no interest in daily human activity and no involvement in worldly affairs. As was the case with Plato, Aristotle would have rejected a BGITS definition of God and, in fact, found it to be a rather ludicrous proposition.

His view of the traditional Greek gods was even less forgiving than Plato's. Plato had allowed for the possibility that the traditional Greek gods were interested and involved in human activities but were unable to intervene because all worldly activities were regulated by the forms in accordance with Logos. For Aristotle, this was a dubious assumption with no proof or logic to back it up, so he rejected the idea out of hand.

He did, however, recognize the need for people to worship gods and goddesses, and he attributed this to the innate human need for emotional satisfaction. In this regard, Aristotle understood human nature and religion in far more subtle terms than did Plato. He clearly understood that human emotions were just as important as rationality and that neglecting one or the other would lead to an incomplete mental image of reality. So although Plato refused to accept the need for poetry, literature, the theater, or any art form that elicited an emotional response, Aristotle believed that they were essential for the good of society. For Aristotle, it was important not only that people think logically and accept an idea rationally, but also that they be emotionally convinced of its validity. To accomplish this, it is sometimes as important to play on emotions as it is to inspire the intellect.

Summary

We have covered a lot of historical and geographical ground in this chapter. I have briefly described three incredible philosophical traditions, as they evolved in different parts of the world, that laid the foundation for later religious, social, and political movements. Many of these philosophical and religious traditions, such as Confucianism and Greek philosophy, continue to have a strong influence on the religious and social fabric of our society, whereas others, such as the Egyptian gods, have been swept away by the tides of history.

Each of these traditions is unique in how it deals with the question of God. They do, however, have some common traits that distinguish them from later Abrahamic traditions. Neither the Chinese nor the Greek religious traditions asked their followers to unconditionally believe in the teachings or writings of their great philosophers and teachers. Quite the opposite—they encouraged a questioning mind that would lay bare the fundamental human questions that the writings were trying to address. For them, it was not a matter of belief in a "revealed word" but rather an open debate in which they themselves had a very clear and poignant point of view. Some of them, such as Confucius, did not even address the question of God, because they felt such questions were irrelevant to a person leading a happy and productive life.

None of the founders of these traditions, with the exception of the Egyptian pharaohs, thought of themselves as prophets, gods, or even sons of God. They all saw themselves as reformers, philosophers, mystics, or poets. They made no claim of divine revelation or paranormal intelligence. Any direct or implied affiliation with God is the product of organized religions that sprang up after their original teachings. It is important to recognize these key points because they are such a radical departure from the core beliefs of Semitic religions—Judaism, Christianity, and Islam—which are all based on the revealed word of God.

Socrates, Plato, and Aristotle deviated substantially from every other conception of God in this period of human history. They were the only ones brave enough to conjecture that the ultimate reality, whatever it might be, was discoverable and understandable through human experience and reason. No longer were metaphysical and supernatural explanations necessary. The power of the gods had been usurped by logic and human intellect, which now had the ability to systematically uncover the many layers of the ultimate reality. In many ways, Aristotle set the tone for the Western intellectual tradition. His ideas and influence would pervade Western thought for the next 2,000 years and would lead to the next big change, the scientific revolution. But before we discuss that, we need to understand the Semitic traditions.

4

The Age of Belief: Judaism, Christianity, and Islam

Well over half the world's population nominally associates themselves with one of the Abrahamic religions: Judaism, Christianity, and Islam. I say *nominally* because many state they are not practicing members. These religions are, by far, the dominant faiths today and our religious, literary, social, and political dialogue revolves around them. I have grouped them together because of their common roots, their common history, and their many common beliefs. This chapter, titled "The Age of Belief," reflects a period of human history where belief in religious doctrine was formalized into religious texts that are still accepted today by believers to be the word of God. Religious doctrine and the clergy were organized on a scale never seen before or since. God's word, as delivered in holy scripture in each of these faiths is a matter of deeply held *belief*. *Faith* in the primacy of the word of God, as spelled out in these scriptures, became paramount in all three Abrahamic religions.

Every sentence, every word, in the Old Testament, the New Testament, and the Koran—the Holy Scriptures of Judaism, Christianity, and Islam, respectively—have been scrutinized, analyzed, and written about in elaborate detail by religious scholars for many centuries. It is not my intent to get into such detailed interpretations and analytics. My goal is more modest: It is to present, in broad brushstrokes, the conception of God and his relationship to mainstream believers of the three faiths and to put these conceptions into the context of the historical evolution of other faiths and philosophies.

One more caveat—each religious tradition has a rich and diverse history, and many religions allow for and have a diversity of beliefs. Sometimes, differences exist between the way the religion is practiced today and some of the writings in the original religious texts, given that many diverse offshoots have emerged over the years. It is not my intent to define in detail each denomination of each religion (that would require several volumes of text by an author much more qualified than I am) but to broadly define how, in the practice of these religions, God is perceived by a vast majority of the adherents of each religion and how each dominant religious belief has evolved over time.

The religions are discussed in historical progression. Our exploration begins with the analysis and discussion of the concept of God within the Jewish tradition since it is the forerunner, in some sense, of the concept of God within Christianity and Islam. To respect this chronology, the analysis of the Christian concept of God follows that of the Jewish ideal. This arrangement not only accurately introduces the developmental sequence of these major world religions, but also helps explain from a doctrinal and cultural perspective the world in which Jesus and Muḥammad shaped and preached their faiths.

Judaism

Abraham: The Common Link Between all Three Abrahamic Religions

The story of all three religions begins with the story of Abraham. The legend as related in the Book of Genesis tells the story of Abraham, a tribal leader of nomads who worshipped the one true God, Yahweh. This was in contrast to the worship of many gods, which was common practice at the time. He was a resident of Ur (what is now northern Iraq and Syria). God appeared to Abraham and promised him that his people would be as numerous as the grains of sand and that he and his people would have a promised land. The only thing asked of Abraham was that he continue to exclusively worship the one true God and that all males in his tribe be circumcised on the eighth day after their birth. This covenant, which is central to the story of Abraham, permeates the holy books of all three Semitic religions. Jews and Christians would later come to believe that

Abraham received the covenant simply because he was an obedient servant of the one true God.

Abraham and his wife, Sarah, did not have any children and, therefore, no heir or successor. Sarah suggested that Abraham allow Hagar (their handmaid) to bear his child so that succession could be ensured. Soon enough, Hagar bore Abraham a son named Ishmael. Although this was originally Sarah's idea, as you might imagine, she did not take kindly to either Hagar or to the heir apparent, Ishmael. At Sarah's bidding, Hagar and Ishmael were banished from the tribe and sent out to wander in the Negev desert. The Old Testament suggests that God was responsible for their survival in this hostile and unforgiving environment and that Ishmael and Abraham (who came looking for him later) built the Kaaba, a small cubical structure (now in the city of Mecca), which was destined to become a focal point for all three Abrahamic religions.

Later in the story of Abraham, Sarah miraculously gives birth to a son, Isaac. The Old Testament tells us that God ordered Abraham to sacrifice this son. Abraham went to the desert determined to follow Yahweh's command, but at the last moment, God intervened, asked Abraham to spare Isaac's life, and rewarded Abraham for his unquestioning obedience. This story is clearly meant to demonstrate Abraham's devotion to the one true God.

Isaac had two sons, Esau and Jacob. Esau was the firstborn, but there are biblical stories about how Jacob (whose name God changed to Israel) stole the role of the firstborn and became the forebearer of the Israelites. Jacob had twelve descendants, who went on to become the founders of the twelve tribes of Israel. This now-large family of Abraham—the Israelites—flourished in Egypt. However, over time, the pharaoh enslaved them, and they remained in his service for over 400 years. This was clearly retribution for the Israelites' worship of Yahweh, their one true God. The pharaoh was, the Egyptians believed, the son of God, and all his subjects were expected to pray to him in elaborate temples constructed in his honor. Egypt was too small to accommodate both Yahweh and the pharaoh.

The Book of Exodus brings the character of Moses center stage. In about 1250 BCE, he was chosen by the Israelites to go to the pharaoh to seek permission for the Israelites to leave Egypt. The pharaoh was not pleased but conditionally conceded. One dark night, Moses led the Israelites across the Sinai as the Egyptian army pursued them. Many of us in the West know the famous story of the parting of the sea and how God protected the Israelites from the pursuing Egyptian armies. The Book of Exodus tells many stories of the miracles that Moses performed to ensure their safe passage and conquest of the Promised Land. It also tells us that Joshua led the Israelite armies into Canaan, destroying all the Canaanite towns and killing every man, woman, and child and establishing the rule of Yahweh in the process. Moses, therefore, played a central role in delivering his people safely from their enslavement in Egypt to Canaan, the land of their ancestors. It would take many heroic battles and many decades of war before the Israelites would ultimately conquer the tribes of Canaan and establish the larger and more prosperous Kingdom of Israel in the north and the Kingdom of Judah in the south. The exodus of the Israelites from Egypt is mentioned in both the Old Testament and the Koran, although the Koran mentions it only in passing.

There is some doubt about the historical accuracy of the Old Testament version of events. Archaeologists have found no evidence to support the theory that the Israelites migrated to Canaan from Egypt or that they conquered the region. We shall not delve into or try to resolve this controversy. What is true beyond a shadow of a doubt is that the region we now know as Israel, Syria, and Jordan was inhabited by a large number of tribes who were frequently at war with each other in a bid to establish supremacy and that these tribes shared many common gods and religious and social customs.

El and Yahweh: Early Gods of the Israelites and the Transition to Monotheism

El had been the historical God of the inhabitants of Canaan. Biblical texts indicate that Abraham and his ancestors all worshipped El and his retinue of lesser gods. These divinities formed an assembly of gods in El's divine court that included the king of the Canaanites, who on his coronation was accepted as one of the sons of El. These sons included Yahweh and Baal, who were both warlike gods, among others who were less prone to aggression.

Theirs was not yet a single, monotheistic religion. Indeed, it can best be described as a diverse group of cults that prayed to one or more divinities.

Some tribes preferred to worship Baal, a fiery storm god who led them in battle and helped vanquish their enemies. Curiously, Baal wielded a thunderbolt, just as the ancient Aryan god Indra did. Perhaps this is a coincidence; perhaps it is an Aryan influence that has not yet been established. By no means the only gods, Yahweh and Baal did dominate the early Canaanites' worship. One or the other of these sons of El would ascend in popularity, depending on the success of a tribe on the battlefield.

The Israelites, regardless of whether they were an invading force returning from exile in Egypt or a congregation of local tribes, changed the religious landscape by insisting on allegiance to their one true God, Yahweh. The Arc of the Covenant was a physical symbol of the unwritten treaty among the different tribes who accepted Yahweh as their supreme God. If one tribe were under attack, the other tribes who were part of the group— the *Am Yahweh*—were duty bound to support their brethren. Temples were erected to honor Yahweh, and the Arc of the Covenant went from temple to temple to renew the common religious bonds. This solidarity among a few select tribes that sprang from a suddenly-discovered monotheism gave them a distinct advantage over any other tribes on the battlefield. As they won territory and subjugated other tribes, their power grew and so did the power and influence of Yahweh, although the tribal elders would probably have put it the other way around.

According to the Old Testament, King David and King Solomon consolidated the Israelite tribes into a monarchy in Canaan around the tenth century BCE. They rebuilt the temple in Jerusalem and, for the first time in many decades, brought peace and order to the region. The traditional covenant that Abraham had made with Yahweh was now part of legend and lore, but the one that King David made with Yahweh to extend his dynastic rule for perpetuity was placed center stage. Festivals and rituals now celebrated the glory of Yahweh, the fierce war god, who made the world tremble with his footsteps as he descended from his abode on Mount Zion to ensure victory for the Israelite armies as they carried the Arc of the Covenant into battle.

By the sixth century BCE, El was no longer the dominant god of the people of Canaan as he had been for over six centuries. El and Baal had all but disappeared and had by now been completely replaced by Yahweh, whom we can see in writings eschewing his greatness and how he had led the Israelites to victory and vanquished its enemies. El and Baal were not completely forgotten, but rather, they had been combined into Yahweh. The Old Testament recognizes that Yahweh is no other than El, transformed to protect the Israelites in the Promised Land. Many hymns and legends attributed to El were now used to describe the legendary accomplishments of Yahweh. Baal and all the other nature gods had been replaced with this single, jealous God. Anyone who "whored after other Gods"[1] was severely punished by Yahweh. Victory or defeat in battle was determined by Yahweh's graces. Floods and famine were attributed to Yahweh's wrath, and when he was pleased, he led his armies to victory and provided bountiful harvests. Yahweh was very much a BGITS God.

Ilam: The Power Behind the Gods

Before the Israelite tribes joined forces under Yahweh, the people of Canaan had long believed that the gods derived their divinity and characteristics from being associated with *Ilam*. This association gave them their purity, their everlasting goodness, and their effulgence. Indeed, not only the Gods, but anything associated with Ilam could derive these qualities.

The Akkadian word for holiness was *ellu*, meaning "cleanliness, brilliance, luminosity." It is related to the Hebrew *Elohim*, which is often simply translated as "God" but originally summed up everything that the Gods could mean to human beings. The "holy ones" of the Middle East were like devas, the shining ones of India. In the Middle East, holiness was a power that lay beyond the gods, like Brahman. The word *ilam* ("divinity") in Mesopotamia referred to a radiant power that transcended any particular deity. It was a fundamental reality and could not be tied to a single distinct form. The gods were not the source of ilam, but like human beings, mountains, trees, and stars, they participated in this holiness. Anything that came into contact with the ilam became sacred too: a king, a priest, a temple, and even the ritual utensils became holy by association.

It would have seemed odd to the early Israelites to confine the sacred to a single divine being.[2]

This concept is similar to the concept of Rtá, which, as we saw in chapter 2, was the core concept in the Rig Veda. We know that the concept of Rtá was highly regarded by the Hittite rulers, who adopted it in their royal names. Could it be possible that this idea, in a modified form, was adopted by the priests and rulers in Canaan? The many common links between the languages and customs of the Indo-European people of this age suggest that they had a lot more in common than we currently know.

The Torah: Judaism's Holy Book

All ancient traditions, whether they be Indian, Chinese, or Greek, started out as oral traditions. Religious practices, rituals, legends, and stories were passed down from one generation to another in hymns learned by rote recitation. Starting in about the eighth century BCE, many of these oral traditions began to be put down in writing. It was a slow and painstaking process, since only a few of the educated elite knew how to read and even fewer would claim to be able to write.

Recording the ancient traditions of the Israelites had three profound effects: first, these ancient legends and rituals were preserved; second, a more uniform set of religious doctrines were more widely adopted by the different tribes; and third, these traditions were less likely to be altered by future generations. With a written text to point to, it was increasingly difficult for new monarchs or priests to change customs and practices that had the blessing of ancient divinity.

The Torah, the Holy Scripture of the Jews, consists of the first five books of the Old Testament: Genesis, Exodus, Leviticus, Numbers, and Deuteronomy. It begins with the origin of mankind and ends with the death of Moses. Traditionalists believe that the Torah is based on revelations that Moses received directly from God. Most current scholars think that the Torah was compiled by many authors over a period of five or six centuries. These five books, often referred to as the Pentateuch, originally contained a written record of the legends, traditions, and religious doctrines not only of the Israelites, but also of the Canaanites, who preceded them. Many religious scholars subsequently edited and added to these texts. These additions might include descriptions of rituals, narratives of ancient legends, historical events, and interpretation that highlighted not only the specific physical events, but also the metaphysical meaning of those events. It is difficult to place an exact time, place, or name on the different editions of the Old Testament. As best we can tell, they came into being from about the eighth century BCE to about the fifth century BCE.

Since we do not know the identity of the scholars who modified the editions, they have been assigned letters that represent a single author or group of authors. In about the sixth century BCE, a religious scholar referred to as P edited and modified the original texts of Genesis, Exodus, and Numbers. Another scholar, referred to as J because of his use of Yahweh to represent God, added the religious traditions of his time. For J, Yahweh was an anthropomorphic god, a god that humans could aspire to know, to be with, and to interact with. Finally, another scholar or group of scholars, referred to as E, used the more formal and universal name *Elohim* for God. E's God was much more distant and difficult to comprehend. This was probably a later group of scholars, and their additions and edits reflect the growing trend among the Israelites toward a more abstract and transcendental definition of God.

It is common to find differences in the versions of the texts presented by J and E, even in some of the most important aspects of these stories. For example, J's most important historical character in the story of the Israelites is Abraham. His covenant with Yahweh and the promise he received for a homeland for his people is central to J's narrative. On the other hand, E places Moses as the central character in the history. He never mentions Abraham's covenant, but instead focuses on the return of the Israelites from Egypt. Neither scholar mentions the Ten Commandments. It is, therefore, no surprise that contemporary Jewish scholars have debated the validity of the differing accounts of history, legend, and moral and ritual requirements that a practicing Jew must follow.

As we know, the five books of the Torah tell the story of Abraham and Moses. But in addition to telling the story of the Israelites, the books open with the story of the origin of mankind through the legend of Adam and Eve. In certain versions, other legends and tales familiar to a Judeo-Christian audience follow, such as those of Cain and Abel, the Ten Commandments, and Abraham's near sacrifice of his son Isaac at Yahweh's command. Moral and social directives merge with history and legend to tell the story of the people of Israel.

The texts are almost certainly not historically accurate, and I don't think they are meant to be. In many instances, historical figures and events are combined with legends and myths, primarily to drive home a point. One story tells of Moses going to Mount Sinai and receiving from God the Ten Commandments—the laws by which all Israelites must lead their lives and which form the ethical basis of the Judeo-Christian faiths. Whether it is historically accurate or not is, in some sense, beside the point. The belief that these ethical rules came directly from God provided the ultimate authority and legitimacy to convince common people to follow them. Some of the other assertions of the Old Testament are not as easy to accept and have been the subject of some debate among modern Jewish scholars, as we shall see later in this chapter.

In addition to the Torah, a great oral tradition prevailed among the Israelites that was, for centuries, forbidden to be committed to writing. After their exile from Jerusalem and the dispersion of the original tribes of Israel, it became clear that the oral tradition had to be written down if it was to survive. This compilation of the oral tradition came to be known as the Talmud, which consists of the Mishnah and the Gemara. The Talmud lays out the ethical and moral laws and the socially acceptable norms that all Jews must adhere to.

The Books of Joshua and the Book of Kings tell the story of the Israelites after the death of Moses. The Israelites settled down in the Promised Land and became a thriving kingdom, with a complex, settled social structure. The most famous kings mentioned in these texts are King David and his son, King Solomon. Stories about King Solomon are now part of the folklore that any child raised in the Judeo-Christian tradition in the West will know. Most important for our discussion is the fact that David began construction on the famous temple in Jerusalem dedicated to the one true God, Yahweh, but he died before it was completed. His son, King

Solomon, completed the temple in about the tenth century BCE. The temple and the associated priests and rituals adhered strictly to the newly compiled Torah. The temple stood for over four centuries, until the Babylonians destroyed it in the seventh century BCE. King Solomon is probably the most popular folk hero in all three religious traditions because of his wisdom and his role in the completion of the temple.

The Babylonian Exile

The Canaanite land where the Israelites settled was in a perilous location, flanked by two large and well-established civilizations: the Mesopotamians on one side and the Romans on the other. The Assyrians and Babylonians (the two prominent civilizations of Mesopotamia) had thrived for many centuries and had their own pantheon and religious rituals, as did the Romans. More important was the fact that they both had powerful armies that could, at will, overrun the small and newly formed kingdom of the Israelites. This is indeed what happened—over and over again—for many centuries.

By about 730 BCE, the Assyrians amassed the largest army in the Middle East. They systematically conquered the smaller states in the region and appointed vassal governors to rule the satellite states. The king of Assyria quickly imposed his own administrative and religious leadership. The Assyrian high god, Ashur, held a status similar to that of Yahweh among the Israelites.

The conquest of Israel by the Assyrians was quick and brutal. It seemed that the smaller kingdom of Judah would be next. The prophet Isaiah declared that Israel had abandoned Yahweh and therefore incurred his wrath. But he reassured his people that no harm would come to them and Jerusalem and its temple would remain safe as long as the people of Judah remained loyal to Yahweh, The miraculous and unexpected withdrawal of the Assyrians before they sacked Jerusalem significantly enhanced the stature of Yahweh in the eyes of the Judeans and the Israelites.

However, the battles between Judea and the Assyrians continued for the next two decades and left the once-thriving monarchies of Israel and Judea in ruins. With most cities in these kingdoms reduced to rubble, and large populations of refugees flowing into Jerusalem, the Judean king

Hezekiah ordered the destruction of all shrines to Yahweh outside the main temple in Jerusalem. He hoped to centralize the clergy's power and thereby reduce the possibility of rural revolt, but the conditions of people outside Jerusalem was grim. Hezekiah's dynastic rule came to an end a few years later in a palace coup, and his grandson Josiah was placed on the throne at only eight years of age. Josiah's reign is interesting, because he was convinced early in his life that he wanted to follow the teachings of Yahweh to the letter. He had some flexibility to do this since the Egyptians and the Assyrians were preoccupied with other matters.

When the Babylonians conquered the kingdom of the Israelites in the seventh century BCE, they looted and destroyed the temple. As a part of their loot, they took back with them the Arc of the Covenant and members of the most prominent Israelite families. These families were allowed to practice their faith in Babylonia but were influenced by their new hosts. During their period of exile, these Israelites formed and formulated a different system of worship and ritual that represented an evolution from the original version.

Judaism Formalized

King Cyrus, one of the greatest Persian emperors, inherited and expanded the vast Persian Empire. He was a practicing Zoroastrian but also worshipped Amun-Ra, who was regarded as the patron god of the great Persian Empire (clearly inherited from Egypt's dynasty of pharaohs). As the son of Amun-Ra, he had godlike stature, and the prayers and rituals associated with him are well documented in Egyptian hieroglyphs. He was also a tolerant emperor who let his subjects practice their faith and maintain their traditions. He decreed the Israelites be allowed to return from their exile in Babylon to Jerusalem and to rebuild their temple. It is unclear how many Israelites made the journey back to Judea. The estimates vary from over 40,000 to less than a thousand. Judea was, in this period, under the control of Persia. All Judeans paid taxes to the Persian governor and were politically and linguistically under the authority of the Persians, even though they were allowed to practice their faith freely. The history from this time was documented by Second Isaiah , who was given this name because his writing appears in the same scrolls as the writings of Isaiah (from a few decades earlier).

The returning Judeans brought with them a Jewish faith that had been transformed in important ways from what they had practiced when they left. They rebuilt the temple in Jerusalem and reestablished the traditional offerings of prayers and sacrifices, but with a Babylonian twist. The offering of prayers and sacrifice could now be done not only in Solomon's temple, but also in other temples or synagogues. More than ever, Yahweh dominated the religious landscape. Second Isaiah viewed the return of the exiles to Jerusalem after seventy years as being part of Yahweh's grand plan to deliver his people to the rightful land of Abraham. The returning exiles were but servants in his grand scheme. The kingdoms of the north (Israel) and south (Judea) were reunited. But while these precepts applied to Israelites dealing with each other, Second Isaiah's message to non-Israelites was rather harsh. All nonbelievers (those who did not profess their unconditional devotion to Yahweh) were to be put to death.

It is ironic that having been given the freedom to practice their religion by the Persian emperor and being allowed to return home to practice their faith, the exiles chose an intolerant, monotheistic society and a jealous god that harked back to the warlike, chest-thumping, aggressive version of Yahweh that had nearly destroyed the early Israelite tribes.

The Age of Belief

The early religion of the Israelites, all the way to about 300 BCE, had been based on the belief in a revealed scripture and a BGITS God: El, Baal, or Yahweh. The fate of humans was intimately linked to the gods, who played a direct and vital role in everyday life. The legends, rituals, and customs in this early religion were based on pleasing the gods to ensure that they would be kind to all believers. The consequences of not following the word of God were calamitous.

But how did one know what the word of God was? It was revealed by God directly to the chosen ones—Abraham, Moses, their descendants—and to the sons of God (royalty). It was not a matter that was up for debate. The scriptures, oral to begin with and written in the form of the first five books of the Old Testament (the Torah), would form the core set of beliefs for the faithful. There was no logical explanation needed or provided for these beliefs.

Although there was room for interpretation of the Abrahamic beliefs—unlike in the Vedic traditions of India, the Confucian ideals of China, and the rationalist approach of the Greeks—questioning the scriptures was not an option. The age of belief is defined as belief (or faith) in oral and written scripture, belief that a given scripture is the word of God, and belief that the scripture must be obeyed without question. A transcendental God and the ability to question even the most fundamental beliefs in scriptures would only arise for the Jewish faithful in later centuries, as scholars and rabbis explored the nature of reality and the relationship between man and God. As we shall see in the next section, this process began with the arrival of the Greeks.

The Believers Face Off with the Rationalists: The Hellenic Influence

In about 300 BCE, the Greek general Alexander defeated the Persians and established Greek hegemony over a large swath of the Middle East, including Judea. The Greeks, with their unique culture and philosophical influence, left a lasting cultural and religious impact on the nascent Jewish culture. While the Judeans were believers in the one true God as revealed to Abraham, the Greeks had no such belief. In fact, their philosophic traditions clearly led them to a more rational view of God, one that was based on the notion that man should be allowed to infer and deduce truths about God—not from belief in any revelation or scripture—but from logic and philosophical argument. This clash between belief and rationality, which was by no means the first or the last, led to some fascinating religious and social conflicts that lasted well into the time of Jesus, over 300 years later.

The Greeks established city-states in territories from Judea to Israel to Constantinople. Life under Greek rule was no longer centered around temples, worship, and rituals dedicated to Yahweh. Instead, the Greeks had no trouble with people worshipping any God they pleased—or not worshipping at all. Theirs was a secular state, with a religious ethos quite unlike that of the monarchs who preceded them. There was no royal mandate to follow Yahweh and certainly no state support of such activities. As a result, the power and influence of the priests declined, and people began to view themselves as increasingly capable of determining their own destiny.

The Greeks also brought a broader worldview to the residents of Canaan, who had been relatively isolated from the outside world. Because the area did not lie on any major trade routes or garner attention for its riches or mineral wealth, it was an intellectual and commercial backwater. The Greeks under Alexander the Great had conquered a good part of the known world, and their leaders brought ideas and products to the people of Canaan that they had never seen or experienced. Within a century, the area was transformed into a bustling center for commerce and learning. That process would continue for another 300 years.

The Greeks—and later, the Romans—posed the single biggest threat to the core beliefs of the early Jewish monotheists. The Jews believed that God had been revealed to them and them alone, through Holy Scripture. God spoke to his believers through the Messiah, or messenger, who had direct or indirect communication with God. Abraham and Moses both spoke directly to God. God spoke to Muhammad through the angel Gabriel and dictated the entire Koran, word for word. The true nature of God's creation and his instructions to humanity were thus revealed in the holy texts from which the faithful derived their prayers, rituals, ethics, and social norms. This belief was an act of faith; no rational explanation was needed.

The Greeks, by comparison, were of a different mind altogether. They believed, in a very fundamental way, that human beings can, through rational and philosophical discourse and discovery, ascertain the will of God and the nature of his creation. For them, God emerged as a result of rational philosophical discourse. This was a tradition that had been established over the course of many centuries of philosophical dialogue and debate. The traditions of Plato and Aristotle were at complete odds with the Abrahamic system of belief. As these diametrically opposed traditions coexisted, both sides were influenced by the other.

It was during this period that many philosophers and some of the earliest scientists began schools of thought based almost entirely on logical reasoning, with no recourse to divine intervention. Euclid and Archimedes, who provided the first elements of formal scientific writing, lived and did their work in Alexandria. Epicurus set out to explore the limits of logical explanations of the world around us. He postulated that the material world and even the gods were made up of atoms that could be combined in different ways to form the various objects we perceive. Great advances were made in astronomy, medicine, and physics. Remarkably during this period, these different philosophical developments continued unfettered without any action by the polis to shut them down because they were against some existing religious scripture. We see the development of a secular system of government in the Middle East that did not interfere with the religious or philosophical beliefs of its subjects.

People in the area gravitated toward systems of philosophy that relied increasingly on logic and less on ancient beliefs and scripture. This is not to say that the older traditions were disappearing. In fact, the common man continued his religious practices in much the same way as the ancients did. The activity continued in parallel with the development of the new philosophies, with one influencing the other. For the educated elite, the traditional scriptures were increasingly viewed as a combination of ancient history and legend—not the absolute word of God.

Modern Conceptions of God in Judaism

Judaism went through a transformation about the same time as Jesus of Nazareth was preaching his message of love and equality. It was brought about by rabbis and scholars who did not see the Torah as the literal word of God but as a guide and companion that would help all human beings lead ethical lives. Taken in this spirit, the Torah could be reinterpreted, and the lessons learned from it could be refreshed.

The decline of Greek influence and power and the rise of the mighty Roman Empire meant that Israel and Judea once again had new rulers. In 70 CE, the Roman emperor Vespasian conquered Jerusalem and set about to destroy all important symbols of Jewish heritage. The temple was razed and lay in ruins for many years to come. Since the Jewish faithful could no longer perform their rituals in the temple, several sects emerged that either did not feel the need for the temple or had no choice but to do without. In fact, some of these sects were formed even before the destruction of the temple as a protest against the perceived corruption of the temple priests. The most important sect was the Pharisees, who were perhaps at the leading edge of reinterpreting scripture.

Two major lines of interpretation emerged that had not previously been central to Jewish liturgy. The first was a strong emphasis on selflessness, kindness, and service to all of humanity. According to Rabbi Hillel, the central message that emerged from the Torah was that we should treat every human being as we ourselves would like to be treated. He did not regard the literal interpretation of the Old Testament as the word of God. Instead, he asked his disciples to focus on the spirit of the Torah and to look deeply into the hidden meaning of the legends and fables within it. It was the duty of every Jew to seek the true meaning and extract the central message of the story and the characters in it. Nothing was sacred any more. People were encouraged to question each tenet of the Torah and to accept it only when they were intellectually satisfied. According to these rabbis, even the word of God should be questioned. This way of looking at the ancient texts was remarkable for the time, because it represented a radical departure from what the conservative temple priests were preaching.

The second line of interpretation saw the conception of God change dramatically from the warlike Yahweh to a much more abstract God that was beyond human comprehension. Gone was the anthropomorphic god of war, who was responsible for every aspect of human existence. Since humans do not know what he looks like and how to describe him, giving God a name was viewed among the new traditionalists as sacrilege. You will remember that the concept of God within Judaism begins within the Old Testament book of Exodus. The name God is given when he identifies himself to Moses in the Book of Exodus is *YHWH*. Thereafter, while faithful Jews avoided naming God outright, they substituted words such as *Adonai*, "my lord," or *Elohim*, "gods" or "the children of El."[3]

Other substitutions that Jews have made throughout their history reflecting the general prohibition against mentioning God by name are *HaShem*, which translates merely as "the name," as well as more pedestrian substitutions like "the forbidden" or "the unutterable name."[4] It might be said that this transcendental God, whose name cannot be uttered, has contributed to the stiff formalism within many of the Jewish religious practices that persist to this day. It is difficult for any individual Jew—and certainly within the Orthodox divisions of the religion—to establish a personalized relationship with God other than one based on absolute subservience in recognition of his supreme authority both in heaven and on earth.

Regardless of a specific term developed to replace the name of God within the Judaic tradition, the emphasis on God as an absolute authority is readily apparent. God is an absolute authority and a revered deity that can be approached only within the most formal rules and considerations. This concept of God within the Jewish tradition is one that has never been lost or changed, regardless of which name is used to describe him. The concept of God in Judaism consistently illustrates the extreme reverence that faithful Jews have for the very concept of God as one that exists apart from any other reality.

The Pharisees believed that the offering of prayers and the performance of rituals should not be restricted to the priests. Instead, every Jew had a moral responsibility and the right to perform these prayers and, therefore, the ability to communicate with God. Prayer did not have to be offered in the temple but could be offered anywhere, including in the home. As long as the prayer was offered sincerely, God would accept it just as much as he would a prayer conducted in the temple in Jerusalem. In fact, there was no need for elaborate rituals. Acts of kindness and compassion toward other human beings were the ultimate prayer. The dedicated and silent study of the Holy Scripture, alone or in groups, pleased God, and he would sit with the faithful, guiding their study.

This newer, humanistic approach to Judaism and transcendental conception of God has now become an integral part of the Jewish tradition. The old traditional conception of an anthropomorphic God, who was fundamentally based on the fear of retribution, was now pushed to the background, and what emerged was an abstract conception of God that appealed to the philosophically inclined. For the faithful who still needed a personal God, there were now clear limits to how this personalization could be achieved. In keeping with the ancient tradition of a fearful and all-powerful God, it was decreed within Hebraic scripture that no one could ever gaze upon him and survive.[5] God must, therefore, be both feared and revered. However, the abstract nature of God was still preserved: He has no equal and no tangible form.

Since this abstract conception of God within Judaism was now difficult for the lay Jew to envision, the importance of the rabbi grew, not only within the faith's religious practices, but also especially within the Jewish community, where the rabbi was and is seen as God's authority on earth. Although Christianity has its priests and ministers, these figures lack the absolute authority that the Jewish community traditionally affords the rabbi as God's secular representative.

With this abstract definition of God, it is clear that Judaism was becoming even more firmly monotheistic as it elevated the status of God to one who is supreme above all else—earthly or divine. This abstract monotheism was, however, distinct from the monotheism of Yahweh, which decreed that all nonbelievers should be punished and that no other God was to be worshipped. Later, rabbinical tradition, except for some conservative sects, rejected this point of view, In fact, it is clear that within the main body of Judaism—since the concept of God was now increasingly abstract, transcendental, and too difficult for humans to comprehend—no single entity could lay exclusive claim to the title. This allowed individuals and sects within Judaism to personalize God within these broad parameters. The conception of God, therefore, has slowly evolved to become one who is still supreme and to be feared in some respects but is also now increasingly viewed as a loving God as well.[6] This has led to several major denominations within Judaism that embrace the different versions of this transcendental concept of God.

All Jewish sects maintain the concept of God as one who is remote and abstract, one who needs to be revered for his divine and his secular authority. However, it is clear that, on the whole, Judaism has slowly come to view God in a much more humanistic way. Although this view adheres to traditional canon within the church, God has become somewhat more accessible to the general population.[7] Therefore, where in earlier eras of Judaism the development of individual notions of and relationships with God may have been impossible or discouraged, the current concept of God within Judaism has become much more personalized.

The Jewish faith is integrated into Jewish culture, which creates a rich and sophisticated religious matrix. To be Jewish implies as much a cultural association as it does a religious association, although Jews comprise different racial and cultural backgrounds. In essence, the concept of God might very well shift somewhat from one of these Jewish groups to another, but one of the unifying aspects of the religion is that the core doctrine and practices associated with the religion are universally held among all Jewish groups.

The Jewish religion carries very strong cultural implications because the Jews believe that they were originally God's chosen people, and therefore, theirs is a unique relationship with God. Theirs is a God who, for the most part, Christianity and Judaism share, and that Islam partly embraces. Furthermore, this relationship with and concept of God in Judaism also relates to the Jewish relationship with God, a divine covenant that demands that all Jews live according to God's divine laws and that all Jews reflect God's holiness at all times.

> God is known through relationship and action. . . . The ultimate reason why various Jewish approaches to God can agree upon the identity of the God they worship . . . is that Judaism is not constituted through theological definition. . . . The identity of the God of Judaism is established through this common worship more than through any of the theological statements made by these different Judaisms.[8]

As with almost every ancient religion, Judaism has many distinct sects, each with their own interpretation of the Tanach (the twenty-four books of the ancient Bible), the Torah (the first five books of the Old Testament), and the Talmud (oral commentaries and traditions). Traditional or conservative Jews retain belief in the literal meaning of the Pentateuch (the five earliest books of the Old Testament), whereas liberal Jews consider it an important guide to the way they live their lives but do not believe that it is meant to be followed literally.

It is impossible for us to do justice to all the varied interpretations and beliefs that Judaism now encompasses. In this section, I have discussed the historical, traditional, and current views of God in Judaism, from the time of the Israelites (even before the term *Jew* was used to describe the religion of the people of Canaan) to the present day. Recent and more liberal sects in Judaism increasingly view God as a transcendental being from which to derive inspiration and scripture, who acts as an important holy guide in their daily lives, but not whose texts are meant to be interpreted literally. This has been a difficult, important, and vital journey for most of the faithful of this ancient religion.

Christianity

The Historical Perspective

The first century BCE was a time of great political and social uncertainty and upheaval in Judea. Its political domination by the Romans had lasted for about two centuries since the death of Alexander the Great. Political and economic power was centered around the local Roman rulers and their appointees and minions. The local Roman governor had no sympathy for Judean customs or beliefs. His chief task was to ensure that the peasants and the common man, who constituted over ninety percent of the population, paid their taxes and recognized the authority of their Roman overlords.

Social and religious life revolved around the temple and the scribes and priests who formed the religious and social elite. There was a select group of Jewish priests, administrators, and officials who helped the Romans administer Judea. These collaborators were despised by the locals, who saw them as part of the oppressive regime and as deserters of the faith.

Corruption, injustice, and intolerance were part of everyday life. A peasant's life was subsistence living at best, with periods of famine when the periodic drought forced many farmers into debt or indentured servitude. Centuries of Roman subjugation had reduced the people to abject poverty, and a sense of hopelessness pervaded the mind of the common man. The writings from this time reflect this sense of despair, and doomsday predictions were commonplace.

To fully understand the origin of Christianity, it is important to view the life of Jesus from this historical and cultural perspective. It was into this atmosphere of conflict and despair that Jesus of Nazareth (the version of his name given in the King James Bible in 1629) was born. His name in his native Aramaic would have been *Ishu* or *Eshu*, a shortened version of the Hebrew name *Yehoshewah*, which has now become *Joshua*. His parents were of modest means and were probably peasants or craftspeople.

Many conflicting stories surround his birth, so it is difficult to create a detailed historical picture of it. What we know for sure is that such a person did exist in Galilee during this period, and that Jesus was born in Bethlehem and raised in neighboring Nazareth. The stories of his birth in a manger and the arrival of three wise men from the East bearing gift are well known to the Christian community. The gospels say very little about his life until he began to preach in public at about the age of thirty. As his following grew, the Romans accused him of insurrection, and he was crucified at the age of thirty-three. This bare-bones sketch of Jesus is just about all we know historically about his life.

Many other legends about his life, documented in the synoptic gospels of Mark, Matthew, and Luke, form the main source of our knowledge about him. However, we are not sure which parts of the legends are historically accurate. We know that they cannot all be accurate, because many of them contradict each other, but we do know that these differences almost always enable the author to make a doctrinal point. We will not dwell on these details here, since they are not central to our discussion. We will, instead, focus on his teachings, as recorded mainly in the gospels of Mark, Matthew, Luke, Thomas, and John the Baptist, about the nature of God and what it means to be religious.

Jesus, John the Baptist, and the New Testament

The words of Jesus have, perhaps more than anyone else in human history, been interpreted and reinterpreted so many times and in so many ways that it is sometimes difficult to separate them from the commentary of later scholars and saints.

It is hard to separate the teachings of Jesus from those of John the Baptist, for instance. John began his sermons about a decade before Jesus did, and his main message was "Repent, for the kingdom of God is at hand." The people of Judah clearly believed him, since many of them came to him to be baptized in the Jordan River. The ritual of baptism was a symbol of repentance and was meant to purify the soul and wash away past sins and prepare the body, mind, and soul for the coming Kingdom of God. Jesus, himself, was baptized by John before he began preaching his sermons.

A few years later, John was imprisoned by King Herod for marrying the wife of his half brother. As soon as Jesus found out that John had been imprisoned, he set about preaching John's message.

This is an odd sequence of events and needs some explaining. Why is it that John would baptize Jesus if the latter was the son of God or perhaps even God himself? There are two possible explanations for this: The more plausible one is that Jesus was John's disciple and continued his tradition when John was incarcerated. The fact that he began preaching as soon as John could no longer do so indicates that he believed in John's message and wanted to ensure that his work was continued. It is also clear that the message that Jesus preached was virtually identical to the one that John had preached. This explanation is not, however, the preferred interpretation of most Christian theologians.

The alternate explanation is that John was the harbinger that trumpeted the coming of the Messiah, Jesus. By adopting this explanation, theologians avoid the difficulty of placing Jesus as following in the footsteps of John. Whatever explanation you prefer, it is clear that the message preached by both Jesus and John the Baptist form the basis of the Christian faith. We will discuss this message in some detail, since it forms the core of Christian concepts of God, morality, ethics, and what it means to be religious.

The Message of Jesus of Nazareth

During his life, the central message that Jesus preached was simple yet profound: The kingdom of God was at hand, and every individual should prepare for this transformation as if it were imminent. This simple and hopeful message has been the subject of intense debate and interpretive commentary for the past 2,000 years.

Although, on the face of it, this message seems simple, it begs several important questions, each of which were answered by Jesus in his sermons:

- What is the Kingdom of God?
- How should we prepare for it?
- When will it arrive?

In answer to the first question, Jesus preached that the current deplorable state of humanity, where the rich and powerful continually perpetuate injustice on the poor and the weak, was only temporary. The present unjust and oppressive system (meaning the Roman system) would be replaced with God's kingdom, where there would be justice for all. The poor would be rewarded with their due; the sick and the weak would be uplifted; men and women of all races and creeds would be treated as equals, regardless of their economic or social status; and the rich and the powerful would be punished for their greed. This was a hopeful, utopian vision of a just, egalitarian, and pious world at a time when people had lost all hope of any change in their way of life.

Jesus laid out in very clear terms what the Kingdom of God would look like, described in the gospels of both Luke and Matthew. The term *kingdom* does not imply any geographical territory or empire. It was, in fact, an idealization, a utopia that every common person could relate to. To understand Jesus's concept of the Kingdom of God, it is best to quote a translation of a portion of the Sermon on the Mount that is referred to as the Beatitudes, one of the most beautiful, poetic, and well-known passages from the gospel of Matthew. He said:

> "Blessed are the poor in spirit, for theirs is the kingdom of heaven.
> "Blessed are those who mourn, for they will be comforted.
> "Blessed are the meek, for they will inherit the earth.
> "Blessed are those who hunger and thirst for righteousness,
> for they will be filled.
> "Blessed are the merciful, for they will be shown mercy.

"Blessed are the pure in heart, for they will see God.

"Blessed are the peacemakers, for they will be called children of God.

"Blessed are those who are persecuted because of righteousness, for theirs is the kingdom of heaven.

"Blessed are you when people insult you, persecute you, and falsely say all kinds of evil against you because of me. Rejoice and be glad, because great is your reward in heaven, for in the same way they persecuted the prophets who were before you."[9]

In Luke's version of the Sermon on the Mount, the same blessings are followed by a set of curses for the rich and powerful, who "will be punished for their ill deeds."[10] In Luke's telling of this sermon, Jesus sees the rich and powerful in the Kingdom of Man as selfish and unjust and—as such—deserving of punishment in the Kingdom of God.

To answer the second question regarding how we should prepare for the Kingdom of God, we must remind ourselves of the context in which these words were spoken. The Roman Empire held sway over Palestine. The common people—mostly peasants, artisans, and the destitute—were systematically persecuted, with no hope for change. Into this atmosphere of hopelessness, Jesus brought a message of hope and redemption for the poor, the hungry, the persecuted, and the downtrodden, a vision of justice for those who had seen none. God's kingdom was exactly what the Romans had not provided and what the people thirsted for. The Kingdom of God was what the Kingdom of Man was not.

It is important to note that the Kingdom of Heaven is something that will come to people on earth, not something they will go to after death. In other words, this is not a concept of heaven guarded by angels. Instead, it is a better life that can be brought about by those who believe and who are virtuous. This is expressed in the well-known verse from the Lord's Prayer, "Your kingdom come, your will be done, on earth as it is in heaven."[11]

The answer to the third question (When will the Kingdom of God arrive?) is a matter of some debate and controversy among preachers and scholars. What did Jesus mean when he said that the Kingdom of God was upon us? Did he mean it was imminent, or was it already here? Some scholars believe that Jesus specifically told his followers that the coming of the Kingdom of God was imminent—as in, expected within their lifetime. This belief is based on specific statements in each of the gospels that explicitly say as much. Clearly, this did not happen.

Other scholars have interpreted his sermons to mean that the Kingdom of God is already here and that we need to better align ourselves with God to fully recognize and appreciate it. When enough people abide by the rules of the Kingdom of God in their actions and in their thoughts, the Kingdom of God will be upon us. Jesus, as a messenger of God, conveyed this message to initiate the process.

For those who believe in the former interpretation, Christ could be looked upon as the son of God, who foretold the future and wanted to forewarn humanity of the impending event. In the second interpretation, Jesus could be viewed as the Messiah, a messenger, who was ensuring that God's message was clearly communicated to the people. This difference in interpretation affects our view of who Jesus really was: Was he God himself, the Messiah, or the son of God? The answer will remain a matter of belief, not a logically derivable or universally accepted fact.

Jesus asked his followers to be kind, compassionate, just, and humble— exactly the qualities he saw lacking in the Kingdom of Man. He did this in parables throughout the New Testament. Perhaps the best known of these is the parable of the Good Samaritan. A sick and dying person on the side of the road is ignored by his countrymen as they walk right past him, oblivious to his pain and suffering. A Samaritan, a person of a different faith and from a different place, sees the sick man, picks him up, and transports him to the nearest place that could care for him, leaving instructions that the sick man was to be cared for and that he would pay for his care. This parable, more than any other, reflects Jesus's central message of compassion and kindness, even toward those who are different from us. It is a powerful story that reminded the people of Palestine that service to humanity is our fundamental duty in the Kingdom of God. The New Testament is full of such parables that both surprise readers and force them to rethink their preconceived notions of God and our relationship to him.

Accumulation of wealth and possessions was considered to be immoral and unacceptable in God's kingdom. Instead, Jesus preached that generosity to the less fortunate was expected of every Christian. Jesus also preached the virtues of forgiveness, repentance, and nonretaliation. These virtues were essential to prepare a person for the Kingdom of God. They are also qualities he clearly saw lacking in the rulers of Israel who had caused their people so much pain and suffering.

In addition to these parables, the New Testament also contains many stories about the acts of kindness and compassion that Jesus performed. A great many of these stories describe miracles. There are stories of Jesus curing people of blindness, leprosy, and other illnesses, simply by his touch. Other stories tell of him bringing people back from the dead and conducting exorcisms to free people of demons. People came from all over Palestine to witness his miraculous healing powers. Indeed, his healing power was the primary reason so many people came to see and to hear him speak when he first began preaching. And, of course, most of us know the famous story of Jesus turning water into wine at a wedding when the wedding party was running short.

For many biblical scholars and for faithful believers, these stories are proof of the divinity of Jesus. If we were to regard the gospels of Luke and Matthew as historical, this may be a reasonable conclusion to arrive at. If Jesus actually did perform these miracles and was resurrected from the dead himself, he clearly was divine.

But for others, these stories serve a different purpose altogether. They are allegorical and therefore serve to establish and reinforce the message that Jesus, as God's messenger, was conveying to humanity. The acts of healing are meant to illustrate what would happen in the Kingdom of God when the downtrodden were uplifted, the impure purified, the sick healed, and the good resurrected to heaven.

The Basic Tenets of Christianity

Christianity, as we know it today, is not simply the preaching of Jesus. Jesus died preaching his message of love, humility, and service to humanity. His followers and disciples were left with the arduous task of summarizing those teachings and, in many cases, adding to them to form what we now call the New Testament. Christianity is therefore influenced as much by the interpretations of Matthew, Mark, Luke, Paul, John, and the other authors of the gospels as by the teachings of Jesus and John the Baptist. They are the authors of the history, the legend, the rituals, the ethics, and the morality embedded in the scripture, which together form the essential and authoritative canon of the Christian faith.

To understand the impact of the writers of the gospel, we must remember that these texts form the basis—both historical and religious—of the teachings of Jesus and his life. As we pointed out earlier, some of the passages in the gospel are clearly historical, others allegorical, and yet other stories or legends are meant to illustrate the teachings of Jesus. Separating one from the other is difficult and often a matter of interpretation and faith. There is no conclusive proof to authenticate the historical validity of any portion of the gospel. The death and resurrection of Jesus, an event that is central to the doctrines laid out by Paul, provides an excellent example to illustrate this point:

Jesus was preaching in Galilee at the age of thirty-three and had led a procession of followers into Jerusalem. The Roman governor, Herod, led a procession of Roman infantry into Jerusalem from the opposite end of the city. Jesus was fully aware that the festival of Passover was being celebrated by Jews throughout the city, and therefore a significant Roman army presence was on hand to maintain order.

Jesus's message to the Romans was clear: He represented the vast majority of people, peasants, workers, and the coming of the Kingdom of God. They, on the other hand, represented tyranny and oppression. By the end of that evening, he finished preaching his message to his followers, ate his last supper with eleven of his disciples, was betrayed by Judas, was arrested, and was sentenced to death by crucifixion by the Romans.

The New Testament tells us that after his death Jesus rose from the dead. The many accounts of this in Christian scripture differ in substantial ways. The gospel of Mark simply says that the body of Jesus disappeared from his tomb and that he had been resurrected.

The gospels of Matthew and Luke present much more elaborate

versions of the incident. Matthew records that the women who went to Jesus's tomb and eleven apostles saw him on a hill in Galilee. Luke reports that the apostles saw Jesus in Jerusalem, not Galilee. Another well-known story states that the apostles initially thought Jesus was a ghost. They were struck by fear, then terror, and finally wonder when they touched him and realized he was flesh and bone. They then watched Jesus ascend into heaven in an event well known in Christianity as the Ascension.

In the gospel of John, the person to first see Jesus was Mary Magdalene, who mistook him for a gardener. Later, Jesus was seen by all the apostles except Thomas, who saw him a week later and was able to convince himself of Jesus's existence by touching his physical being.

The varied stories of the death and resurrection of Jesus must be taken at face value, without questioning their historical basis, since we have no way to verify any of them. For the faithful believers, this is a no-brainer. For the skeptic or the more scientifically minded, it is hard to imagine any of these versions of events being historically accurate. How could a person return from the dead? If he was resurrected, why are the accounts so entirely different in the gospels? Perhaps the accounts are simply stories meant to glorify Jesus—who was clearly a person of great charisma and wisdom. Perhaps the writers of the gospel did have mental experiences—perhaps dreams that made them believe that they had met Jesus after his death. These explanations would appear to be more reasonable. Believers in the literal interpretation of the New Testament will, of course, continue to believe the story as presented in the scriptures.

The resurrection of Jesus is important from a biblical point of view because it represents the later Christian belief that all of us will be resurrected on Judgment Day. Paul, in his gospel, views the resurrection of Jesus as only the beginning of the resurrection of every human being with the coming of the Kingdom of God.

> I declare to you, brothers and sisters, that flesh and blood cannot inherit the kingdom of God, nor does the perishable inherit the imperishable. Listen, I tell you a mystery: We will not all sleep, but we will all be changed—in a flash, in the twinkling of an

eye, at the last trumpet. For the trumpet will sound, the dead will be raised imperishable, and we will be changed. For the perishable must clothe itself with the imperishable, and the mortal with immortality. When the perishable has been clothed with the imperishable, then the saying that is written will come true: "Death has been swallowed up in victory."[12]

The gospel of Paul had such a decisive impact on the development of Christian traditions and ideas that some regard Paul as the true founder of Christianity. It is said that Paul was visited by Jesus as a bright light as he traveled on the road to Damascus and was instructed by Jesus to spread his message to the people in the Holy Land so that they could be directed away from sin in preparation for the coming of the Kingdom of God. Paul had never met Jesus in person; his claim that he saw him in his resurrected form came many years after Jesus's death.

What Paul preached was different in important ways from the teachings of Jesus, although it was clearly based on the principles that Jesus had laid out. Jesus preached God's kingdom. Paul declared that the forgiveness of sin was centered in Jesus, who was now called *Christ*. According to Paul, if we believe in Jesus, we will be saved from the wrath of God. Paul said, "If you declare with your mouth, 'Jesus is Lord,' and believe in your heart that God raised him from the dead, you will be saved."[13]

It is obvious that this message is quite different from the one that Jesus preached. The focus has shifted from making this world a better place by improving human behavior to accepting Jesus as our savior and thus achieving salvation. Paul's version of the scripture has become a dominant point of view in modern Christianity. Although the focus of Jesus's message was the misery and injustice under Roman rule and how this would be transformed in the Kingdom of God, Paul's message elevated Jesus to the status of the Messiah, or the son of God.

Jesus, himself, probably never thought of himself as divine. Gods in human form were not part of the Jewish tradition, so it is unlikely that Jesus—a devout Jew—would have construed himself as the son of God.

In his own writings, Jesus wrote of himself most often as the son of man. It is only later gospels that elevate him to Christ the Savior. Subsequent theological writings even tried to establish proof that Jesus was God in human form and therefore deserved our prayers. This transition from Jesus's representation as a son of man to God incarnate happened over a period of several decades and has been hotly debated among theologians and scholars ever since.

The Concept of God in Christianity

There is little to suggest that Jesus viewed God in terms any different from those in which Abraham, Moses, and all the Jewish faithful of his time regarded the Supreme Being. For Christians, God is also the Supreme Being and the creator of everything in existence. In this regard, the Christian concept of God is monotheistic, just like the Jewish and Islamic versions. In all these traditions, God is not only the omnipotent creator of this universe but is also intimately involved in its well-being. He was very much a BGITS God who needed to be appeased both by prayer and by our actions. Failure to repent and follow the moral laws laid out in the Kingdom of God meant that one ran the risk of his wrath and eternal damnation.

However, Christianity is unique among these Abrahamic traditions, because the concept of God evolved in a somewhat different manner than it did in Judaism and later in Islam. The Christian faith, more than any of the other Abrahamic religions, made God accessible to the common man. In ancient Jewish traditions, Yahweh ultimately came to be viewed as the only true God of the people of Canaan. In modern Jewish traditions, God has been viewed in rather abstract terms, as a transcendental being that humans are not fully capable of comprehending. Jesus was raised in the Jewish tradition, with this remote concept of God, which he accepted without question.

Jesus, however, transformed this abstract concept of God into a much more personal one, and he repeatedly referred to God as *father* in his sermons. In fact, his reference to God in Aramaic is probably more closely translated into a more informal term for father, such as *papa*. This anthropomorphic God is unique among the Abrahamic religions and it makes the Christian concept of God one that is much more approachable than others. Therefore, it is conceivable within the Christian faith to view God as an elderly patriarch who cares deeply about the well-being of his flock. In Christianity, God remains the supreme lord of the universe, but Jesus is viewed as the savior; in Judaism and Islam, these ideals of God and savior remain combined within the same Supreme Being.

This allocation of authority allows Christianity to split the conception of God into three unique components, referred to as the Holy Trinity: God, himself; Jesus, who is viewed by most scholars as the son of God; and the Holy Ghost, or the Holy Spirit, which is a reference to God's work within the human realm.[14] This conception of God as a trinity is uniquely Christian in origin and character. In fact, it might be argued that the only way Christianity, from a theological perspective, could have remained a true monotheistic religion was to divide godhood into three components. Otherwise, the religion would have been accused of being polytheistic. Theologically, different Christian denominations and sects argue to exhaustion about the exact characteristics of this trinity and of Christ's position in the pantheon. However, the overarching conclusion among Christians is that there is one God, one Holy Son, and one Holy Spirit, which together constitute the conception of God in totality.

Another unique aspect of Christianity is that its founder never intended to create his own religion, nor did he claim to be divine. Did Jesus consider himself to be God? The answer, according to most scholars, is almost certainly no. Jesus viewed himself as *the Messiah*, a term in the Jewish tradition that refers to someone anointed by God. However, after his death Jesus's followers took his self-identified role of Messiah one step further and claimed that he was the son of God. Some even claimed he was God incarnate. His followers believed that, as the son of God, he came to deliver them from their oppressors and enemies—the Romans, who controlled Palestine during this period, and the priests who collaborated with them.[15] It was this message of hope and redemption that made him so popular during his life and contributed to his fame, adoration, and canonization following his death.

Perhaps more than any other religious leader of this time, Christ emphasized the importance of justice and equality among all human beings. At a time of terrible inequity and injustice, Jesus preached his message of nonviolence, pacifism, kindness, and compassion toward all human beings. These essential human traits, he preached, were highly regarded in the Kingdom of God. He demonstrated his commitment to these ideals through his sermons but also through personal action. He would dine with the impure, regardless of their social or religious background. He tended to the sick and dying himself and asked his followers to do the same. This ideal of service and sacrifice for a fellow human being is an integral part of many religious traditions. However, for Jesus, it formed the fundamental basis of his religiosity.

His was a very earthy religion, where the Kingdom of God would come to his people rather than his people seeking to achieve eternal bliss in heaven. For Jesus, heaven and hell existed within this earthly domain. This pragmatic and people-centered approach is also unique to Christianity. Each individual was responsible for cultivating these qualities and refraining from greed, avarice, and lust. This contributed to the individualistic nature of Christians and their respect for individual rights and responsibilities. Out of this expanding religious movement, it was actually the writings of his followers that created the unifying doctrine of Christianity as it has become known over time.

By and large, the concept of inclusivity is the characteristic that is most often associated with the Christian concept of God. This is because of the approachability of the Christian God to the average person. Christianity essentially adopts the stance that an individual can become a recognized member of the Christian faith simply by accepting Christ as the individual's personal savior. This openness to membership, despite any particular doctrinal differences, is the principle of the Christian faith that remains one of the reasons for the faith's historically rapid and widespread growth. The Christian faith is less associated with any particular racial, cultural, or ethnic connotations than either Judaism or Islam. In this sense, New Testament tracts, such as the gospel of John, reveal the highly personalized approach to faith that Christianity supports.

Islam

Islam (which translates to "surrender") is the youngest of the three Abrahamic religions. Its roots are deeply connected with the prophets of Christianity and Judaism. But it differs significantly in its interpretation of monotheism by introducing a new prophet, Muḥammad, and a new revelation documented in the Koran, which is what the faithful believe is the last and most authoritative word of God. As with our discussion of the other religions, we will place the teachings of its founder in a historical context in order to more fully appreciate their meaning.

Gods in Pre-Islamic Arabia

Arabia was (and is) a harsh, inhospitable desert environment. At the time of Muḥammad, it was considered by most people—and certainly by the powerful kings of Persia and Rome—to be a wasteland, with no strategic or economic value. There were no foreign invasions, because no empire was particularly interested in annexing a large swath of desert with warring tribes that would be difficult to govern. This tribal, nomadic culture flourished, uninterrupted, for many centuries and developed its own cultural and religious identity. The Bedouin tribes were frequently on the move in search of food and water, living in a few permanent settlements nurtured by spring-fed oases dotting the desert. Mecca and, later, Medina were such settlements. Caravans of merchants carrying goods from one settlement to another were common, and historical records describe great bazaars and festivals for trade and commerce. Society was dominated by tribal allegiances and loyalties. Feuds and bloody wars between tribes were common, and it was not considered unethical or immoral to raid another tribe to satisfy the needs of one's own.

We know very little about pre-Islamic Arabia. Our primary sources are inscriptions on the cubic structure known as the Kaaba in Mecca and the remnants of the oral poetic tradition practiced in Arabia for many millennia. What we do know is that for hundreds of years before the birth of Muḥammad, the Arabs had robust, diverse, and dynamic religious traditions. The focal point of both pre-Islamic and Islamic religious traditions was the Kaaba, at the center of which is a large black rock with special religious significance. Legend has it that the Kaaba was built by Adam, the first man, and was subsequently discovered by Abraham, Ishmael, and Hagar as they wandered through the Arabian Desert. Abraham, the patriarch of all three Abrahamic religions, established the monotheistic tradition of worshipping Yahweh, the one true God, at the Kaaba. Since then, the Kaaba has become home to over 300 religious deities worshipped by Arabs of different tribes. Although the tribes had cultural and political differences, they were clearly quite accepting of each other's religious beliefs and, in a remarkable show of religious tolerance, their favorite deities coexisted peacefully with each other for over 1,000 years.

Deities referred to in the Kaaba included many who were remnants of historical associations made by Arab tribes with neighboring Byzantine and Egyptian empires. We find shrines to Jesus and Mary, and to Hubal, the moon god and the ancient god of the Quraysh tribe, the keepers of the Kaaba. The most prominent of the shrines were reserved for the three daughters of Allah, the primary goddesses in the Arab pantheon: Al-lāt, Al-'Uzzá, and Manāt. Al-lāt was the goddess associated with the devil and evil spirits; Al-'Uzzá was a fertility goddess who was often called upon to bless the warriors before they set out for battle and was probably an adaptation of the Egyptian goddess Isis; and Manāt was the goddess of fate. Although Allah was considered the creator God and the supreme deity, he was seen as rather remote, and it was these lesser deities that people worshipped as a part of their everyday rituals, to ask for favors and forgiveness. Besides the many deities, the Arabs believed in supernatural beings called *djinns*. These were formless, ghostlike creatures involved in everyday human activities. They could lead people astray and were generally feared. People communicated with the djinns through *kahins*, their priests.

So what religion did pre-Islamic Arabs follow? There is evidence that many Arabs were Jewish and Christian. The Roman Catholic Church actually had a bishop assigned to the region, and parts of Arabia and northern Africa were ruled by a Jewish king. These well-established traditions were mixed in with local customs, gods, and rituals, which had been adopted over the course of many centuries. Many Arabs worshipped the gods and goddesses enshrined in the Kaaba, and modern writers would refer to these tribal religions and polytheistic traditions as *pagan*. In modern parlance, this word is used to refer to the religious traditions of people before the coming of Christianity or Islam. It implies a backward or uncivilized people who had no well-developed religious traditions. This characterization is unfortunate, because it is clearly incorrect. Any religious tradition that allows people of different faiths to coexist in peace for hundreds of years deserves our respect, not our derision.

Muslims refer to this pre-Islamic period, when Arabs worshipped many gods, as *jahiliyyah*, the time of ignorance. This Arabic term derives from the words *jahl* ("ignorance") and *jahaalah* ("foolishness") to denote the utter ignorance of pre-Islamic Arabs who had strayed from the monotheistic path of Abraham and foolishly worshipped many gods. One may choose to agree or disagree, but it is clearly the point of view of believers in the Islamic tradition.

The Historical Origins of Islam

The prophet Muḥammad was born into this society and into the powerful and well-respected Quraysh tribe of Arabia in about 570 CE. He was born into the prominent Banū Hāshim family, which at the time of his birth was of very modest means. The most reliable sources of information about the life of Muḥammad are the Koran and the Hadith, an oral compendium of stories and sayings of the Prophet that was put in writing about a century after his death. The Hadith was subsequently added to and edited by several scholars over the years, which resulted in over 300,000 Hadiths, most of which were very unlikely to be the word of the Prophet. Muslim scholars, over the centuries, have attempted to whittle down this collection to quotations that can be reliably traced to the Prophet himself, and so there are many edited compilations of the Hadith today, some accepted by the Sunnis and some by the Shia communities.

As is the case with the Bible and the Buddhist and Confucian texts, neither the Koran nor the Hadith was meant to be a historical account of events. Biographies of the Prophet were written a few centuries after his death, the oldest being penned by Ibn Ishaq in about the eighth century CE and translated later by Ibn Hisham. Many of these biographies were influenced by the passage of time and were in keeping with the prevailing legends of their time. As a result, much of what we know today is a combination of history and legend.

As with the other prophets who came before him, the circumstances of Muḥammad's birth portend his future greatness. Stories describe angels dressed all in white descending to earth from heaven—in one instance blessing him, and in another ripping open his chest and removing something from it. We know with much more certainty that Muḥammad's father died soon after his birth and that his mother died when he was six. His grandfather immediately took over his care and raised him until he too died, when Muḥammad was eight.

Before his grandfather died, he asked his son, Abu Taleb, and his daughter-in-law, Fatimah (Muḥammad's uncle and aunt), to take good care of Muḥammad and to raise him as their own son. The fact that Muḥammad lost so many loved ones and was orphaned by the age of six clearly had a profound effect on his thinking and his teachings later in life. He developed a particular empathy for the weak and underprivileged, and it is this sense of affiliation with the downtrodden that informs Muḥammad's later ethics.

As he reached adolescence, Muḥammad began to develop a reputation for wisdom and fairness and his ethical nature and his sense of justice are well documented. When he was still a young man, he participated in a meeting of the tribal elders to establish a code of conduct by which all tribes would agree to abide. This seventh-century alliance created by various Meccan tribes is referred to as the Alliance of the Virtuous, or *Hilf al-Fudul* in Arabic. Even though Muḥammad was young, he played a key role in negotiating this alliance. The consequences of the alliance were immediate: fair and uniform dealing in trade and the elimination of decades-old quarrels and vendettas between tribes. Muḥammad saw the benefits of instituting a code of ethics which would bring all the Arabs together under a uniform code of law. This early success may have played an important role in his development of the strict code of conduct expected of all converts to Islam.

At the age of twenty-five, Muḥammad was asked by a prominent, wealthy widow named Khadija to lead her caravan of goods and supplies to market. With his reputation of honesty and fairness, Muḥammad was able to successfully complete the trip and return with unexpectedly large financial returns. Khadija was so impressed by his success that she asked, through a friend, if Muḥammad would be open to marriage, even though she was quite a bit older than he was. Khadija and Muḥammad were soon married and remained in a monogamous relationship for the next twenty-five years. Every account of the Prophet's life indicates that they were happily married and devoted to each other and their children. Some sources claim that they had one daughter, Fatimah, whereas others claim they had six or more children, some of whom may have been adopted. It was common practice in the day for wealthy families to adopt and raise orphans and less fortunate children. One of the children he adopted was Ali, the son of his uncle Abu Taleb. Ali was the first male to convert to Islam and later married Fatimah, the Prophet's daughter.

Muḥammad spent long hours and sometimes days alone in nature, in contemplation of the creator's bounty. On one of these lonely retreats, in about 610 CE—Muḥammad must have been about forty—he had a terrifying experience, as told in the Koran. As he lay in a cave, ready to retire for the day, he heard a loud voice command him, "Read!" When he protested that he did not know how, the voice insisted and again commanded him, "Read!" Muḥammad had no choice but to repeat the words that he heard from this divine presence.

He raced home and told Khadija what had happened. She at once consulted with wise and trusted people around her, who apparently reassured her that these were nothing other than messages from God and that Muḥammad was the chosen one through which God had decided to convey his messages to mankind. For a while, the messages stopped, and Muḥammad was concerned that God had lost faith in his ability to communicate his message. When they began again, Muḥammad shared the revelations with Khadija and a few close associates, increasingly convinced that they were indeed the words of God. The revelations continued for over twenty years. The scriptures tell us that there were more than a hundred such revelations, which Muḥammad recited word for word to his small group of followers. Sometimes, these experiences were aural; other times, the message was conveyed directly to his mind. In some instances, Muḥammad actually saw a vision of the angel Gabriel reciting God's message to him. In still other situations, Muḥammad would go into a trance-like state and even lose consciousness.

To the faithful, Muḥammad's experiences are entirely real, and the messages he received, as recorded in the Holy Koran, are the words of God, with no human interpretation. To the faithful, the Koran constitutes God's commands and therefore represents the absolute guide to life and religion.

To the nonbeliever, Muḥammad's experiences may seem unbelievable and self-serving. It is difficult to provide a logical explanation for them. This is particularly true because Muḥammad was by no means the only one during this time claiming to be communicating with gods. Numerous *kahins* (a class of Arab priest), faith healers, soothsayers, and religious leaders had made similar claims. What then was so special about Muḥammad's revelations? According to some historians, Muḥammad may have been experiencing periodic hallucinations or epileptic seizures resulting from intense periods of spiritual meditation in contemplative solitude. This would suggest that the recitations were a product of his own mind. This is quite remarkable, given the incredibly beautiful poetry of the revelations.

Such experiences are not unheard of among religious sages who have spent many years contemplating the nature of God and his creation. The Buddha, Jesus, and many others who sought enlightenment are believed to have received divine inspiration—if not overt revelation—after spending years in its pursuit. What is unusual about Muḥammad's revelations is that they occurred on so many occasions and over such a long period of time.

Indeed, when Muḥammad convened a meeting and revealed his experiences to the leadership of the Quraysh, his tribe, they were incredulous. Many of them openly laughed at him, whereas others thought he had lost his mind. During his first three years of preaching, Muḥammad attracted a relatively small number of mostly young and poor converts. They appreciated his message of compassion, equality, and justice and his insistence on simple living. They also appreciated the fact that Muḥammad practiced what he preached. He gave generously and lived simply.

Before he proclaimed his revelations from God, he was widely respected for his honesty and wisdom, and most members of the Quraysh thought that he would assume a leadership position in the tribe. When he declared that his followers would worship Allah, most Quraysh assumed he meant that they should regard Allah as the supreme deity. Muḥammad's message, however, was much more restrictive: They were to not only worship Allah but reject all the other tribal gods that the Arabs had revered for many centuries. Most followers found this entirely objectionable and, at the end of five years of preaching, Muḥammad had converted less than fifty Quraysh to Islam. Even his uncle Abu Taleb did not convert, although as a senior member of the Quraysh, he remained Muḥammad's primary protector.

As Muḥammad's revelations in the hills above Mecca continued, he became more vocal in his preaching of God's word. The tribal leaders were alarmed by his claims and saw him as a distinct threat to their way of life. They were concerned about the potential wrath of the deities that Muḥammad had asked them to abandon and the fact that abandoning them went against the age-old traditions of the tribe. His pronouncements of the equality of slaves and women were just as threatening to the status quo. Finally, as keepers of the Kaaba, the leaders were in no mood to offend the other tribes who traveled to Mecca, each to pray to their own tribal deity.

The tribal leaders appealed to Abu Taleb to ask Muḥammad to refrain from preaching his faith. Despite his uncle's pleas, Muḥammad insisted on speaking his mind. He would surely have been killed or driven out of Mecca had his uncle not protected him from the rage of the Quraysh. Seeing they could not stop Muḥammad, members of the tribe began to systematically persecute his followers. They went as far as to place a three-year ban on anyone associating with Muḥammad's Banū Hāshim clan.

Muḥammad had been attempting to convert tribes in neighboring cities for many years, but he had been unsuccessful. Finally, in about 618 CE, he successfully converted a group of visiting pilgrims from Yathreb to his faith. Two years later, they returned and joyfully announced that both tribes at the Yathreb oasis had converted to Islam.

Unfortunately, Muḥammad's uncle, Abu Taleb, and Khadija, his wife of twenty-five years, also died that year. These deaths were a severe setback for Muḥammad, both politically and personally. Interestingly, at this time also, Muḥammad received a revelation from Gabriel, who asked him and his followers to move out of Mecca—where Muḥammad's situation had been growing increasingly precarious and tribal elders had actually decided to kill him. On the night of the planned assassination, Muḥammad and a few of his faithful followers escaped from Mecca through the back roads and headed to Yathreb. On his arrival in Yathreb, renamed Medina in 622 CE, Muḥammad was given a hero's welcome. This journey from Mecca to Medina, referred to as the *Hijra*, has a special significance in Islam.

Muḥammad eventually remarried, and although it was a tradition among the Quraysh to have no more than four wives, Muḥammad received a revelation from Gabriel that granted him God's authority to have additional wives because of his status as the Prophet. He ultimately took between eleven and thirteen wives. Some marriages were arranged to cement tribal allegiances, and others were marriages of charity to particularly needy women, such as widows. His favorite among these latter wives was Aisha, who was forty-one years his junior. She remained his wife until his death in 632 CE. By all accounts, Muḥammad was a loving and caring husband, who spent many hours with his family discussing and preaching the word of God.

In his early sermons, Muḥammad preached the greatness of Abraham, Moses, Jesus, and many of the other prophets of the Jewish and Christian faiths. He regarded them all as messiahs, or messengers from God, with a common lineage dating back to Adam. However, as time went on, it became obvious to many of the Jewish and Christian tribes that Muḥammad's message contained elements that were incompatible with their ancient beliefs. Many of them began to reject Muḥammad as a messenger of God and his strict monotheistic teachings, which clearly denied their own tribal gods and goddesses.

Muḥammad made no secret of the fact that he was offended by the refusal of the Jewish tribes to accept his status as the messenger of God. He instructed all Muslims to pray five times a day facing Mecca—not Jerusalem, as had been the custom in the past. This decree represented a growing schism between the Muslims and the followers of Abraham and Jesus regarding both their temples and their gods. The rift between Muslims and their Jewish and Christian neighbors resulted in battles for control of the local lands. Muḥammad, at the head of a Muslim army, defeated the rulers of two Jewish tribes and took prisoners. They were eventually allowed to walk free, but in conformance with the traditions of the day, Muḥammad confiscated their land and property.

Muḥammad's revelations in Mecca had been primarily concerned with ethical and religious issues, but in Medina, a distinct shift occurred in Gabriel's subject matter; the revelations began to have more to do with social and political issues than with matters of religion. Muḥammad's teachings in Mecca had focused on compassion and service to the poor, uplifting the downtrodden, peaceful resolution of conflict, and speaking the truth. In Medina, the Prophet preached the right of the faithful to take up arms if they had been wronged and to recover by force what had unjustly been taken from them. This teaching was taken by some as justification to raid caravans carrying food and supplies to Mecca.

The early caravan raids were unsuccessful, but as the Muslims learned the ways of war, it soon became apparent to other tribes that they were dangerous. The Muslims achieved a significant victory in the battle at the oasis of Bader when their small army of 300 defeated the Quraysh, who outnumbered them three to one. A year later, a large army of Quraysh soldiers marched toward Medina and was met at Ehud by an army of Muslims led by Muḥammad. This time, Muḥammad was defeated and barely escaped with his life.

Muḥammad often led his troops on raids and into battle to defend his faith. Although the religion espoused nonviolence, Muḥammad had received a revelation that a Muslim was allowed to resort to violence if his faith was threatened. The faithful were expected to respond to calls for *jihad*, or "struggle," when called upon by the Prophet. He instructed his soldiers to spare the lives of prisoners, women, and children, and to divide the spoils of battle equally among themselves. The years in Medina had transformed the Muslims from a small religious group to a politically and militarily viable city-state that was a serious threat to the tribes around it.

After his defeat at Ehud, Muḥammad was convinced that he had to do everything to protect his followers from another impending attack. The Meccans were as determined as ever to defeat the Muslims once and for all, and Muḥammad sent out messengers and emissaries to tribes surrounding Medina to ensure that they did not form alliances with the Meccans. The Meccans, meanwhile, amassed a huge army—over 10,000 soldiers—and marched on Medina in 622 CE.

One of Muḥammad's advisors was familiar with the military tactics of the Persian Empire and came up with the idea of building a massive trench outside Medina. Within a few days, the Muslims had finished digging the trench, which effectively prevented a direct assault by the Meccan cavalry. When the Meccans arrived, they were unable to break this unusual fortification and instead laid siege to the city.

After a few weeks in the desert, as their supplies dwindled and the alliance that they had put together began to waver, the Quraysh decided to withdraw. This was a historic victory for the Muslims, who saw themselves as protected by the divine will of Allah.

During the siege, a Jewish tribe near Medina, the Koreza, had joined the Meccan alliance, even though they had signed a treaty with Muḥammad. After the siege was over, Muḥammad accused the Koreza of betraying the Muslims and used this as a reason to attack and conquer them. All 700 males in small Jewish community were executed and the women and children were taken as slaves. Muslim scholars have gone to great lengths to provide adequate justification for this unusually barbaric act.

In 624 CE, Muḥammad had a vision that directed him to plan a pilgrimage, or *hajj*, to Mecca. He immediately sent word to the Quraysh of his plans and sought a peace treaty with them. By then, the Quraysh must have known that the Muslims were a fully capable military threat to them, and they chose peace and appeasement over what they thought might be a bloody and risky battle. The Treaty of Hudaybiyyah, between the Quraysh and Muḥammad, was signed in 626 CE, and it directed both sides to maintain peace for the next ten years. It provided for all children and young adults who had been separated from their families to return to Mecca should they wish to do so. It also provided the Muslims an opportunity to make a pilgrimage to Mecca while the Meccans retreated to the hills above the city. In accordance with the treaty, 1,500 unarmed Muslims set out from Medina for the *hajj*. The Quraysh allowed them to return home without incident and to honor the age-old tradition of praying at the Kaaba.

What followed were a few years of relative calm. The Quraysh now regarded the Muslims as equals in political and military terms, and neither side was anxious to provoke the other. Muḥammad continued to receive regular visits from Gabriel that increasingly focused on political and social issues.

In 728 CE, a tribe that was allied with the Quraysh attacked a tribe that was under the protection of Muslims. Muḥammad asked the Quraysh to pay war reparations to the attacked tribe or to consider the Treaty of Hudaybiyyah invalid. The Quraysh considered paying the Muslims for actions taken by an independent tribe not only unjust, but also humiliating. Their leader, Abu Sufyan, fully recognized the military superiority of the Muslims and attempted to diffuse the situation by traveling to Medina to restore the peace. Muḥammad, however, was in no mood for compromise. He mustered an army of over 10,000 Muslims and marched on Mecca. Abu Sufyan, recognizing that the Meccans were going to be defeated and potentially massacred, made a last-ditch effort to save his tribe by converting to Islam.

Muḥammad informed the residents of Mecca that anyone who converted to Islam would be spared; everyone else would be put to the sword. The Muslims walked into Mecca without a fight, and most residents—willingly or otherwise—converted to Islam. Muḥammad's conquest of the Arabian Peninsula was now complete. He was not only the Prophet, but also the king of Arabia.

As one of his first acts after the victory over the Meccans, Muḥammad entered the Kaaba and removed and destroyed every image of the deities who had resided there for many thousands of years. He announced to the residents of Mecca that the Kaaba had been cleansed and that Allah now had blessed the holy shrine and that it was purified for all Muslims to worship in. Many of the residents of Mecca who had very reluctantly converted to Islam continued their traditional Arab practices in private even though any public displays of images of old deities or prayers offered to them were considered the ultimate sin and severely punished. Nonetheless, over time, Islam completely replaced the traditional religions of the Arab tribes.

After the successful conquest of Mecca, Muḥammad returned to Medina and began the process of consolidating his political, military, and religious power. He continued to receive revelations from the archangel Gabriel. In a revelation in 632 CE, Gabriel commanded Muḥammad to go on his final pilgrimage to Mecca. As Muḥammad traveled back to Medina, he gave his last famous sermon at Kum, which turned out to be of immense historical significance.

Muḥammad turned to his son-in-law Ali and said, "Whoever's mawla I am, Ali is also his mawla."[16]

Many of the faithful took this to mean that Ali was the anointed successor of Muḥammad as leader of the Muslims. The Shia (meaning "the followers") regard Ali as the first caliph in Islam. Many of the other Muslims felt that the logical successor to Muḥammad was his closest confidant and elder statesman of the religion, Abu Baker. We now know the followers of Abu Baker as the Sunnis (or "followers of the word of God"). Sunnis make up about 80 percent of the world's Muslims today.

This split in Islam happened almost immediately after the death of Muḥammad, in 632 CE at the age of sixty-two. He was buried where he died, in Medina, and his tomb is now the second holiest place in Islam. He was survived by his many wives and children, who continued to practice and preach his faith. Some of his wives, in particular Aisha, played a crucial role in compiling many of his words and sayings. His wife Hafsa helped compile the first complete Koran and remained involved in religious and political matters for many decades after his death.

Muḥammad's later disciples did not try to elevate him to divinity. His teachings were clear in this regard. God was beyond all earthly beings; Muḥammad was simply a messenger. Muslims do regard Muḥammad as the ideal human being, who as a messenger of God had no faults and made no false statements. This implies absolute belief in the Holy Koran and invites no argument or discussion. For the believer, Allah is the one and only God, and the Koran is his revealed word transmitted through Gabriel to Muḥammad. This truly was the age of belief.

We have spent several pages discussing the historical account of Muḥammad's life and times. My purpose here is simply to put into historical context the teachings of Muḥammad and to clearly identify the sources of his inspiration. Within this context, both believers and nonbelievers can see the origins of the religion and how and why the principal scriptures came to be. They can judge their relevance for themselves in today's world.

The Basic Teachings of Islam: The Holy Koran

The basic teachings of Islam are codified in the Koran, which Muslims believe to be the written word of God. The importance of the Koran therefore cannot be overemphasized because it occupies a significantly more central place than the Bible does for Christians. The New Testament announces the coming of Jesus, the Son of God, and proclaims his message; Jesus is the focus of their belief. In Islam, Muḥammad is just the messenger who introduces the primary player—the Koran—to the faithful.

The Koran consists of 114 chapters, or surahs, and 6,000 verses. They are not ordered in the sequence in which they were revealed to Muḥammad but rather by the length of the passage. The longest verses appear first and the shortest ones at the end, as Gabriel instructed Muḥammad to do. According to the Koran, Muḥammad memorized and repeated God's words as transmitted by Gabriel, and not until fifty years after the Prophet's death were these verses written down. This oral tradition required the repeated rendition of the verses by the faithful. Indeed, Muslims believe that the Koran must be recited specifically in Arabic and cannot be translated into any other language. They believe that the beauty of the poetry and composition in the original language gives the passages in the Koran a unique ability to inspire and motivate the faithful.

Because the goal of every Muslim is to prepare his mind and body to submit to the will of Allah, Muḥammad and later Islamic scholars prescribed some fundamental practices that every Muslim must perform. These constitute what we now refer to as the Five Pillars of Islam:

- *Shahadah*: the declaration that there is no god except Allah and that Muhammad is God's messenger
- *Salat*: the ritual prayer performed five times a day
- *Zakāt*: the giving of a percentage of one's savings to the poor and needy

- *Sawm*: the fasting and self-control performed during the holy month of Ramadan
- *Hajj*: the pilgrimage to Mecca that Muslims must make at least once in a lifetime if they are able

The Conception of God in Islam

In Islam, Allah is the only true God. The roots of the name *Allah* can be traced to the Arabic definite article *al* and the word *ilāh*, meaning "God," so *Allah* literally means "the God." The monotheistic implication of this term was brought into sharp focus by Muḥammad when he insisted on Allah being the only one worthy of prayer. Using the name *Allah* to refer to God was not new. As we saw earlier, several religious texts in Hebrew and Aramaic refer to God as *Eloah* (or more commonly its plural, *Elohim*) or *'Alāhâ* in Syriac, both meaning simply "God." The name *Allah* can be found on inscriptions on Babylonian tablets dating as far back as 1700 BCE, and there are many more such references in Christian and Jewish scriptures.

So it is clear that the name *Allah* predates Islam by many centuries. Indeed, the Islamic conception of God actually predates Islam itself. Muḥammad's insistence on praying to a single God, with no exception, was in fact part of the old Hebrew tradition. Muḥammad himself said that what he was proposing was nothing new. He repeatedly stated that the message that God conveyed to him went back to the way Abraham asked the people of Canaan to worship the one true God. In this sense, *Allah* was meant to signify the one true God that Abraham had worshipped in the Kaaba. Abraham, of course, did not refer to his God as *Allah* but as *Yahweh*. Over the years, the Arabs had forgotten this monotheistic tradition and had begun to worship many gods, including Allah.

The Jews and Christians had preached the oneness of God as well. Muḥammad, however, went one step further in his insistence that Allah was the only god worthy of worship. This meant the complete rejection of all other deities. This concept is probably best represented by the Arab word *Tawhid*, which translates into "the oneness of God." It also implies the absolute nature of that God. He is without beginning or end, never created or destroyed, all-encompassing and beyond human comprehension. He is the singular and absolute reality that transcends the material world that he created. This uncompromising monotheism is central to Islam in its absolutism and rejection of any representation of God in images, or idols, and its absolute rejection of all other names or forms of God.

The Koran speaks of the divine essence, which cannot be humanly comprehended, and divine attributes that we can use to speak about this ultimate reality. What attributes can be assigned to God? Here are a few: He is the creator of all that we perceive; the mover behind all that is moved; he sees and knows all, never makes mistakes, is not part of but rather is independent of his creation. We can use these attributes to talk around him, to describe his greatness without being able to directly describe him as an entity. The Hadith speaks of ninety-nine attributes of Allah that can be used to describe him. Two of these attributes, *all-merciful* and *all-compassionate*, are included in the *bismillah*, which is the sequence of words that begin the daily prayers of most Muslims.

This description of God is similar not only to the concept of God in the other Abrahamic religions, but also to those in the Eastern religions of Confucianism, Taoism, and Hinduism. However, unlike these religions, Islam tolerates no deities other than Allah. To represent him through idols or images would diminish his greatness. To assign any attributes to Allah that would limit his infinite nature or to pray to any other god is a grave sin, known as *shirk* in Islam.

The concept of God within the Islamic tradition is highly abstract and does not allow for individual interpretations or revelations. Whereas God in Christianity is patriarchal and loving and, for some, exists in three parts, the Islamic God is absolute and uncompromising in its monotheism. He is completely dissimilar to anything we know in this material world. He is beyond description and comprehension and, as such, should not be represented through any human depictions. Idols and images of Allah are specifically forbidden in Islam. Indeed, this has resulted in the unfortunate destruction of many magnificent idols and sculpture in many parts of Asia and Europe. Islamic invaders and conquerors systematically destroyed idols and images of gods throughout the regions they conquered, even if they were not of Allah.

In places where this destruction could not be completed, the faces of the idols were disfigured by one stroke of a hammer. One cannot but notice the missing noses and parts of faces in otherwise exquisite sculpture that exists in historic temples and churches. Later Muslims went one step further and insisted that the name Allah could only be applied to their monotheistic God and not to any other concept of Allah, such as the ancient creator-God worshipped by Jews, Christians, and pre-Islamic Arabs.[17]

This literal and abstract absolutism is not found within Judaism or Christianity, and it leads to the idea that it is sacrilegious for any adherent to engage in an interpersonal manner with God. This literal inference of God and his supremacy within the Islamic tradition is characterized in the following passage:

> In the realm of supernatural beings Allah stands alone as the "Real" depriving all other so called gods of all possible reality. These were now "mere names," not corresponding to any real entities existing outside of language ... the term *ilah* ... when applied to anything other than Allah Himself is nothing but a word.[18]

Therefore, although the concept of God within Judaic and Christian traditions is supreme, the concept of God within Islam is both supreme and absolute. Prayer in Islam is highly structured and required at specific times throughout the day. Although God is ultimately unknowable, his will is readily apparent through the Koran, and it is this will that Islam's adherents must submit to.

This abstraction of God within Islam is manifested within the actual text of the Koran itself. The Koran is seen as the direct thought and doctrine of God as if he himself wrote it:

> The Qur'an is at once the most ... determining principle and the primary source of the Islamic system of beliefs, laws, ethics, behavior and even emotions and attitudes. It has been the dynamic force behind the rise of Islamic culture and civilization ... and regarded by Muslims as the very word of God Almighty, therefore normative and binding in nature.[19]

Prayer and Traditions in Islam

The ritual prayer that all Muslims are required to perform is not only recited in words but requires that a definite set of physical actions be performed as prescribed by the Koran. Prior to the prayer, the person is expected to cleanse themselves by washing their face, hands, and feet. During the prayer, the faithful are expected to kneel and prostrate themselves while facing in the direction of Mecca. These gestures symbolize their complete submission to Allah, as do the words of praise in the prayers.

This combination of physical ritual combined with the rendition of the prayers is not unique to Islam but is, in fact, practiced in just about every faith. What is perhaps unique about Islam is the frequency of prayer and the importance of communal praying. Muslim scholars tell us that the number of times a Muslim must pray in the day has varied from two to fifty. These numbers were revealed to the Prophet by Gabriel, and the number five was arrived at as a compromise.

The clergy's reminder and call to prayer is called the *adhan*. In modern times, this has translated into loud and sometimes disruptive chants over loudspeakers that are music to the ears of the believers but potentially disruptive to non-Muslims. There have been instances where mosques, churches, and temples have competed with each other over which could be louder in calling their faithful to prayer. Ultimately, the city governments had to ask them all to refrain from disturbing the public at odd hours of the day. As you might imagine, this can and has led to social conflict in several secular countries around the world.

What is Islam's view of the human condition, and what ethical precepts are its followers expected to follow? Interestingly enough, the Koran's view of the human condition starts at the same place that the Old Testament does—with Adam and Eve—it occurs in a paradise, in heaven. Because of this original sin, humanity was banished to earth and will continue to remain here until Judgment Day, when the followers of Allah, the righteous, will enter paradise and be rewarded for their good deeds and their faith in the one true God. Others who have forgotten their true purpose in life and who have not submitted to the will of Allah will forever be banished from heaven, as Adam and Eve were because of their forgetfulness and love for material possessions.

As in any other religion that relies on scripture and the revealed word of God, the Koran spends a good bit of time and effort defining the will of Allah, since this prescribes the behavior and ethics demanded of a true believer. Many surahs in the Koran spell out basic ethical behavior: truthfulness, honesty, justice, fairness, fidelity, humility, modesty, prayer, fasting, and respect for others. These expectations are no different from those of the world's other major religions.

Ethical and Social Dimensions of Islam

One of the unique aspects of Muḥammad's teachings was his emphasis on equality. This was something that was quite revolutionary at the time, when differences between the rulers and the peasants and between tribes and religions often led to segregated societies. Muḥammad insisted that everyone, regardless of their tribal or national affiliation, was equal in the eyes of God. He did, however, reserve this equality only for the faithful who had submitted to the will of Allah. Those who had not or had committed *shirk* did not deserve to be treated in the same manner as the faithful until they changed their ways. God was forgiving and all merciful only toward those who would repent and accept Muḥammad's claim that the Koran was God's word. This posed some serious problems for the nonbelievers, who had deep historical and social ties to their own religions and gods.

Muḥammad attempted to apply this concept of equality to both men and women. The Koran went a long way in improving the status of women in Arabia at a time when women had very few rights. Prior to the teachings of Muḥammad, women were regarded as property of their father or their husband. Muḥammad, for the first time, established inheritance rights for women, who would receive half as much as a male heir. In addition, any bride price paid by the groom for a bride was to remain the property of the bride until she died. Polygamy was common at this time and perhaps justified by the large number of men lost in battle. Widows and servant girls were often married to ensure their security in a family. Divorce was regarded as a last resort, although a man could simply divorce his wife by repeating the word "divorce" three times. Women, on the other hand, had to ask for their husband's permission for a divorce or had to seek it in a court of law that was entirely male. These rights, although unacceptable by today's standards, were substantial improvements at that time.

There is no question that the Koran was written in a male-dominated society and is directed almost entirely at men, with instructions and commands provided on how they should act. Women were not expected to act at all, and therefore there are very few directives to them except in their manner of dressing. The Koran does not require women to be completely veiled. Instead, it asks women to dress modestly and to cover themselves appropriately in the presence of nonfamily members.

The Prophet's wives began wearing veils presumably at his direction, even though it was not a common custom among the Arabs at the time. This practice was subsequently adopted by a large proportion of Muslim women. The hijab has been the subject of some controversy in the West. Although the Koran does not specifically require it, some Islamic scholars and social and cultural traditions have interpreted a portion of the Koran as insisting that Muslim women be almost completely veiled.

Summary and Observations

In this chapter, we explored the various concepts of God within three of the world's prominent religious traditions: Judaism, Christianity, and Islam. The concept of God within Judaism, the oldest of these three religions, greatly influenced the fundamental concepts of God within the other two. Since they are so closely tied together by geography and history, it is not surprising that many aspects of these religions are similar. First, let us focus on what all three religions have in common.

- All three religions view the Old Testament as a foundational text, and Abraham is an important figure in all of them (hence the name *Abrahamic religions*).

- All three are based almost exclusively on the revealed word of God, as documented in a Holy Scripture: the Old Testament, the New Testament, or the Koran.
- Each of the Abrahamic faiths has at its center a patriarchal figure that can be identified as the founder of the religion. Jesus and Muḥammad in Christianity and Islam, respectively, were historical figures about whom we know very little. We know even less about Abraham and whether he actually existed or whether he was a legendary figure.
- The patriarch of each of the faiths is believed to have brought to humanity a divine, revealed message that forms the basis of that specific religion's core beliefs. In Christianity, he was considered to be the Son of God or even God incarnate.
- God in all three of these religions is a supreme being and all powerful. In Judaism and Islam, and for some denominations in Christianity, God is remote, abstract, and, for all intents and purposes, beyond human comprehension. It is, therefore, not acceptable to portray him in words, images, or idols, because this would unfairly limit or prescribe him.
- Some denominations of modern Judaism and Christianity have allowed for a less literal and more liberal interpretation of scripture. They have encouraged open discussion, dialogue, and even debate on some of the basic tenets of their faith.

Despite similarities, significant differences in the three faiths exist in important areas relating to both theology and what constitutes God's being, existence, and interest in the physical world. Although they share similar concepts of God, each religion has delved differently into what constitutes it:

> From the God of the biblical Old Testament who . . . expresses a full range of human emotions to the Christian assertion that God was incarnated in human form to the theological struggles between the Mu'tazilites and the Ash'arites, the difficulty about

a transcendent deity in anything other than anthropomorphic terms has been a central issue for all three Abrahamic faiths.[20]

As this passage illustrates, each of the traditions has maintained a unique concept of God in their religious canon. In the Jewish faith and tradition, the oldest of these three major traditions, God is so venerated that he cannot be named. There are numerous terms, such as Adonai and HaShem, that make indirect reference to him. These are always used from a position of deep reverence and submissiveness. Despite remaining unnamed, the authority of a God within Judaism is supreme and absolute. Although God may be somewhat abstract and obscure to the typical Jew, his authority is not, and this Supreme Being is highly revered, if not feared. The Jewish concept of God is that of a supreme being who chooses not to dictate the actions of his followers, does not decree the particular choices that his followers might make, and does not regulate their behavior on earth.[21]

The Christian concept of God is more anthropomorphic. Jesus himself preached the vision of God that was more of a loving, fatherly figure than an abstract and incomprehensible entity. The Christian God is much more accessible and immediate than the Jewish or Islamic God. For most Christians, Jesus is an integral part of the Holy Trinity, in which Christ is seen not just as God's son but also as an aspect of God himself. This tripartite God is unique to the Christian faith and an inherent aspect of Christian theology.

God, in Islam, is remote and abstract and must remain so. Any attempt to limit his infinite nature is considered blasphemy. The Islamic concept of God has deep cultural and historical roots within ancient Arabic tribal culture, yet it deviated substantially from it by insisting on an uncompromising monotheism. This meant that all the ancient gods that the Arabic tribes had worshipped for thousands of years were removed from the Kaaba and replaced by Allah, as directed by the word of God revealed to Muḥammad and enshrined in the Koran. Mainstream Islam still interprets the Koran quite literally, and the few attempts to develop modern interpretations have not had a significant impact on most parts of the Islamic world.

All three religions are a product of an age of belief. The three competing concepts of God reveal the incredible power of belief in the revealed word of God as documented in scripture. The concept of God in these major religious traditions are not mutually exclusive but are certainly viewed this way by many fundamentalists. To large segments of the population, the differences are significant enough to cause people to wage war, time and again, to protect their faith. Religious institutions and conflicts within and between these Abrahamic religions have dominated social and political life in the world for centuries and do not appear to be near a resolution.

5

The Age of Reason: Development of the Scientific Method

> *"I believe in a Spinoza's God who reveals himself in the harmony of all that exists, but not in a God who concerns himself with the fate and actions of human beings."*
>
> —Albert Einstein

Judaism, Christianity, and Islam completely dominated the religious and political landscape in Europe, the Middle East, and large swaths of South Asia and North Africa for many centuries, until about 1400 CE, when the long period of human history sometimes referred to as the Dark Ages began. Even during the European Renaissance, any arguments against the teachings of religious clergy were punishable by death or worse. Questioning the authority of the Pope or the Imam was heresy and the consequences dire. It is, therefore, remarkable that in the middle of such challenging times for new ideas (from about 1450–1700 CE), or perhaps because of it, a remarkable new way of thinking developed that was to dominate human history until the present day.

A small group of rationalists and empiricists on the fringe of religious discourse consistently made the point that it was important to have a rational discussion based on empirical evidence about all matters, including religion. The voice of this very small minority of intellectuals was, for many centuries, drowned out by the constant drum beat of the religious establishment, who clearly saw them as a threat—and rightly so. Over the course of 400 years, the period of European history known as the Renaissance, entirely new ideas and discoveries surfaced about the world and forced us to reexamine long-held beliefs. This age has sometimes been termed the *Age of Reason*, and it sowed the seeds of a new way of thinking and ultimately led to the development of the scientific method.

How did this new way of thinking emerge? How did this new approach lead philosophers and scientists to rethink God, and how did they reconcile their ideas with the common BGITS concept of God? Indeed, the realm of defining God was no longer limited to religious leaders, priests, and pundits. In this chapter, we'll highlight the development of the scientific method through the writings of a select few leading philosophers of the time. These ideas emerged in Europe from the old Aristotelian ideas and evolved over four centuries into a highly structured and well-defined way of thinking whose development is far more important in human history than any single scientific discovery or technological breakthrough.

The Renaissance

Starting in about the second century CE, the mighty Roman Empire was in decay, and the order and organization imposed by this central authority began to disintegrate. For the next few centuries, "almost imperceptibly the Empire passed into the Papacy."[1] Will Durant succinctly describes this period:

> The Church, supported in its earlier centuries by the emperors whose powers it gradually absorbed, grew rapidly in numbers, wealth and range of influence. By the thirteenth century, it owned one-third of the soil of Europe, and its coffers bulged with donations of rich and poor. For a thousand years it united, with the magic of an unvarying creed, most of the peoples of a continent;

never before or since was an organization so widespread or so pacific. But this unity demanded, as the Church thought, a common faith exalted by supernatural sanctions beyond the changes and corrosions of time; therefore dogma, definite and defined, was cast like a shell over the adolescent mind of medieval Europe. It was within this shell that scholastic philosophy moved narrowly from faith to reason and back again in a baffling circuit of uncriticized assumptions and preordained conclusions. In the thirteenth century, all Christendom was startled and stimulated by Arabic and Jewish translations of Aristotle, but the power of the Church was still adequate to secure, through Thomas Aquinas and others, the transmogrification of Aristotle into a medieval theologian. The result was subtlety, but not wisdom . . .

After a thousand years of tillage, the soil bloomed again; goods were multiplied into a surplus that compelled trade; and trade at its crossroads built again great cities wherein men might cooperate to nourish culture and rebuild civilization. The Crusades opened the roots to the East and let in a stream of luxuries and heresies that doomed asceticism and dogma. Paper now came cheaply from Egypt, replacing costly parchment that had made learning the monopoly of priests; printing, which had long awaited an inexpensive medium, broke out like a liberated explosive and spread its destructive and clarifying influence everywhere. Brave mariners armed now with compasses, ventured out into the wilderness of the sea, and conquered man's ignorance of the earth; patient observers, armed with telescopes, ventured out beyond the confines of dogma, and conquered man's ignorance of the sky. Here and there, in universities and monasteries and hidden retreats, men ceased to dispute and began to search; deviously, out of the effort to change baser metal into gold, alchemy was transmuted into chemistry; out of astrology men groped their way with timid boldness to astronomy; and out of the fables of speaking animals came the science of zoology.[2]

These dense paragraphs beautifully summarize the incredible developments occurring in Europe that ultimately led to the scientific and technological revolutions that transformed all of humanity forever.

Before we trace the development of the Renaissance through the philosophical teachings of some of the most prominent philosophers of this period, let me say a few brief words about the primary characteristics of the sea changes in religion, politics, and society over this period. The Renaissance, which began in Italy and eventually spread to all of Europe, had four important characteristics.

Humanism

The term *humanism* implies an emphasis on the human condition and away from metaphysical speculation in all aspects of literature, the arts, society, and politics. It represented a shift away from unquestioning religious faith. The plays of Shakespeare, the poems of Chaucer, and the social commentaries of Machiavelli all deal with human emotion—love, anger, jealousy, lust, and ambition—not with the path to discovering God. These were universal human themes requiring no tether to religion.

Rationalism

Rationalism saw a significant and sustained effort to justify religious traditions and scripture through rational arguments. Beginning with Thomas Aquinas and going all the way to Locke, the rationality of Christian belief was defended by a few and debated by others. Rationality was increasingly important in religious and social debate.

Education

A great deal of emphasis began to be put on education, particularly of the elite. Most kings and queens of this era were highly educated, and many of them could speak several languages, having been educated by the finest teachers in their kingdom or even by superior foreign tutors. With the coming of the printing press, in some nation states, even ordinary people had a chance to educate themselves.

Equality

More individuals demanded rights and the sort of freedom that would have been inconceivable in all of previous human history.

We do not have the luxury of delving into the historical details of these broad trends in this book, but they are covered in many volumes of some excellent references (many cited in this chapter). Instead, we highlight important developments through the ideas and philosophies of some key individuals. We will be even more limited in our discussion, which will focus only on how these philosophical contributions resonated with and were often in conflict with the religious traditions of the time. In the process, our concept of God, at least at the philosophical level, was transformed by the writings of these original and prolific authors. Their impact went far beyond the religious themes we'll discuss here.

Perhaps the most important set of ideas, and ones that have direct implications for our discussion, was the development of an entirely different way of thinking about the acquisition and organization of knowledge of the world around us. These ideas ultimately matured and coalesced into what we now refer to as the scientific method, an idea so powerful that it transformed the human condition through revolutions in science and technology—truly the crowning achievement of this age of reason.

Francis Bacon

At a time when it was blasphemy to question the authority of the scriptures or to challenge the Aristotelian system of knowledge, Francis Bacon took on the superhuman task of reassessing all human knowledge and how it is acquired, analyzed, and assimilated. He proposed an entirely new system of how we learn and organize information, based on empirical and inductive principles.

Francis Bacon was born in 1561 into a prominent English family in Elizabethan England. The British Empire was expanding and had cast its substantial influence over every corner of the world. England had begun to emerge as a world power, and it was a time of big economic and intellectual ideas. His father, Sir Nicholas Bacon, was Lord Keeper of the

Great Seal of England; his mother, Lady Anne Cooke, was the daughter of the tutor of King Edward VI. Lady Cooke herself was a highly educated woman, a linguist, and a theologian, who without any doubt had a great early influence on the young Francis.

At the surprisingly young age of twelve, Francis was sent off to Trinity College, Cambridge, where he, as a young prodigy, came into contact with the some of the most brilliant thinkers of the time. It is clear from his writings that he came away rather underwhelmed by the penchant for Greek philosophy that was the norm at the time. At the age of sixteen, he accepted a position with the English ambassador to France. In 1579, his father suddenly passed away, leaving the young Francis with a taste for the good life, no money, and little to fall back on.

He took to the practice of law, both to make a living wage and with the intention of entering politics. In 1583, Bacon was elected to Parliament and, for many years afterward, was reelected to his seat, a clear testament to his ability to influence people with words. He was an outstanding orator and spoke with a depth of knowledge and gravity that impressed even his most vocal critics. His intellectual ability and fondness for debate and dialogue made him a popular figure, not just in intellectual circles but among political cohorts as well.

In 1606, he was appointed solicitor general, and in 1613 became attorney general. Finally, in 1618, Bacon was appointed Lord Chancellor, a position he believed was rightfully his because of its historical connection with his father's function as Keeper of the Seal. With his incredibly hectic and successful political life, it is a wonder that he had time at all for philosophy.

Bacon's philosophical foundations were laid in Cambridge, where he was exposed to the established intellectual tradition of the day. Greek philosophers—in particular, Aristotle and Plato—had been rediscovered after the European Dark Ages and were revered as never before. His early education convinced him that humanity's quest for knowledge had not been well served by the classical Greek methods. In his mind, the Greek philosophers had spent too much time and effort on theory and too little on observation. He felt this was the primary reason humanity had not made much progress over the millennia in understanding the world around us and expanding our spheres of knowledge.

Indeed, the word *knowledge* has a very special place and meaning in Bacon's writings. He did not accept the teachings of the classics or of experiential findings as the basis for what humans knew; he believed humanity must set a higher standard. Bacon asked us to abandon all our current learning and start all over again. We must do this so that errors, prejudices, and misconceptions that have crept into our conscious and subconscious mind are forever expunged from our knowledge base. Next, we must recognize the sources of our errors so that we can systematically and consistently avoid them in the future. In Bacon's words, we must destroy the *idols of the mind*. The term *idol* refers to religious idolatry, which mistakes things or objects for ideas. This imagery probably arose from Abrahamic religious traditions, which discouraged the worship of images or idols.

He defined the most common sources of error in our accumulation and organization of knowledge. For example, man tends to find order where none exists. This is a tendency that emanates from our desire to organize and simplify the world around us. Bacon referred to this kind of error as *idols of the tribe*.

As we observe in everyday life, different people organize their thoughts in different ways based on their intellectual inclinations. Some will find connections and correlations where none exist. Bacon cautioned us to be acutely aware of errors in our knowledge that can easily be created by the infusion of our biases into an objective truth that should form the basis of our knowledge. This is particularly dangerous when we generalize from one limited set of observations. Any such generalization must be tested and retested by multiple independent observations and observers. Only if the generalization holds up in every single instance can it be accepted as a valid theory. We can see the basis of the scientific method articulated clearly for the first time in this reasoning.

Man tends to believe what he is predisposed to believe on the basis of his prejudices, his past experience, his nature, and his preconceived ideas. Observations of nature and the world around him are then viewed with a biased lens that can easily distort the truth. Bacon referred to this second set of potential errors as the *idols of the cave*. We are all products of our environment, each with our own unique but limited perspectives. As Bacon put it, "For what a man had rather were true, he more readily believes. Therefore, he rejects difficult things from impatience of research; sober things, because they narrow hope; the deeper things of nature, from superstition; the light of experience, from arrogance and pride; things not commonly believed, out of deference to the opinion of the vulgar."[3] True knowledge should transcend such personal prejudices.

Bacon defined *idols of the marketplace* as the third set of errors introduced into our common knowledge base through misunderstandings induced by imperfect communication. Recognizing the limitations of language and of communication between groups of people, Bacon warned of errors that might be induced simply by interpreting words in different ways. Different terms can mean significantly different things to different people, particularly with abstract ideas. One of the primary difficulties in understanding and interpreting religious and philosophical texts is our inability to place their words in the proper context. The innumerable commentaries, interpretations, and essays written to explain the Talmud or the Bible are a great example of the confusion and rich diversity of interpretation that can result from the same text. There was no room for such personal interpretation in Bacon's universal knowledge base.

Finally, Bacon warned us against the *idols of the theater*. These are errors thrust upon us through systems of philosophy or religious dogma that have pervaded our society for generations. These systems of thought are a world unto themselves and quite often result in the creation of systems of logic that make sense only within the confined ideological spaces of the philosopher's mind. For example, the Greek philosophical tradition forces us to organize our knowledge in ways that are consistent with the rules set forth by Plato and Aristotle. Religious dogma is often justified as logical because we begin with the premise that scripture is the word of God and so must not be denied. Such a system of logic was not acceptable to Bacon, since it is based on false premises. These preconceptions artificially limit the validity of our knowledge.

It is tempting to force reality to conform to the elegant but artificial structures that allow us to explain the world. Many such edifices have been created only to be left by the wayside in favor of more modern and fashionable ones. Bacon wanted to construct a system that would withstand the test of time and would not be subject to the limitations of philosophical traditions. He argued that we must wipe away these cobwebs of our past.

After describing the potential pitfalls in the accumulation of knowledge, Bacon described in some detail what we now know as the method of scientific inquiry. He distinguished between our everyday experiences and deliberate experimentation to prove or disprove a hypothesis. Everyday experience does provide the basis for empirical evidence and is a valuable tool in helping establish reasonable hypotheses. However, as Bacon put it, "The true method of experience first lights the candle and then, by means of the candle, shows the way. Commencing as it does with experience duly ordered and digested, not bungling nor erratic, and from it educing axioms and from established axioms again new experiments."[4]

But the deliberate and careful accumulation of data is not sufficient to build knowledge. We must use this data to ferret out the essence of a phenomenon, what Bacon called its *form*. The data must be assimilated and organized, and general conclusions must be drawn on the basis of an inductive method to obtain more general rules and laws. These general rules, or *hypotheses*, must then be retested with additional data. Only those that remain valid after repeated retesting will survive to become part of our knowledge base. This is the definition of the scientific method.

Bacon sought not the simple enumeration of data but the development of the laws that explain and, indeed, *govern* the observed phenomena. For example, we can make observations about the motion of heavenly bodies and compile this information into volumes of astronomical data, but without Newton's laws of motion (modified by Einstein), we would never fully appreciate the order in the universe. The universal laws are verifiable by anyone and are not a matter of personal opinion or bias. The laws of motion are the form, the essence, of the concrete observations we can make. This form is always based on an accumulation of observations and is usually an abstraction that allows us to generalize beyond the original observations. We avoid the errors Bacon warned us against by constantly testing and retesting the *form* of a phenomenon with additional observations.

Sometimes, our understanding of the *form* is modified to account for new information. Newton's laws of motion, for example, held sway for over 400 years before Einstein showed them to be valid only under certain conditions. Why did it take so long for the *form* to be proved incorrect? Because the conditions under which the laws were violated were so unusual and rarely encountered that all observations were in complete accord with the proposed laws. It took a rare event—a solar eclipse—and teams of scientists all over the world making observations to prove that Einstein's ideas were, indeed, observably correct. Without this confirmation, Einstein's hypothesis would have remained exactly that—an unconfirmed hypothesis. With experimental and verifiable confirmation by independent observers, the hypothesis became an accepted theory—Einstein's theory of general relativity. Bacon would have been proud!

Bacon lived to the ripe old age of eighty-three, and he was a prolific writer. He wrote commentaries on the importance of the inductive method and of testing hypotheses with observations—not just in the physical sciences, but also in the medical and psychological sciences. His writings on analyzing and integrating observations of human behavior (both in real life and in deliberate experimentation) were the precursor to what is now the immense field of behavioral and clinical psychology.

Bacon was a man who saw himself as a seeker of truth, wherever it might lead him. He was unfazed by tradition and not limited by trends. By challenging established thought, which relied too much on complex logical conundrums, he saw the incredible value in the back-and-forth between logical reasoning and direct observation. One cannot—and should not—live without either of them. Those of us used to the scientific method don't give it a second thought today, but it was a profound change in the thinking of the time.

The greatness of Bacon lies not in his originality or in his contributions to science but in laying down in clear, concise, and understandable prose the basis for the scientific method.

Galileo Galilei

Perhaps no scientist, living or dead, exemplifies the struggle between reason and belief as poignantly as Galileo Galilei. He has been called the father of modern astronomy or even of modern science. What I find most fascinating, besides his accomplishments as a scientist, is his struggle for acceptance by a society that was unaccustomed to empirical observations and the scientific method. Sadly, Galileo's struggle 400 years ago is a microcosm of the struggle of science within society even today.

In 1615, as the Roman Inquisition was beginning to investigate his heretical heliocentric model of the universe, Galileo wrote a lengthy letter to Christina of Lorraine, the Grand Duchess of Tuscany, that has become a classic text in the history of science. It is brilliantly written and captures a moment when a proponent of the age of reason collided head-on with the well-entrenched establishments of the age of belief. The letter is too long to reproduce in its entirety, but I have quoted from parts of it below.

> Some years ago, as Your Serene Highness well knows, I discovered in the heavens many things that had not been seen before our own age. The novelty of these things, as well as some consequences which followed from them in contradiction to the physical notions commonly held among academic philosophers, stirred up against me no small number of professors—as if I had placed these things in the sky with my own hands in order to upset nature and overturn the sciences. They seemed to forget that the increase of known truths stimulates the investigation, establishment, and growth of the arts, not their diminution or destruction. . . .
>
> Showing a greater fondness for their own opinions than for truth they sought to deny and disprove the new things, which, if they had cared to look for themselves, their own senses would have demonstrated to them. To this end they hurled various charges and published numerous writings filled with vain arguments, and they made the grave mistake of sprinkling these with passages taken from places in the Bible which they had failed to understand properly, and which were ill suited to their purposes. . . .

> These men have resolved to fabricate a shield for their fallacies out of the mantle of pretended religion and the authority of the Bible. These they apply with little judgment to the refutation of arguments that they do not understand and have not even listened to. . . .
>
> They go about invoking the Bible, which they would have minister to their deceitful purposes. Contrary to the sense of the Bible and the intention of the holy Fathers, if I am not mistaken, they would extend such authorities until even in purely physical matters—where faith is not involved—they would have us altogether abandon reason and the evidence of our senses in favor of some biblical passage, though under the surface meaning of its words this passage may contain a different sense. . . .
>
> But I do not feel obliged to believe that the same God who has endowed us with senses, reason, and intellect has intended us to forego their use and by some other means to give us knowledge which we can attain by them. He would not require us to deny sense and reason in physical matters which are set before our eyes and minds by direct experience or necessary demonstrations.[5]

These passages demonstrate the frustrations of a man steeped in the scientific tradition, where hypotheses are verified through empirical observation, trying to convince an audience of believers who regarded their interpretation of the Bible as the final word on everything—regardless of the evidence presented to them, literally by their own eyes. He goes on to say that the Bible is open to interpretation, whereas the laws of nature are immutable and verified by observation. He is, of course, correct with regard to any religious text.

> It is necessary for the Bible, in order to be accommodated to the understanding of every man, to speak many things which appear to differ from the absolute truth so far as the bare meaning of the words is concerned. But Nature, on the other hand, is inexorable and immutable; she never transgresses the laws imposed upon her or cares a whit whether her abstruse reasons

and methods of operation are understandable to men. For that reason it appears that nothing physical which sense experience sets before our eyes, or which necessary demonstrations prove to us, ought to be called in question (much less condemned) upon the testimony of biblical passages which may have some different meaning beneath their words. For the Bible is not chained in every expression to conditions as strict as those which govern all physical effects; nor is God any less excellently revealed in Nature's actions than in the sacred statements of the Bible.

Hence I should think it would be the part of prudence not to permit anyone to usurp scriptural texts and force them in some way to maintain any physical conclusion to be true, when at some future time the senses and demonstrative or necessary reasons may show the contrary. Who indeed will set bounds to human ingenuity? Who will assert that everything in the universe capable of being perceived is already discovered and known? Let us rather confess quite truly that "Those truths which we know are very few in comparison with those which we do not know."[6]

Galileo next addresses the problem of a lazy and apathetic general population who would rather seek simple but perhaps erroneous conclusions. This group seeks the path of least effort and is anxious to criticize those who have worked tirelessly to learn more about the wonderful universe we live in;

> People who are unable to understand perfectly both the Bible and the science far outnumber those who do understand them. The former, glancing superficially through the Bible, would arrogate to themselves the authority to decree upon every question of physics on the strength of some word which they have misunderstood and which was employed by the sacred authors for some different purpose. And the smaller number of understanding men could not dam up the furious torrent of such people, who would gain the majority of followers simply because it is much more pleasant to gain a reputation for wisdom without

> effort or study than to consume oneself tirelessly in the most laborious disciplines.
>
> Now if the Holy Spirit has purposely neglected to teach us propositions of this sort as irrelevant to the highest goal (that is, to our salvation), how can anyone affirm that it is obligatory to take sides on them, that one belief is required by faith while the other side is erroneous? Can an opinion be heretical and yet have no concern with the salvation of souls? Can the Holy Ghost be asserted not to have intended teaching us something that does concern our salvation? I would say here something that was heard from an ecclesiastic of the most eminent degree: "That the intention of the Holy Ghost is to teach us how one goes to heaven, not how heaven goes."
>
> In my opinion no one . . . should close the road to free philosophizing about mundane and physical things, as if everything had already been discovered and revealed with certainty. Nor should it be considered rash not to be satisfied with those opinions which have become common. No one should be scorned in physical disputes for not holding to the opinions which happen to please other people best.[7]

Finally, he makes the case for all rationalists and scientists as he lays out the standard protocol of the scientific method, so everyone can independently test and verify observations and conclusions.

> Those who believe an argument to be false may much more easily find the fallacies in it than men who consider it to be true and conclusive . . . The more the adherents of an opinion turn over their pages, examine the arguments, repeat the observations, and compare the experiences, the more they will be confirmed in that belief.[8]

When he was finally found guilty of heresy, Galileo was placed under house arrest—a surprisingly light sentence for the time. His apology to the Church is a coerced confession:

I have been judged vehemently suspect of heresy, that is, of having held and believed that the sun is the center of the universe and immoveable, and that the earth is not at the center of same, and that it does move. Wishing however, to remove from the minds of your Eminences and all faithful Christians this vehement suspicion reasonably conceived against me, I abjure with a sincere heart and unfeigned faith, I curse and detest the said errors and heresies, and generally all and every error, heresy, and sect contrary to the Holy Catholic Church.[9]

The conflict between the advancement of science and religious doctrine continues to this day, and the lack of public understanding—or even awareness—of scientific results is almost as bad today as it was at the time of Galileo. His comments about the apathy and lack of intellectual curiosity of the public at large still holds true. What has changed, however, is the extent of authority of religious institutions—particularly in secular, democratic countries—and the ability of people to speak their minds without being persecuted for it. Unfortunately, many countries remain where religious zealots rule and, in those unfortunate circumstances, there is no room for religious tolerance or deviation from a given cleric's interpretation of the holy book.

Baruch Spinoza

Most Western philosophers would agree that Benedictus de (or Baruch) Spinoza laid the foundation for the period we now call the Enlightenment. His uncompromising rationality provides us with a framework where we can construct a definition of God. As we shall see, his definition of God is remarkably similar to the ancient Aryan view of the Rtá discussed in chapter 2.

Spinoza was born into a Jewish family in Amsterdam in 1632. All indications are that he was intellectually gifted and not prone to follow in the established traditions of the Sephardic Jews of the time. His disregard for traditional teachings and his refusal to recant blasphemous words that he uttered as a teenager led to his excommunication from the

Jewish community. Isolated from his faith and abandoned by his family and friends (who no doubt considered him an unrepentant sinner), Spinoza first went to live on the outskirts of Amsterdam with a family of Mennonite Christians, who were perhaps sensitive to his predicament. He lived a Spartan and isolated lifestyle. He immersed himself in reading and writing, earning his keep by teaching children and polishing optical lenses. In 1660, when his hosts moved to Rhynsburg, Spinoza moved with them. His home still stands on the street that now bears his name.

He was a dedicated and uncompromising philosopher. Although he may have been socially ostracized, Spinoza was not particularly deterred from his intellectual pursuits by his excommunication. He immediately set to work on a series of essays and treatises on complex social and philosophical issues of the time. Although he wrote extensively, only a single book was actually published under his name during his lifetime—*The Principles of Cartesian Philosophy*, in 1663. His crowning achievement was his four-volume masterpiece, *Ethics*, in which he explored, among other things, the rational basis for a definition of God. Spinoza completed this work well before he died, but he was fully aware of the dangers of publishing anything that could be viewed as heresy. The Catholic Church and the heads of state in Holland and Germany did not tolerate challenges to their authority. His friends and colleagues had suffered prison sentences or worse, and Spinoza knew well how far he could push the envelope.

A Treatise on Religion and the State, which he published anonymously in 1670, was banned and its sale prohibited as soon as it appeared. Even though it was anonymous, Spinoza received many letters accusing him of being an atheist, a man who would surely burn in hell for his denial of the common interpretation of scripture.

Spinoza made the bold—certainly for the time—assertion that the language of the Bible is not meant to be taken literally but is allegorical and metaphorical in nature. Taken literally, the stories and the claims in the Bible violate common sense and seem too fantastical to be true. This made perfect sense to Spinoza, since any religious text that is meant to inspire an entire people must provide a sense of wonder and amazement that appeals to the common mind. An unimaginative story that simply states the facts as they happened may not be inspirational at all. In fact, it would probably be a bit dull and uninteresting. In Spinoza's words,

> Scripture does not explain things by their secondary causes but only narrates them in the order and style which has the most power to move men, and especially uneducated men, to devotion . . . Its object is not to convince the reason but to attract and lay hold of the imagination.[10]

This may seem perfectly reasonable to a mind of the twenty-first century, but it was revolutionary and bordering on heresy in the sixteenth century. Spinoza did not stop there. He went on to provide examples of how the Bible presented beautiful allegorical tales of the parting of the sea and the resurrection of Jesus. He regarded the Old Testament and the New Testament as parts of the same canon and applied the same logic to both. The stories of the superhuman achievements of Moses leading his people to the Promised Land were put in the context of imaginative tales that offer inspiration and hope. The power of these stories, said Spinoza, was not in their factual content but in the lessons learned from beautiful tales that excite the human imagination and make us all believers in the power of good over evil. When God intervenes to save the chosen ones, he does this as an act of mercy and as a blessing to true believers. Why else would the common person believe in the power of the Almighty?

For the rationalists among us, this is inconsistent with any logical explanation we can provide and is therefore unacceptable as fact. Spinoza claimed that this is not the point of the scriptures at all. As he says in the quote above, the scriptures are not meant to satisfy people of reason; they are meant to provide a basis for faith.

Ethics and the Nature of God

The reaction to Spinoza's first work would have forewarned him of the reaction he would receive if he were to have published his masterpiece, *Ethics*, during his lifetime. When he was ready to publish it in 1674, after ten years of writing, his friends warned him of the dangers, and he acquiesced. The book was published in 1677, after Spinoza's death, and was almost immediately banned in Holland, attacked as being "profane, atheistic, and blasphemous."[11]

Ethics is a masterpiece of philosophy presented in four parts. Spinoza describes his system in a style that is clearly inspired by Euclid's geometry. He explores the relationship of man to God and to his fellow human beings. In laying out the logical framework for discussing such complex topics, he starts with enumerated axioms and works his way through proofs of theorems complete with corollaries and appendices. The terse, Euclidean style of presentation of his ideas is deliberate and ensures that the rigor of rationality is preserved throughout his philosophical deliberations. Anyone reading *Ethics* should not expect to see the same level of rigor and logical clarity as you might expect in mathematical proofs today. The logical progression is full of holes and missed steps. In fact, a modern reader would have a hard time making his way through the logic without some confusion and doubt.

In the first part of *Ethics*, titled "Concerning God," Spinoza begins by defining three key terms that were commonly used and understood by philosophers of his time: *modes*, *attributes*, and *substance*. By *modes*, Spinoza means individual objects or events; human beings or human thoughts. Mountains and rivers are all specific, transient manifestations of some underlying, eternal reality. What is this eternal and unchanging reality? Spinoza calls it *substance*, literally the underlying foundation on which all modes are based. We shouldn't regard substance as the elemental or physical makeup of objects—for example, we shouldn't think of trees being made up of wood and leaves, or even the formative elements carbon and hydrogen. Instead, Spinoza uses the term *substance* in a way that transcends the material world. It is meant to define the essence of the object, its underlying principles and laws. Each substance has a set of *attributes*, which he defined as the essence of the material substance.[12]

At the end of his logical exercise, Spinoza arrives at his definition of God as an infinite, necessarily existing (that is, uncaused) substance of the universe. "There is only one substance in the universe; it is God and everything else that is, is in God."[13] If God is the only substance and whatever exists is either a substance or in a substance, then everything must be in

God. Those things that are "in" God (or, more precisely, in God's attributes) are what Spinoza calls *modes*.

This definition of God has profound ramifications and is more complex than it first appears. Spinoza claims that God is not only the underlying substance of all things, but also the universal cause of all that exists.

He is careful to distinguish between what he calls the *infinite* modes or attributes of God—those that flow directly from God's nature—and the *finite* modes, which are specific instances that result from the application of the infinite modes. The laws of nature and the principles governing everything that exists in nature are the infinite modes of God, while the motion of bodies and the growth of living beings are examples of finite modes that result from the specific application of these infinite modes.

His definition also, in effect, eliminates the possibility of God existing as an entity outside anything that we see, experience, or conceive. Everything around us is an attribute of God. This includes all objects, living or inanimate, and the laws that govern them. This definition of God then includes all of nature and the laws that govern nature. Perhaps more important, this definition excludes an anthropomorphic God or a supernatural God that is outside the realm of the laws of nature.

In the words of Steven Nadler,

> Spinoza's fundamental insight in Book One is that Nature is an indivisible, uncaused, substantial whole—in fact, it is the only substantial whole. Outside of Nature, there is nothing, and everything that exists is a part of Nature and is brought into being by Nature with a deterministic necessity. This unified, unique, productive, necessary being just *is* what is meant by "God." Because of the necessity inherent in Nature, there is no teleology in the universe. Nature does not act for any ends, and things do not exist for any set purposes. There are no "final causes" (to use the common Aristotelian phrase). God does not "do" things for the sake of anything else. The order of things just follows from God's essences with an inviolable determinism. All talk of God's purposes, intentions, goals, preferences, or aims is just an anthropomorphizing fiction.[14]

Do we then conclude that for Spinoza, God and nature are one and the same? Spinoza goes to great lengths to say that this is not so. To highlight the difference, Spinoza takes some effort to distinguish between two aspects of nature: the essential and productive attributes of God. By making this distinction, Spinoza distinguishes between the essential components of nature, such as its laws, and the rest of creation—which essentially must follow as a consequence of these laws and the way they interplay and act on matter and energy.

He goes on to establish the equivalence of God and the essence of nature, *Natura naturans*. It is this essence of nature—the underlying laws of the universe, not the commonly observable manifestations of nature—that defines God. The transient elements of nature, such as the trees around us and the thunder and lightning in the skies, are manifestations of the underlying permanent and essential laws that govern these transitory phenomena.

Mind, Matter, and Free Will

Many other philosophers, before and since Spinoza, have accorded the human mind a special place outside the bounds and laws of nature. Descartes, for example, believed that to preserve the concept of free will, the human mind and soul must be exempt from the deterministic laws that rule over the material universe. In effect, the human spirit transcends the laws of nature. This ensures that we are separate and distinct from nature, not one with it, and therefore have the ability to control and manipulate it by our actions. Spinoza rejects this. In books III and IV of *Ethics*, he clearly lays out his point of view that nothing stands outside nature, not even the human mind and soul. Our actions and our thoughts are determined by the same laws of nature as everything else in the observable universe. We are very much a part of nature and everything we think and do is subject to the very same laws of nature.

Spinoza's aim in the third and fourth volumes of *Ethics* is to place the human mind and soul firmly in nature's domain. Nothing stands outside of the universal laws of nature—not even the human mind. Human thought and emotion are the most difficult to fit into this depiction, because they seem to transcend logic. Not so, says Spinoza. Nature and the laws of nature are always and everywhere the same, even within our minds. Much like the Vedic Rtá, Spinoza's God is not mind or matter; he is the immutable laws of nature that control both.

What is truly remarkable about Spinoza's writings is their radical departure from the conventional wisdom of the time. To suggest that God is not a supreme being outside the realm of nature was nothing short of blasphemy. It is no wonder that *Ethics* was not published until after his death. Spinoza's ideas threatened the elemental foundations of Judaism and Christianity of his time. His books were banned in Holland and remained in intellectual obscurity for many decades after his death.

Spinoza clearly recognized that his ideas had societal consequences. His ideas led directly to democratic and egalitarian ideals. Nature does not distinguish between the rich and the poor, between the pious and the agnostic, or between the ruling and the working class. Neither the clergy nor the royalty have any God-given right to their position—and this fact directly undermines their claims to power.

Spinoza's ideas would have resonated with the authors of the Upanishads. The Advaita philosophers of ancient India saw only one underlying reality—a supreme consciousness that pervaded all. The Chandogya Upanishad speaks clearly and consistently about the oneness of humanity, God, and all creation. The Atman (the essence of us as human beings) is one with the Brahman, Spinoza's *Natura naturans*. To understand God, we must understand its substance, the universal laws of nature—that is, the Rtá of the Rig Veda. In doing so, as Einstein put it 400 years later, we are "reading the mind of God."[15] We are beginning to come full circle in the history of our philosophical traditions. We will come back and discuss this in much more detail in chapter 8.

John Locke

Thomas Jefferson wrote,

> Bacon, Locke and Newton, whose pictures I will trouble you to have copied for me: and as I consider them as the three greatest

men that have ever lived, without any exception, and as having laid the foundation of those superstructures which have been raised in the physical & moral sciences.[16]

John Locke is generally regarded as the torchbearer of Francis Bacon. He was born into a Puritan family in 1632, just outside Bristol, England. He was baptized and raised in the typical Puritan tradition and attended the prestigious Westminster school in London, and Oxford University. Oxford was at this time on the leading edge of knowledge in science and medicine. Noted scientists such as Robert Boyle and Robert Hooke were there, laying the early foundations of physics. Locke later earned a degree in medicine and began his practice as a personal physician for Lord Ashley. Later, he continued his medical studies under the direction of Thomas Sydenham, who played a significant role in shaping his views on social issues, as well as medicine.

Locke wrote extensively about social issues and, in particular, made arguments against absolute monarchy and the importance of individual freedom and consent as the basis for a democratic system of government. His outspoken writings and speeches forced him to flee to Holland in 1683. He spent five years there, in the company of freethinking Protestant groups that were greatly influenced by Spinoza. The rationalist ideals in *Ethics* shaped Locke's ideas on political and religious freedom and the separation of church and state. It is here that he composed his essay titled "Letter on Toleration," which was published upon his return to England.

Locke's religious convictions were very conservative, consistent with his Puritan upbringing. He considered the Bible to be divine revelation and the word of God. Miracles and superhuman efforts were not regarded as parables but as proof of the divine origin of the Bible. The laws of nature that science was beginning to discover were no different from revelations in the Bible, since both had their origin in God. Indeed, according to Locke, the laws of nature could only be unveiled through the teachings in the Bible. Without it, man would be reduced to an immoral, ignorant being. He was a firm believer in creation by intelligent design.

Rationalists had begun to question scripture with thinly veiled concerns about the infallibility of what was claimed to be the word of God. Locke stood firmly by his beliefs. In his view, a conflict between reason and scripture was not sufficient motivation to abandon scripture. He claimed that there were two ways of gaining knowledge and establishing facts: One was with reasoning and observation, and the other was through revealed scripture. The revealed word did not need to be proved with logic or shown to be valid through rational argument. However, logical arguments must be made to establish whether a claim of divine revelation is real.

Revelations could only be made by messengers of God, and in Locke's view, a person could be shown to be a messiah only if he had performed a miracle. Locke reasoned that Jesus was clearly the Messiah because so many miracles had been ascribed to him. He used this same questionable logic to reject the claims of other potential messiahs, such as Muḥammad. As a Protestant, he also criticized the clergy and held them responsible for not suitably using reason to judge what part of the Holy Scripture was God's word and what was not.

Despite his conservative religious views, Locke is often referred to as the father of liberalism because of his belief in the basic equality of all human beings. He derived this philosophy through biblical texts (Genesis 1:26–28).

The other major theme of Locke's writing is religious tolerance. His Puritan beliefs notwithstanding, he was a firm believer in the individual's right to choose their religion. He recognized that different religions provided different points of view. Human beings, he said, were not in any position to pass judgment over these belief systems, and even if they could, it would not be wise to enforce a single "state religion" on the people because "beliefs cannot be compelled by violence."[17] Imposing a state religion could only lead to massive social unrest and war. His opinions were clearly shaped by the European Wars of Religion from 1520 to 1650 following the Protestant Reformation. When his book *Letters Concerning Toleration* was published in 1689, he had seen firsthand the mayhem and bloodshed that religious intolerance could lead to. Religious tolerance also meant that there had to be a clear separation between church and state so that the state would not impose its will and its religion on a free people. This was a radical idea for his time and one that was adopted by the American colonies in the following century.

Despite his extensive writing about equality, Locke was a major investor in the slave trade through the Royal African Company. He participated in crafting the Fundamental Constitutions of Carolina, which formalized the absolute power the slave master had over his slaves. In doing so, he very deliberately created a systematic process for the enslavement of tens of thousands of Africans. This disconnect between his writings and his actions have led to accusations of hypocrisy. Some critics have said that Locke cared about liberty, freedom, and equality only when it applied to white English gentry.

Thomas Hobbes

Several prominent thinkers of this same period, such as Thomas Hobbes, felt and wrote quite differently from Locke. Hobbes was much more skeptical about revealed scripture, organized religion, and the existence of a supernatural God. In 1651, Hobbes published his well-known master-work, *Leviathan*, in which he laid out his view of God and religion.

Hobbes saw human beings as fearful, insecure, and brutish and in need of an "earthly God" who had the authority to impose ethical, moral, and therefore social order in the world. In his view, humanity had created gods to comfort themselves when they faced hardship and adversity.

This, in his view, made matters worse. It led to religious intolerance and conflict. This was all too real for anyone living in Europe at the time. The Thirty Years' War (1618–1648) had just ended in Germany, and decades of conflicts between Catholics and Protestants had cost millions of lives all over Europe. For Hobbes, God should not be defined by religious scripture or doctrine but by social and political factors—by relationships between people.

Social contracts should define relationships between people, and this, in turn, should define God. This God, whom he dubbed *Leviathan*, was an all-powerful entity who would ensure that social contracts between people were respected and enforced, with two consequences: First, religious teachings would be divorced from politics and the social order. Second, the right of a ruler to rule his people would no longer be sanctioned by the Church or a religious establishment. A king would not have any God-given right to rule; his authority must come from social contracts that the people had established.

This was the beginning of a political system in which the democratic representation of the people formed the basis of a ruler's power. In some ways, this was a throwback to the old Hellenistic ideas of democracy. According to Hobbes, this was the only way to ensure that the belief in God did not lead to intolerance and war. Hobbes's God is based not on revealed scripture but on a logical interpretation of human psychology and social and political reality.

The rather different points of view of Locke and Hobbes illustrate the intellectual climate in England at a time of transition from the age of belief to the age of reason. Even the brightest of minds struggled to define their beliefs to bring them in line with rational thought. One thing is, however, clear: The importance of reconciling religious belief with rational thought was on everyone's mind. It was no longer sufficient to simply believe and accept the word of God as revealed in scripture and religious dogma without question.

Voltaire

François Marie Arouet was born in Paris in 1694 to an upper-middle-class family. He barely survived his birth; his mother did not. His early poor health would dog him for the rest of his eighty-four years, a remarkably long life for his time. François showed his penchant for poetry at an early age. He was only a teenager when he began composing poems of some repute. This convinced his father that he would be good for nothing and in fact would cause nothing but trouble. His fears were confirmed when François announced his intention to pursue a career in literature.

It didn't take long for his writing to land him in trouble. In 1717, at the age of twenty-three, he found himself imprisoned in the Bastille. During that year behind bars, he took to the task of writing poetry seriously and inexplicably took on the name Voltaire. His first full-length poem, "Henriade," was followed in 1718 by his first successful play, *Edipe*, which ran on Paris stages for well over six weeks. Parisian playwrights, critics, and intellectuals raved and congratulated him on its brilliance and wit. For the next eight years, Voltaire wrote both successful and (many) unsuccessful plays and poems. In the process, he became a well-known and highly acclaimed author and wit. Royalty and commoners alike flocked to hear him speak. He was irreverent and blunt, clever and irascible in his criticism of whatever he saw as being inconsistent with his egalitarian and liberal views. His passion was palpable to his audiences and his logic and satirical wit biting to the core.

These were perilous and uncertain times. King Louis XVI had just died, and the political establishment was in no mood for criticism or humor. His satire and wit caught the attention of the regent and he was banished to England in 1728, where he lived for three years. He used this opportunity to learn about the ways of the English and very quickly realized the remarkable changes that had transformed England from a monarchy to a country ruled by a parliament—a parliament that was more powerful than any European monarch. In England authors, political pundits, philosophers, and poets spoke without fear of imprisonment or the guillotine. In a remarkably short time, he understood the renaissance in England and penned one of his early masterpieces, *Letters on the English*. He was living in a truly remarkable time in England: Locke and Hume had begun to apply Baconian methods and logic to well-established religious dogma and superstition. The teachings of the Church were being openly debated and questioned and in many cases abandoned by not only the intellectuals, but also by large swaths of the middle class.

Isaac Newton died while Voltaire was in England, and he made it a point to attend his funeral. He was deeply impressed by the respect given to such thinkers, scientists, and men of arts. He contrasted the open and accepting atmosphere in England with the aristocratic and papal tyranny in France at the time, where the path of any challenge to religious dogma led to the Bastille. There was no room for new ideas and certainly no room for political or religious dissent.

Letters on the English remained unpublished for a few years until a publisher in France distributed it widely without the consent of its author, who did not wish the contents of the book to be made public. In the book, Voltaire urged his countrymen, particularly the middle class, to rise and demand their rights to free expression and their fair place in running the country. This was revolutionary for the time—indeed, it was the beginning of the long philosophical road to the French Revolution.

Voltaire was once again on the run after the regent ordered him confined to the Bastille. This time, he did not escape alone but eloped with the Marquise du Châtelet, a highly educated and intellectually gifted woman who was well versed in mathematics and physics. Together, they spent many years working in the chateau at Cirey, conducting scientific experiments, writing, and entertaining friends and dignitaries. It was during this time that Voltaire wrote his classic novels *Candide*, *Zadig*, and *Micromegas*. These novels combined Voltaire's fantastic flights of imagination with humor and political satire, and were meant to simultaneously amuse, entertain, and incite the audience. It was a productive time and one that drew him the attention of some of the most powerful monarchs in Europe.

One of Voltaire's admirers was none other than the young ruler of Germany, Frederick the Great. He was a freethinking product of the Enlightenment. He invited Voltaire to be his guest at his palace in Berlin and in 1750, Voltaire obliged and ended up staying two years—joining him for royal occasions and for private parties where the "conversation was more interesting than any book of philosophy of the day."

However, Voltaire was too independent and free with his words to last too long in a royal court. After two years, he returned to France to settle down in a small town named Ferney at the French–Swiss border. Ferney was sufficiently far away from Paris for the political establishment to care too much what he did, and he could find a home in France if he upset the Swiss. Ferney, for a short while, became the center of European intellectual discourse. Voltaire graciously received a constant string of prominent visitors but tired of them quickly and complained loudly about not having enough time to himself.

Voltaire, the Church, and God

Voltaire was already in his mid-sixties and at the peak of his literary career when the ongoing feud in France between Protestants and Catholics took a turn for the worse. Persecution, murder, and lynching motivated primarily by religious differences were becoming commonplace, driven by an overzealous clergy. Voltaire was incensed. For the first time in his career, his writings took on a serious and urgent tone. They were not the musings of a philosopher but a call to action. He urged all like-minded Frenchmen to join him in the battle against the tyranny of the Church.

In 1767, he published *A Treatise on Toleration*, in which he urged his readers to reject intolerance and clergy-inspired dogma and to be more accepting and open-minded about the beliefs and faith of others. Voltaire believed passionately that the clergy was misusing its authority and its influence to drive people to what he considered the two greatest enemies of French society: intolerance and superstition. Voltaire presciently wrote, "The man who says to me, 'Believe as I do or God will damn you,' will presently say, 'Believe as I do, or I shall assassinate you.'"[18]

These words still ring true. For Voltaire, it was a matter of personal liberty and individual freedom—freedom from the clutches of dogma, which he regarded as intellectual slavery. For him, it was obvious that any attempt to force people to believe in ideas against their will was sure to lead to social upheaval and incessant feuds, if not all-out war. He urged people to learn to accept different religious, political, and philosophical opinions.

In the years following the publication of *Treatise on Toleration*, Voltaire unleashed hundreds of short booklets that ranged from poetry to real-life drama and fiction, all with the single-minded purpose of questioning the integrity of the Church. He questioned the authenticity of the Bible and those who believed in its literal interpretation. He skewered the clergy by pointing out the gaping holes and inconsistencies in their sermons and in their interpretation of scripture. Voltaire reserved his most vitriolic writing for the tyranny of religious dogma and the priesthood. Finally, he took on the persecution of religious minorities brought on by the Church's preached intolerance, which in his mind had no place in Christianity.

Despite his strident criticism of the church and the clergy, Voltaire was no atheist. In many of his writings, he professed his belief in a supreme being that created and maintained this world and was eminently worthy of worship. He fervently embraced the teachings of Jesus but rejected the clutches of organized religion, which he saw as corrupt and fundamentally flawed. In his view, the church had become too political, self-serving, corrupt, and powerful to truly lead humanity to God. For him, the simplicity of prayer and devotion, the leading of an ethical life in accordance with the teachings of Jesus, and service to humanity constituted true religion. It was the trappings of ritual and blind faith, untamed by reason and amplified by the teachings of a self-serving clergy, that ultimately led to superstition and intolerance, the two most dangerous of evils perpetuated on mankind.

Voltaire was wildly popular among literati, philosophers, and the common man. A large number of people clearly agreed with him but were too afraid to speak up. They did not have his status or the resources to protect themselves from the wrath of the Church. It is a testament to the change that occurred in Europe that Voltaire was not arrested and sentenced to death. His blasphemous writings and his persistent opposition to both the Church and the political establishment would surely have ended violently a few decades earlier. His influence in France and in the rest of Europe led to a significant reduction in the authority of the Church and, ultimately, to the French Revolution. Voltaire laid the groundwork for a political and religious infrastructure based on reason rather than dogma and intolerant beliefs.

Emmanuel Kant

No discussion on the transition from faith to rationality would be complete without a discussion of Emmanuel Kant, one of the most influential philosophers of the eighteenth century.

Kant was born and lived his whole life in the small town of Königsberg, in East Prussia, now a part of Russia. He led a highly structured and regular life as a university professor far from the intellectual capitals of Europe. He chose not to travel and was quite content with an academic pursuit of philosophy. Unlike most philosophers during the Renaissance, Kant did not write his most important work, *The Critique of Pure Reason*, until he was over fifty-five years old.

Kant was most influenced by the writings of skeptics such as David Hume. The skeptics had argued that neither the rationalists nor the empiricists had the tools to adequately address philosophical questions about the world around us, particularly those related to religion or God. According to Hume, we have only two sources of knowledge: direct sensory observation and relations between objects. Inferences about the future made on the basis of past experience have no rational basis. For example, if you have observed the sun rising in the morning every day of your life, you could not conclude that the sun would rise tomorrow based on any rational argument. This meant that no prediction of the world around us was possible through pure reason. The conclusions and predictions of science, which were beginning to have a profound influence on philosophy, were therefore in serious question under this skeptical view.

Kant agreed with most of Hume's arguments and hypotheses, but he reasoned that we have one more source of knowledge: the ability of our own mind to construct relationships. These relationships were independent of the definitions of the objects and also independent of direct experience. This was a profound insight, and it led to a complete rethinking of how knowledge could be acquired and what the differences were between reality and our perception of reality.

The basic arguments that Kant presents in his seminal work, *Critique of Pure Reason*, revolve around these three ways in which we acquire knowledge of the world around us—either through direct observation, through relations between objects, or through our own mental constructs. Kant claimed that the knowledge we acquire is not simply a passive reception of information from our sense perceptions. Instead, the perception and understanding of the information received is also a function of how each individual processes, organizes, and comprehends this information. Our minds are more like an inquisitive lawyer or judge, demanding and assimilating data, than like a passive pupil receiving information from a teacher.

Knowledge acquired is, therefore, not just a product of our direct sensory perceptions but filtered by our mental ability to absorb this information into a form that is unique to our mind. For Kant, synthetic, a priori knowledge was possible.

In the context of modern science, this is clearly true in many obvious instances. A person who is color-blind will perceive the world differently than one who is not. Our visual, auditory, and olfactory perception of the world differs substantially depending on our sensory organs and how their signals are interpreted by our brain. Physiological experiments conducted in the past few decades clearly show that our feelings of physical pain are determined largely by how our brain interprets the signals coming to it from the cells on our skin. In a very interesting version of such an experiment, a person who has lost a limb continues to feel pain in the limb even though he no longer has it. Given the evidence provided by modern science, there is very little doubt that Kant's claim that our perception of the world around us is determined both by the sensory input we receive and our mind's interpretation of this input is valid. Even higher-level conceptualizations, such as space and time, are constructs of our mind and are, therefore, not an inherent part of reality.

Kant argues that our brains construct hypotheses to make rational sense of our perceptions. Our knowledge of the world is, therefore, informed by the organization we impose on the information we receive. How does this affect our concept of God? We have no direct perception or sensory experience of God. However, our minds naturally postulate the existence of God to make sense of the complex universe around us.

Our minds are inclined to think of relationships between objects. Our tendency to look for cause-and-effect relationships ultimately leads us to seek a first cause for the world in which we live. Kant freely admits that this does not prove the existence of God. Indeed, there is no way to logically prove or disprove the existence of God, but it is perfectly rational for our minds to evolve a concept of God in an attempt to organize and rationalize our reality.

God, therefore, emerges as a natural and necessary consequence of the way our mind assimilates our experiences and our sensory inputs. To postulate the existence of God is rational; however, it is not possible to use rational arguments to go beyond this hypothesis to explore the nature of God. Kant rejected the notion of a God that was justified only on the basis of revealed scripture. He regarded such claims as inconsistent with rationality and, unlike Locke, found this to be sufficient reason to abandon such a notion. Blind faith for him had been replaced with rational faith.

Kant's next important contribution, *A Critique of Practical Reason*, addresses the question of God from the imperative of morality and ethics. Kant claimed that reason alone is sufficient to define a universal code of conduct for man; religion or God does not need to be invoked. It is in our own self-interest and in the interest of those around us that we abide by universal moral laws that will result in a just and peaceful society. However, Kant noted that all human beings have desires and impulses that go against their best interests and against the rational, universal moral code of conduct. To ensure that this is minimized requires a belief in God. God and the promise of immortality provide the incentive for people to act morally so that their actions may be rewarded by a supreme being—either in this life or in subsequent lives.

George Wilhelm Friedrich Hegel

George Wilhelm Friedrich Hegel was born in 1770 in Stuttgart, Germany, into an educated, well-to-do family. He was, by all accounts, a very serious, thoughtful, and successful student in both high school and at Tübingen Protestant Seminary. After several teaching assignments, Hegel accepted a position as professor of philosophy at the University of Berlin, where he served from 1818 until his death in 1831. During this period, he was regarded as the preeminent philosopher of his time.

During his lifetime, Hegel published four books: *Phänomenologie des Geistes* (*Phenomenology of Spirit*) in 1807, which develops a theory for the evolution of the human mind and ideas from sensory perception to absolute knowledge; the three volumes of *Wissenschaft der Logik* (*The Science of Logic*) in 1811, 1812, and 1816; *Enzyklopädie der philosophischen Wissenschaften* (*Encyclopedia of the Philosophical Sciences*), a summary of his entire philosophical system in 1816; and *Grundlinien der Philosophie des Rechts* (*Elements of the Philosophy of Right*) in 1821, a discourse on the application of his philosophical ideas to developing a more just and ideal human society. After his death, his students would assemble his lectures and writings into other compilations of his work.

Hegel's philosophical approach differed from all the major Renaissance philosophers in that he undertook a detailed analysis of the historical development of western thought and used it to develop a general theory for the evolution of human ideas and societies. This philosophical history bore many lessons for Hegel, who was one of the few philosophers who attempted to integrate the teachings of different religious traditions into a universal historical narrative. He saw these historical developments as a progression of ever-improving ideas that culminated in what he regarded as the pinnacle of human accomplishment, an understanding of the absolute reality or universal consciousness.

Hegel's work is generally accepted as being one of the hardest to understand and interpret—particularly through the lens of translation, which can quite easily distort the meaning. Risking oversimplification, I have attempted to distill his complex philosophical discourses into three basic ideas that are central to our discussion: the dialectic process, the concept of the *spirit*, and the integration of the world of objects and the world of ideas—absolute idealism.

The Dialectic Method

Hegel's analysis of Greek and European history led him to the conclusion that the evolution of human ideas followed a dialectic process. Aristotle described the dialectic process as starting with a *thesis*. An *antithesis* emerges, which challenges, contradicts, or competes with the original thesis. This competition of ideas leads to changes, integration, and improvements, and an amalgam arises that is referred to as a *synthesis*. Hegel carried this process much further. According to him, the dialectic process repeats itself *ad infinitum*: A synthesis forms a new thesis, which has inherent contradictions within it along with the seed of an antithesis, which in turn leads to a dynamic process that continuously improves our understanding of the world around us. This process continues indefinitely, until it approaches the *ultimate synthesis*, the absolute knowledge of the spirit.

Hegel, in trying to integrate historical developments into his philosophical framework, was really trying to describe the dynamics of the universe. He wanted to see how the worlds of objects and ideas evolved over time and if this dynamism could be described by some philosophical paradigm. Hegel was, first and foremost, a historian par excellence. He tracked the development of human civilization and presented a theory to explain the dynamic changes through the course of history. He then applied his dialectic theory to these changes to all subjects—physical, metaphysical, and cosmic. His claim is that this theory forms the basis by which dynamic changes occur in the evolution of the worlds of objects and ideas that are a part of the ultimate reality.

Hegel's "Spirit" as God

In 1826, Hegel published his highly regarded book, *Phenomenology of Spirit*, which laid out his thoughts on metaphysics, religion, and the historical development of human societies. He claimed that the dynamic dialectic process described above controls not only the historical evolution of human societies and ideas, but also nature and the cosmos. Hegel called this integrated whole the *Spirit*. The Spirit is the ultimate reality that encompasses all objects, ideas, and consciousness, just like the Rtá.

The Spirit, Hegel claimed, was initially infinite and unmanifested. Out of this thesis arose its antithesis—a finite, substantiated reality of the cosmos. The synthesis of these two gives us the reality we seek to understand today. This process describes not only the evolution of the Spirit, but also the development of humanity and the material universe.

In the beginning, all that existed was this ultimate reality—infinite and without physical form. The Spirit then differentiated itself into the material universe—the world we live in with all its animate and inanimate objects. In a dialectic process, the unmanifested Spirit (thesis) then reunited itself with the manifested reality of the universe of objects (antithesis) to give us the reality we perceive today (synthesis). It is this continuing process of the coming together of the manifested and unmanifested aspects of the Spirit that defines reality, and it is how reality and our perception of it evolve over time. The Spirit then encompasses both the perceived world of objects and the underlying essence of reality, the world of ideas and concepts.

Hegel's Absolute Idealism

Hegel rejected Plato's idea of separating reality into different parts. For him, everything—objects, sensory perception, ideas, and consciousness—were an integral part of the whole of reality, the Spirit. The physical universe and the universe of ideas were simply manifestations of the unmanifested ultimate reality or Spirit. The dialectical process is the evolutionary process that allows us to resolve contradictions in our understanding of this ultimate reality and, over time, develop a more complete understanding of it.

Hegel's Spirit or ultimate reality is his definition of God. It is a universal definition that is not based on any religious scripture, and is consistent with his philosophical framework that unifies the world of objects with the underlying essence that defines the world of ideas or forms. His inclusion of all of reality into the Spirit implies that our minds, bodies, and souls are also a part of this ultimate reality: We are all part of the universal consciousness, as are all living beings and inanimate things.

In this aspect of his philosophy, Hegel was clearly influenced by the Upanishads. He was well aware of this philosophical tradition[19] and incorporated it into his broad philosophical framework. The idea that this finite world of objects and ideas emerged from an infinite, timeless, ultimate reality is central to both Hegel's philosophy and the Upanishads.

Kantian subjective idealism, the idea that interpretations of sense perceptions by the mind are limited to individual minds, leads us to the conclusion that we are incapable of universal knowledge. Hegel rejected this idea. Hegel claimed that even though we use our own minds to understand, organize, and comprehend the world around us, it is possible for us to comprehend the true nature of reality. This was a significant departure from Kant, for it meant that we could use rational thinking and the instrument of our mind to "know" the world around us. This knowledge would be universal and not a matter of subjective belief.

Hegel's absolute idealism allows us to proceed with the development of the scientific method, which relies entirely on the development of universal laws or ideas that are not subjective. Without our ability to construct universal principles, or universal, synthetic, a priori knowledge, we would remain limited to sensory perceptions and tautological definitions, with no possibility of making scientific predictions or scientific laws.

The Scientific Method

Spinoza's ideas were read in whispered tones in intellectual circles in Europe for many years after his death. As more and more people began to accept some of the methods being used by philosophers and scientists of the time, such discussions became increasingly open and animated. The scientific method slowly became much more widely accepted through discussions of epistemology initiated by philosophers such as Bacon, empirical discoveries pioneered by scientists such as Galileo, and an open exchange of ideas in atmospheres of religious opposition and the persecution of scientists.

The progress of scientific discovery and religious and philosophical discourse went hand in hand, one influencing the other. Paralleling the philosophical developments we discussed previously, a tsunami of scientific discoveries and accomplishments was taking place all over Europe. Starting with the early discoveries of Galileo and Copernicus, and the later ones of Newton, Darwin, Boyle, and others, the scientific revolution was well under way. Two centuries of intellectual fervor and scientific discoveries had a profound effect on religious discourse. Our ability to comprehend the mysteries of nature through scientific explanations meant a smaller role for divine intervention and an even smaller role for belief in the supernatural.

The scientists themselves were less concerned with the philosophical basis of their methods and a lot more interested in the fascinating empirical observations they were making. Large volumes of scientific data were being collected and analyzed by different scientists. New theories were being proposed, debated, and either accepted or rejected if further improvements needed be made. Out of this milieu of scientific accomplishment emerged a consensus on how such scientific discoveries should be handled in a systematic manner. This consensus is now widely accepted and referred to as the *scientific method*.

The scientific method is a system of defining true knowledge and distinguishing it from subjective opinion, belief, myth, or fiction. As used in this book, it is a filter that allows us to decide whether a claim or conjecture should become a part of our human knowledge base. That is, it determines whether something is an objective set of facts or a belief unsubstantiated by empirical evidence. Claims that do not pass the scientific method filter are excluded from our scientific knowledge base, because these claims have not or cannot be supported by empirical observation.

Here is the generally accepted, step-by-step process of the scientific method.

1. Conduct experiments or use everyday experience to gather empirical evidence by direct observation.
2. Independently verify this empirical evidence by having others perform the same experiment or make the same direct observations. Check for consistency among independent observations (made by different groups at different times and places).
3. If independent observations and empirical evidence consistently verify the observations, the data is accepted as valid.
4. Propose a hypothesis that explains the observations.
5. Test the hypothesis with all available empirical observations. If the hypothesis consistently explains all available relevant observations and empirical data, it can be accepted as a valid theory or scientific law.
6. Constantly reevaluate existing theories and laws with new empirical evidence that becomes available to ensure that they are still valid. If an inconsistency is found, either modify or reject the theory, and propose a new one to replace the invalidated theory.

There are, of course, many examples of the application of this method throughout our recent history. Some of these are fascinating stories of incredible scientific triumphs; others of false starts and dismal failures. Through it all, the scientific method has survived and provided the bedrock on which all our scientific and technological success stands. Its success stems from its unfailing ability to separate fact from fiction, objective or absolute from subjective, knowledge from belief, and truth from superstition.

Perhaps the greatest early triumph of the scientific method was Newton's explanation of the mechanics of the motion of terrestrial and celestial bodies. Newton's laws of motion and gravitation provided a single elegant theory that explained in precise quantitative terms the motion of a cannon ball shot from any cannon anywhere in the world. Not only that, but it consistently predicted the motion of the moon and planets in ways that were never done before. Most important, it was in agreement with all known empirical observations of the time. Anyone, anywhere in the world, could test the theory's validity.

Newton's theory held its own for over 400 years before Albert Einstein showed that Newton's laws applied in most but not all circumstances. He postulated that at speeds approaching the speed of light, Newton's laws and the concept of time needed to be modified. His postulate was not widely accepted and was greeted with a great deal of skepticism (in the spirit of the scientific method). Some years later, a solar eclipse provided an opportunity to empirically verify Einstein's claims. The world's telescopes were positioned to observe the bending of the sun's rays by the moon's gravitational field (as predicted by Einstein). When the results of all the independent observations came in, Einstein's predictions were verified. His postulate was accepted by the scientific community as a theory verified by direct, independent observations. Since then, many empirical verifications of the theory have been published and until an exception to the theory is found, it will continue to be a part of our scientific knowledge base.

It is possible that many models or laws explain all the limited number of observations available. If this is the case, one model is not better than the other, and we must accept them all. However, over the course of time, as more observations become available or deliberate experiments are performed to test the predictions of the models, one of them will usually emerge as consistent with all observations.

Another example of the application of the scientific method is the fascinating story of the development of the theory of plate tectonics. This is a story about how scientists discovered that continents actually drift on the earth's surface over geologic time—an almost unbelievable claim if there weren't compelling empirical evidence to prove it!

In 1915, Alfred Wegener hypothesized that continents actually drifted across the globe, calling this the *continental drift theory*. Wegener's claim was based on his observation that the outlines of many coastlines (like South America and Africa) are mirror images, like puzzle pieces that fit together. This was not the first time that this observation had been made. Early explorers and cartographers, such as Magellan, had also observed and reported this on their maps. He was, however, the first to make the seemingly preposterous claims that the earth's surface had evolved over time and that the continents may have been joined together at some point in the past.

Further direct observational evidence of continental drift came from paleontologists, who reported that there were fossils of similar species found on continents that are now separated by great geographic distances. Similarities in the glacial past of now-far-removed continents also supported the hypothesis.

A key problem with Wegener's hypothesis was that no one had an explanation for why the continents moved. The observational evidence was compelling but not definitive. To explain the underlying reason for continental drift, several geologists posited that the movement was a result of the earth going through cycles of heating and cooling, which causes expansion and contraction of the land masses, resulting in continental drift. There was evidence of global cooling and warming cycles, although the continents would have to plow through oceanic crustal plates and move across large distances and it was unclear how this could be possible.

With the nuclear race heating up in the 1960s, a worldwide array of seismometers was installed to monitor nuclear testing, and these instruments revealed that earthquakes, volcanoes, and other seismic activity occurred along well-defined boundaries. The regions defined by these boundaries were dubbed *tectonic plates*. Why would seismic activity be so concentrated at the boundary of these plates?

The final piece of the puzzle—and the biggest break—came from an examination of the remotest portions of the earth, the mid-ocean ridges (seismically and volcanically active regions on the ocean floor). It was well established by the 1960s that the earth's magnetic field has undergone several magnetic reversals over geologic time. It was also known that active underwater volcanoes erupt in the middle of the Pacific and Atlantic oceans, spewing out lava that would solidify almost instantly as it hit the frigid temperatures at the bottom of the ocean. A key component of this lava was a magnetic mineral, appropriately called *magnetite*. The crystals of magnetite orient themselves in the direction of the prevailing magnetic field at the time the lava turns to a solid. Paleomagnetic studies revealed a striped pattern of magnetic reversals in the magnetite minerals in the crust of the ocean floor. This could only occur if the lava spewing from the volcanoes was pushing the ocean crust away from the mid-ocean ridges over time. This empirical evidence provided the first clear explanation of how the tectonic plates could move. The active volcanoes on the ocean floor provided the driving force of the continental-plate conveyor belt. At the other end of the plate, seismically active areas were shown to be acting as subduction zones, where the crust was being pushed back under the earth's crust.

As more empirical evidence has accumulated since the 1960s, the theory of plate tectonics has gained widespread acceptance. The theory has provided reasonable explanations for many observations, such as how the Himalayas were formed or in support of paleontological observations about the presence of similar fossil species found on continents far from each other.

In the interests of space, I have provided only a thumbnail sketch of the many puzzle pieces needed to arrive at a widely accepted theory. It all started when Wegener presented a hypothesis that turned out to be only partially correct. It then required fifty years of experimentation and data gathering to come up with a theory that is now consistent with all independently verifiable empirical observations. If observations in the future are inconsistent with the theory, we will have to revisit it.

This is a true triumph of the scientific method, a methodology that has provided us with by far the most robust way to ensure that our knowledge is indeed true so that we can consistently separate fact from belief, conjecture, and superstition. This, in my view, is the most important development in human history.

Summary

The scientific method emerged from a growing consensus among influential thinkers and philosophers that empirical evidence and rational thought must be applied rigorously to all philosophical discussions. The "revealed" word was not sufficient. Belief and unquestioned acceptance of holy scriptures were replaced with a new skepticism that could only be addressed through independently verifiable, empirical data and strict adherence to rational arguments that lead to logical conclusions. The injection of empiricism and logic into social and religious discourse not only transformed science, but also modernized religion. The scientific method has, without question, led to scientific discoveries and technological innovation that have transformed the world as never before in human history.

God According to Scientists and Philosophers

> Larry King: "Do you believe in God?"
> Stephen Hawking: "Yes, if by *God* is meant the embodiment of the laws of the universe."

We started this book exploring the most ancient musings of mankind about God and creation. Our journey took us through an incredible path of human self-discovery and philosophical development. For hundreds of years, people sought answers to questions about God through religious texts thought to be the revealed word of God. As we saw in the last chapter, the Enlightenment led to an alternative view of these questions and laid the foundation for the scientific method. In this chapter we will continue this journey through the lenses of prominent writers, philosophers, politicians, and scientists of the past 200 years.

We begin by attempting to summarize the concept of God put forward by a few chosen political leaders, philosophers, and scientists who lived in the early period of the scientific revolution. Their opinions represent a cross section of opinions among rationalists and scientists. A common theme runs through most of them. They were almost all born to moderately religious families. They were all introduced to and raised in their faith in their younger years. They almost all attended university or were highly educated otherwise. Since they were exceptionally well read (which was not at all common in the eighteenth and nineteenth centuries), they were all influenced by Renaissance philosophers. In this sense, they do not reflect the thinking of the average person on the street, who was much less educated and almost certainly more conservative in their religious beliefs.

During their education and early careers, they all began to question, each in their own way, the tenets of their faiths. They all struggled with reconciling their belief in the scriptures with their natural tendencies toward rationalism. Those who lived and wrote in the eighteenth and nineteenth centuries were clearly more guarded in their skepticism of scripture and religious doctrine. Not conforming to the religious norms of the time was risky. Over time, as democratic and egalitarian ideals spread, religious persecution largely became a thing of the past (in the West). Rationalists, agnostics, and even atheists were able to openly express their ideas without fear of persecution, and this will be apparent as you read the thoughts of the select group below, as we transition from the seventeenth to the twentieth century.

Unfortunately, the changes inspired by the Renaissance in the West did not percolate to all parts of the world. This is particularly true in today's theocracies, where there is no dividing line between religion and politics. Here, the word of the cleric still reigns supreme, and no dissent is tolerated. The age of belief continues unabated in these societies, and the light of rational debate, religious tolerance, and democracy has not yet touched these parts of the world.

There is little doubt that the rapid exchange of ideas across a connected world will lead to changes. The Arab Spring and the rise of democratic movements in the Middle East are clear signs that this process has already begun. Unfortunately, it is not clear whether the chaos and confusion that this change will bring will lead to more secular, democratic institutions or whether the well-organized and politically powerful religious right will be able to reestablish theocracies, as was the case in Iran.

I have chosen to express the opinions of these influential personalities in their own brilliant words rather than paraphrasing or interpreting them and running the risk of introducing biases or errors.

The people I have chosen can be grouped into the following general groups:

- The American Founding Fathers
- Writers and scientists from the nineteenth century
- Contemporary scientists from the twentieth century

George Washington

As the father of one of the most powerful nations that has ever existed, George Washington's religious beliefs have been the subject of great debate and controversy for over 200 years. As an infant, he was baptized into the Church of England. However, since church members were required to swear an oath of allegiance to the British monarch, after the American Revolution, the Episcopal Church became Washington's denomination and the state religion of Virginia.

There are not a great deal of public documents or speeches that imply the private faith or philosophy of this great man. We do have records that indicate his level of religious devotion. For example, despite his substantial involvement in the church's activities, his attendance at services at Mount Vernon was irregular at best. In the years 1762 to 1773, he attended church services an average of about fifteen times in a year. When he traveled, his attendance at places of worship was much more regular. Over the course of his two-term presidency, Washington made it a point to attend religious services in every city he visited. In many cases, he would attend multiple services to ensure that he prayed with various denominations—Catholic, Anglican, or Episcopal. This appears to be a political strategy to reassure his constituents that he was a man of faith, but also that he was a man of religious tolerance.

From what little we have, we can say that he was not an evangelical Christian, nor was he purely a deist—a believer in a creator that doesn't interfere with the laws of the universe. He can perhaps best be described as a Christian deist who was acutely aware of the importance of keeping his religious affiliation out of the public eye to minimize any potential for the appearance of religious bias or conflict. This was true of many of the Founding Fathers, who preferred to remain silent on issues relating to religious doctrine or denomination to avoid any semblance of divisiveness in the new nation. All of them—Washington, Jefferson, Franklin, Adams—preached the path of righteousness and virtue that is common to all religions.

Because of his stature in American history, many quotations have been incorrectly attributed to George Washington—for example, the words "so help me God," at the end of the presidential inaugural oath. Peter Henriques concluded that the claim is a myth and is unsupported by any evidence.[1] Another quote often ascribed to George Washington is "It is impossible to rightly govern the world without God and the Bible." This claim has even less basis in fact, but has been mistakenly repeated so many times that it has become the stuff of legend.

In fact, George Washington rarely used the words *God* or *Jesus Christ*. Instead, he chose to use the word *Providence* repeatedly in his writings. He attributes his victories in battle and the success of the Constitutional Convention to Providence. There is no doubt that Providence carries with it the connotation of divine intervention—or, at least, a grand architect that oversaw the new American Republic. Frank Grizzard Jr. put it this way:

> The qualities attributed to Providence by Washington reveal that he conceived of Providence as an "Omnipotent," "benign," and "beneficent" Being that by "invisible workings" in "Infinite Wisdom" dispensed justice in the affairs of mankind.[2]

In other words, George Washington affirmed to the nation on more than one occasion his belief in Providence—the invisible hand of God, who served not only to nurture the young nation, but also to provide a moral compass that directed us to do the right thing. His message was one of religious tolerance. Belief in one particular god was of little consequence; what mattered was for every man to follow a righteous path.

Washington and the other Founding Fathers enshrined this message in the US Constitution through the separation of church and state in the First Amendment. This message was vital to the success, unity, and sustainability of the nation. We must be deeply grateful to our Founding Fathers for their incredible foresight and exemplary leadership in founding and building a nation on such enduring principles.

Benjamin Franklin

Walter Isaacson described Benjamin Franklin as "the most accomplished American of his age and the most influential in inventing the type of society America would become."[3] So what did a person of such historical significance think about God and about organized religion? As with most people of his time, Franklin's views on God are nuanced and require careful interpretation. It is best for you to judge for yourself based on his writings.

> I had been religiously educated as a Presbyterian; and tho' some of the dogmas of that persuasion, such as the eternal decrees of God, election, reprobation, etc., appeared to me unintelligible, others doubtful, and I early absented myself from the public assemblies of the sect, Sunday being my studying day, I never was without some religious principles. I never doubted, for instance, the existence of the Deity; that he made the world, and govern'd it by his Providence; that the most acceptable service of God was the doing good to man; that our souls are immortal; and that all crime will be punished, and virtue rewarded, either here or hereafter. These I esteem'd the essentials of every religion; and, being to be found in all the religions we had in our country, I respected them all, tho' with different degrees of respect, as I found them more or less mix'd with other articles, which, without any tendency to inspire, promote, or confirm morality, serv'd principally to divide us, and make us unfriendly to one another . . .
>
> I grew convinc'd that truth, sincerity and integrity in dealings between man and man were of the utmost importance to the felicity of life; and I form'd written resolutions, which still remain in my journal book, to practice them ever while I lived. Revelation had indeed no weight with me, as such; but I entertain'd an opinion that, though certain actions might not be bad because they were forbidden by it, or good because it commanded them, yet probably these actions might be forbidden because they were bad for us, or commanded because they were beneficial to us, in their own natures, all the circumstances of things considered. And this persuasion, with the kind hand of Providence, or some guardian

angel, or accidental favorable circumstances and situations, or all together, preserved me, thro' this dangerous time of youth, and the hazardous situations I was sometimes in among strangers . . .

This is the writing of one of the most brilliant minds of his time and a man deeply influenced by the Enlightenment. There is little doubt that he was influenced by the French and English philosophers that he so avidly read. In fact, these lines could easily have been penned by Voltaire or Diderot.

Thomas Jefferson

Thomas Jefferson was a private man who spoke sparingly about his religious beliefs. Being born and raised an Anglican, he attended church regularly but was deeply influenced by the spirit of the Enlightenment. He argued forcefully for and played a leading role in the campaign to separate church and state. Jefferson's religious views became a major public issue during the bitter party conflict between Federalists and Republicans in the late 1790s. His opponents branded him an atheist, and he had to refute allegations that he did not believe in a Christian God. In his religious persuasion, he can perhaps best be described as a *rational Anglican.*

His views were liberal by the standards of the day and are best expressed in his own words. An extensive set of quotations is available at the Robert H. Smith International Center for Jefferson Studies or at www.monticello.org, where the following quotes originated.

> **1787 August 10.** (Jefferson to Peter Carr) Fix reason firmly in her seat, and call to her tribunal every fact, every opinion. Question with boldness even the existence of a God; because, if there be one, he must more approve the homage of reason, than that of blindfolded fear.
>
> **1802 January 1.** (Jefferson to the Baptist Association of Danbury, Connecticut) Believing with you that religion is a matter which lies solely between Man and his God, that he owes account to none

other for his faith or his worship, that the legitimate powers of government reach actions only, & not opinions, I contemplate with sovereign reverence that act of the whole American people which declared that their legislature should 'make no law respecting an establishment of religion, or prohibiting the free exercise thereof,' thus building a wall of separation between Church & State.

1803 April 21. (Jefferson to Benjamin Rush) To the corruptions of Christianity I am indeed, opposed; but not to the genuine precepts of Jesus himself. I am a Christian, in the only sense in which he wished any one to be; sincerely attached to his doctrines, in preference to all others; ascribing to himself every human excellence; and believing he never claimed any other.

1813 May 31. (Jefferson to Richard Rush) . . . the subject of religion, a subject on which I have ever been most scrupulously reserved. I have considered it as a matter between every man and his maker, in which no other, & far less the public, had a right to intermeddle.

The rights of conscience we never submitted, we could not submit. We are answerable for them to our God. The legitimate powers of government extend to such acts only as are injurious to others. But it does me no injury for my neighbor to say there are twenty gods, or no god. It neither picks my pocket nor breaks my leg. . . . Reason and free enquiry are the only effectual agents against error.

1816 January 9. (Jefferson to Charles Thomson) I too have made a wee little book, from the same materials, which I call the Philosophy of Jesus. It is a paradigma of his doctrines, made by cutting the texts out of the book, and arranging them on the pages of a blank book, in a certain order of time or subject. A more beautiful or precious morsel of ethics I have never seen. It is a document in proof that I am a real Christian, that is to say, a disciple of the doctrines of Jesus, very different from the Platonists, who call me infidel, and themselves Christians and preachers of the gospel, while they draw all their characteristic dogmas from what it's Author never said nor saw.

1821 February 27. (Jefferson to Timothy Pickering) No one sees with greater pleasure than myself the progress of reason in its advances towards rational Christianity. When we shall have done away the incomprehensible jargon of the Trinitarian arithmetic, that three are one, and one is three; when we shall have knocked down the artificial scaffolding, reared to mask from view the simple structure of Jesus, when, in short, we shall have unlearned every thing which has been taught since his day, and got back to the pure and simple doctrines he inculcated, we shall then be truly and worthily his disciples: and my opinion is that if nothing had ever been added to what flowed purely from his lips, the whole world would at this day have been Christian. . . . Had there never been a Commentator, there never would have been an infidel. In the present advance of truth, which we both approve, I do not know that you and I may think alike on all points; as the Creator has made no two faces alike, so no two minds, and probably no two creeds. We well know that among Unitarians themselves there are strong shades of difference . . .

1823 April 11. (Jefferson to John Adams) The truth is that the greatest enemies to the doctrines of Jesus are those calling themselves the expositors of them, who have perverted them for the structure of a system of fancy absolutely incomprehensible, and without any foundation in his genuine words. . . . But we may hope that the dawn of reason and freedom of thought in these United States will do away all this artificial scaffolding, and restore to us the primitive and genuine doctrines of this the most venerated reformer of human errors.

Here, again, we find a free-thinking person of the highest intellect who is deeply religious and yet so stridently critical of organized religion that he wrote, " . . . so distorted and deformed the doctrines of Jesus, so muffled them in mysticisms, fancies and falsehoods, have caricatured them into forms so monstrous and inconceivable, as to shock reasonable thinkers."[4] He was a man of faith, a believer in the teachings of Jesus Christ moderated by reason. He didn't blindly accept the teachings of the clergy. It is a well-reasoned faith that preserves the higher principles at the core of Jesus's message but has the ability to sort through interpretations of the message that do not serve humanity. At its heart, his spirit of individual freedom of thought and expression was untethered by the intolerance that invariably arises from religious dogma.

Charles Darwin

Charles Darwin was born in 1809 into a family of Freethinkers. He was baptized into the Church of England and later studied natural history and geology at Cambridge University. While he was a student, he was involved in many early scientific investigations, including meticulously cataloguing a particularly fascinating collection of beetles. His ability to observe nature with care and in exquisite detail, to record his observations systematically, and to draw conclusions based on these observations was key to his later success. Parallel to his scientific work, he also served as an Anglican clergyman and was active in his church's activities.

During his studies, he became a close associate of John Stevens Henslow, a professor of botany. Henslow saw the unique abilities in the young Darwin and invited him to sail on the now famous HMS *Beagle* for a planned two-year expedition to South America. The expedition, which actually lasted five years, was to launch a remarkable scientific career, lead to seminal contributions in geology and biology, and, of course, give birth to the theory of natural selection. Darwin exemplified the scientific tradition with his emphasis on direct observation; his proposed hypothesis on evolution was comprehensively documented and verified.

Today, Darwin's theory has been well established through millions of independent observations by many thousands of scientists around the world. It is unfortunate that the debate between evolutionists and creationists continues despite the mountains of compelling evidence supporting evolution. It is not my intent to delve into this political controversy; our central concern is what Darwin thought of God and his place in this world around us. Here is a letter he wrote in response to this controversy:

> It is impossible to answer your question briefly; and I am not sure that I could do so, even if I wrote at some length. But I may say that the impossibility of conceiving that this grand and wondrous universe, with our conscious selves, arose through chance, seems to me the chief argument for the existence of God; but whether this is an argument of real value, I have never been able to decide. I am aware that if we admit a first cause, the mind still craves to know whence it came and how it arose. Nor can I overlook the difficulty from the immense amount of suffering through the world. I am, also, induced to defer to a certain extent to the judgment of the many able men who have fully believed in God; but here again I see how poor an argument this is. The safest conclusion seems to be that the whole subject is beyond the scope of man's intellect; but man can do his duty.[5]

In 1879, to John Fordyce (a skeptic), Darwin wrote:

> [My] judgment often fluctuates. . . . Whether a man deserves to be called a theist depends on the definition of the term. . . . In my most extreme fluctuations I have never been an atheist in the sense of denying the existence of a God. —I think that generally (& more and more so as I grow older) but not always, that an agnostic would be the most correct description of my state of mind.[6]

His doubts about the teachings of the church were also a source of some concern to his wife, Emma, as is evident from a letter she wrote to him while he was on the *Beagle*.[7]

Darwin had clearly not made up his mind—or perhaps he was just being guarded in his opinion. His theory of natural selection profoundly changed his perception of the world around him. While his family attended church every Sunday, Darwin went for long walks. As best we can tell from his actions and from his letters to his friends and family, his Anglican beliefs changed to agnosticism later in his life.

> Although I did not think much about the existence of a personal God until a considerably later period of my life, I will here give the vague conclusions to which I have been driven. The old argument from design in Nature, as given by Paley, which formerly seemed to me so conclusive, fails, now that the law of natural selection has been discovered. We can no longer argue that, for instance, the beautiful hinge of a bivalve shell must have been made by an intelligent being, like the hinge of a door by man. There seems to be no more design in the variability of organic beings, and in the action of natural selection, than in the course which the wind blows. . . .
>
> In my Journal, I wrote that whilst standing in the midst of the grandeur of a Brazilian rainforest, "it is not possible to give an adequate idea of the higher feelings wonder, admiration, and devotion, which fill and elevate the mind." I well remember my conviction that there is more in man than the mere breath of his body; but now the grandest scenes would not cause any such convictions and feelings to rise in my mind. . . . This argument would be a valid one if all men of all races had the same inward conviction of the existence of one God; but we know that this is far from being the case. Therefore, I cannot see that such inward convictions and feelings are of any weight as evidence of what really exists. The state of mind which grand scenes formally excited me, and which was intimately connected with the belief in God, did not essentially differ from that which is often called the sense of sublimity; and however difficult it may be to explain the genesis of this sense, it can hardly be advanced as an argument for the existence of God, any more than the powerful though vague and similar feelings excited by music. . . .
>
> I cannot pretend to throw the least light on such abstruse problems. The mystery of the beginnings of all things is insoluble by us, and I for one must be content to remain an Agnostic.[8]

Mark Twain

Mark Twain is among the greatest storytellers of all time and a keen observer of the human condition. Besides being a gifted storyteller, he wrote short articles on more serious topics while retaining his penchant for wit and satire. His contempt for the BGITS definition of God and of organized religion is evident in his unabashed writings. I have taken only a few compelling excerpts that leave no doubt about where he stands.

> If I were to construct a God I would furnish Him with some way and qualities and characteristics which the Present (Bible) One lacks.
>
> He would not stoop to *ask* for any man's compliments, praises, flatteries; and He would be far above *exacting* them. I would have Him as self-respecting as the better sort of man in these regards.
>
> He would not be a merchant, a trader. He would not buy these things. He would not sell, or offer to sell, temporary benefits of the joys of eternity for the product called worship. I would have Him as dignified as the better sort of man in this regard.
>
> He would value no love but the love born of kindnesses conferred; not that born of benevolences contracted for. Repentance in a man's heart for a wrong done would cancel and annul that sin; and no verbal prayers for forgiveness be required or desired or expected of that man.
>
> In His Bible there would be no Unforgiveable Sin. He would recognize in Himself the Author and Inventor of Sin and Author and Inventor of the Vehicle and Appliances for its commission; and would place the whole responsibility where it would of right belong: upon Himself, the only Sinner.
>
> He would not be a jealous God—a trait so small that even men despise it in each other.
>
> He would not boast.
>
> He would keep private His admirations of Himself; He would regard self-praise as unbecoming the dignity of his position.
>
> He would not have the spirit of vengeance in His heart. Then it would not issue from His lips.

There would not be any hell—except the one we live in from the cradle to the grave.

There would not be any heaven—the kind described in the world's Bibles.

He would spend some of His eternities in trying to forgive Himself for making man unhappy when he could have made him happy with the same effort and he would spend the rest of them in studying astronomy.[9]

A God who could make good children as easily as bad, yet preferred to make bad ones; who could have made every one of them happy, yet never made a single happy one; who made them prize their bitter life, yet stingily cut it short; who gave his angels eternal happiness unearned, yet required his other children to earn it; who gave his angels painless lives, yet cursed his other children with biting miseries and maladies of mind and body; who mouths justice, and invented hell—mouths mercy, and invented hell—mouths Golden Rules, and forgiveness multiplied by seventy times seven, and invented hell; who mouths morals to other people, and has none himself; who frowns upon crimes, yet commits them all; who created man without invitation, then tries to shuffle the responsibility for man's acts upon man, instead of honorably placing it where it belongs, upon himself; and finally, with altogether divine obtuseness, invites his poor abused slave to worship him![10]

The gods offer no rewards for intellect. There was never one yet that showed any interest in it.[11]

Our Bible reveals to us the character of our God with minute and remorseless exactness. The portrait is substantially that of a man—if one can imagine a man charged and overcharged with evil impulses far beyond the human limit; a personage whom no one, perhaps, would desire to associate with, now that Nero and Caligula are dead. In the Old Testament His acts expose His vindictive, unjust, ungenerous, pitiless and vengeful nature constantly. He is always punishing—punishing trifling misdeeds with thousand-fold severity; punishing innocent children for the misdeeds of their parents; punishing unoffending populations for the misdeeds of their rulers; even descending to wreak bloody vengeance upon harmless calves and lambs and sheep and bullocks, as punishment for inconsequential trespasses committed by their proprietors. It is perhaps the most damnatory biography that exists in print anywhere. It makes Nero an angel of light and leading, by contrast.

It begins with an inexcusable treachery, and that is the keynote of the entire biography. That beginning must have been invented in a pirate's nursery, it is so malign and so childish. To Adam is forbidden the fruit of a certain tree—and he is gravely informed that if he disobeys he shall die. How could that be expected to impress Adam?[12]

Albert Einstein

The best known and perhaps the most respected scientific mind of our age is Albert Einstein. Because he was so well known and so highly regarded for his intellect, he was often asked for his opinion on social, ethical, and religious matters. Since he spoke and wrote in such a nuanced manner, the best way to present his views is to quote him directly. It would be a disservice to the reader if I were to paraphrase his words, since they are so profound and dense in their content.

The most famous of these quotes comes from Einstein's 1930 essay, "What I Believe," in which he tried to explain in simple and clear language his beliefs about religion, God, reincarnation, his Jewish faith, the supernatural, and social issues such as nationalism and bigotry. The publication of this essay was met with immediate and strident criticism from the religious leadership. Boston's Cardinal William Henry O'Connell called Einstein a closet atheist. Herbert S. Goldstein, an orthodox rabbi in New York, sent Einstein a very direct telegram: "Do you believe in God? Stop. Answer paid. 50 words." In response, Einstein sent back a telegram:

> I believe in Spinoza's God, who reveals himself in the lawful harmony of all that exists, not in a God who concerns himself with the fate and doings of human beings.[13]

In later writings, he expanded on this theme many times.

> I cannot conceive of a personal God who would directly influence the actions of individuals, or would directly sit in judgment on creatures of his own creation. I cannot do this in spite of the fact that mechanistic causality has, to a certain extent, been placed in doubt by modern science.
>
> My religiosity consists in a humble admiration of the infinitely superior spirit that reveals itself in the little that we, with our weak and transitory understanding, can comprehend of reality. Morality is of the highest importance—but for us, not for God.[14]

> It seems to me that the idea of a personal God is an anthropological concept which I cannot take seriously. I also cannot imagine some will or goal outside the human sphere . . . Science has been charged with undermining morality, but the charge is unjust. A man's ethical behavior should be based effectually on sympathy, education, and social ties and needs; no religious basis is necessary. Man would indeed be in a poor way if he had to be restrained by fear of punishment and hope of reward after death.[15]

When asked if he was a religious man, Einstein replied,

> Yes, you can call it that. Try and penetrate with our limited means the secrets of nature and you will find that, behind all the discernible laws and connections, there remains something subtle, intangible and inexplicable. Veneration for this force beyond anything that we can comprehend is my religion. To that extent I am, in fact, religious.[16]

Einstein's view of God sprang not from his need for a supernatural power that oversaw the fate of mankind but from his sense of marvel at the incredible beauty, richness, and complexity in nature that he wanted to understand better. What made it all tick? What were the underlying laws of nature? His concept of God was very far removed from the BGITS.

Does this concept of God have a familiar ring to it? It is the Rtá of the early Aryans, the Tao of the ancient Chinese philosophers, the Maat of the Egyptian pharaohs. Although the ancient mystics may not have had the benefit of all the scientific discoveries of our time, they shared one important common thread with these modern thinkers: They were fascinated by nature's incredible complexity and persistently inquisitive about the order in the universe. They knew that they did not understand these universal laws, but it was clear to them that man's ultimate quest was to better comprehend these universal truths.

Linus Pauling

Linus Carl Pauling was a brilliant chemist and antiwar activist who played a part in stopping the atmospheric testing of nuclear weapons. He is the only person to win two unshared Nobel Prizes, one for chemistry and one for peace.

Pauling was raised in a German Lutheran family, but his parents were not especially active in the church. He was born in Portland, Oregon, and attended Oregon Agricultural College (now Oregon State University). In 1922, Pauling graduated as salutatorian of his class and entered the California Institute of Technology (Caltech). The following year, he and Ava Helen were married, and they eventually raised four children. He completed his doctorate in 1925, becoming an assistant professor of chemistry at Caltech in 1927. In 1939, Pauling published his famous book *The Nature of the Chemical Bond*, considered by many to be the most important contribution to chemistry literature in the twentieth century. He also wrote the most popular freshman chemistry text ever—*General Chemistry*—which was first published in 1947 and has since seen several updates and editions. In 1954, Pauling was awarded the Nobel Prize for his work on the chemical bond and the structure of molecules.

As a high-profile scientist, Pauling felt obligated to speak about the growing arms race and the development of nuclear weapons by both the United States and Russia. In 1958, he expressed his very strident opposition to weapons of mass destruction in his book *No More War!* At a time when many scientists were advocating the development of nuclear weapons, Pauling spoke out about the dangers of unleashing them in the world. His activism for peace and his involvement in the peace movement in California in the 1950s and '60s led to his Nobel Prize in Peace.

In an attempt to work with individuals who were all working to better humanity, Linus and Ava joined the Unitarian Church, which was under the leadership of Los Angeles minister Stephen Fritchman. Their stated motivation was that "it accepts as members people who believe in trying to make the world a better place."

Pauling made it clear on several occasions that he was not a follower of any organized religion. In an interview on *The Phil Donahue Show*, he was asked, "Do you believe in God?"

He replied, "No, I do not."

He viewed religion in the same light as he did chemistry: They were both experimental sciences. His views on God and religions were based on what he observed and the conclusions he could draw from those observations.

Linus and Ava, as atheists, clearly did not believe in a BGITS conception of God. They both rejected organized religion at a very young age, and like many scientific minds of that age, they rejected the concept of a God who directly intervened in the fate of humans and belief in revealed religious texts. Instead, it seemed that a religion and perhaps a different definition of God based on reason, ethical behavior, and a desire to make the world a better place was becoming the accepted philosophy of their generation of scientists. The Unitarian Church provided them with an ideal avenue to pursue these goals.

Ava listed seven principles of Unitarianism, formulated by a Unitarian committee in 1930, to highlight the similarities of outlooks in science, Unitarianism, and her own personal beliefs:

1. The use of the scientific method
2. Rationality of the universe and progressive discovery of truth
3. Humility and reverence toward vaster forces of the universe
4. The conviction of the infinite possibility of human progress
5. The free exercise of intelligence in religion
6. The conviction of the self-sufficiency of humanity to solve its problems
7. A sense of human brotherhood

Throughout their careers, the Paulings never deviated from these principles. For them, religious mysticism and dogma had been replaced by a rational expression of belief in the forces of nature. Respecting, understanding, and ultimately utilizing these universal and powerful laws of nature for the good of mankind was, in their minds, the real definition of religion.

Stephen Hawking

There are very few living scientists today who have written on complex and leading-edge matters in physics as eloquently and lucidly as Stephen Hawking. He has made string theory and M theory, which are incredibly complicated from both a physical and a mathematical point of view, more accessible to the layperson. It is therefore interesting to get his take on whether he believes in a God of any kind.

> When people ask me if a god created the universe, I tell them that the question itself makes no sense. Time didn't exist before the big bang, so there is no time for God to make the universe in. It's like asking directions to the edge of the earth. The earth is a sphere; it doesn't have an edge; so looking for it is a futile exercise. We are each free to believe what we want, and it's my view that the simplest explanation is *There is no God*. No one created our universe, and no one directs our fate. This leads me to a profound realization: There is probably no heaven, and no afterlife either. We have this one life to appreciate the grand design of the universe, and for that, I am extremely grateful.[17]

Elaborating on his view of God creating the Universe, Hawking said the following:

> What I have done is to show that it is possible for the way the universe began to be determined by the laws of science. In that case, it would not be necessary to appeal to God to decide how the universe began. This doesn't prove that there is no God, only that God is not necessary.[18]

Steven Weinberg

The opinion of many scientists of our day can perhaps best be summarized in the words of Steven Weinberg, a Nobel laureate in physics, who has written eloquently on this topic.

> Science doesn't make it impossible to believe in God, it just makes it possible not to believe in God. . . .
>
> With or without religion, you would have good people doing good things and evil people doing evil things. But for good people to do evil things, that takes religion . . .
>
> Religious people have grappled for millennia with the theodicy, the problem posed by the existence of suffering in a world that is supposed to be ruled by a good God. They have found ingenious solutions in terms of various supposed divine plans. I will not try to argue with these solutions, much less to add one of my own. Remembrance of the Holocaust leaves me unsympathetic to attempts to justify the ways of God to man. If there is a God that has special plans for humans, then He has taken very great pains to hide His concern for us. To me it would seem impolite if not impious to bother such a God with our prayers.[19]
>
> It used to be obvious that the world was designed by some sort of intelligence. What else could account for fire and rain and lightning and earthquakes? Above all, the wonderful abilities of living

things seemed to point to a creator who had a special interest in life. Today we understand most of these things in terms of physical forces acting under impersonal laws. We don't yet know the most fundamental laws, and we can't work out all the consequences of the laws we do know. The human mind remains extraordinarily difficult to understand, but so is the weather. We can't predict whether it will rain one month from today, but we do know the rules that govern the rain, even though we can't always calculate their consequences. I see nothing about the human mind any more than about the weather that stands out as beyond the hope of understanding as a consequence of impersonal laws acting over billions of years. [20]

Summary

The thoughts and writings of just a select few of the most brilliant and influential minds of the past 300 years provide a fascinating journey of how our attitudes toward God and organized religion have evolved. We have slowly but surely moved away from a firm belief in a BGITS God to one that is based on the rational and empirical thinking of the scientific method. We have moved from the age of wonder to the age of belief and finally to the age of reason. As we shall see in the next chapter, as science expands our understanding of the universe and opens up whole new worlds to explore, we are coming full circle to an enlightened age of wonder.

A Journey Through Time: Coming Full Historical Circle

Over the course of the past six chapters, we have explored man's quest for answers to the eternal questions about the existence and nature of God, his role in our universe, and the purpose of our existence. We've found a rich array of answers that have been proposed over five millennia.

In this chapter, we will step back and take a bird's-eye view of how far we have come in this historical journey. As we shall see, we have come a long way, but this evolution in our thinking has led back to many of the original ideas of our ancestors. We have come one giant circle in history, but this time, we have a much better understanding and perspective of God and his creation than we did the first time we walked this path. This enlightened wisdom of many generations, coupled with a return to our early human sense of wonder, provides us hope that God and religion can be viewed in the proper perspective and can serve us in our ultimate goal: bettering humanity.

God in the Age of Wonder

Imagine yourself as an ancient Aryan warrior sometime around 5000 BCE, living in the steppes of Central Asia or the northwestern part of the Indian subcontinent. You live a nomadic life and forage, farm, and hunt for food. It is cold and dark as the sun goes down, and the light and warmth return as the sun comes up at dawn. The stars in the heavens shine bright as your nomadic tribe settles down for the night. Wild animals and rival tribes are a constant threat, so you must always be on guard. You have no tools except those that you use for foraging, farming, and hunting. You have no sense of how far the forest extends or what lies beyond the faraway mountains. You marvel at the stars that shine down on you, the moon that provides some degree of comforting light in the crisp, clear nights, the sun that breaks through the thick blanket of darkness every morning, and the beauty of the blue sky that seems to cover you like a dome. You are thankful for the rain that nourishes your crops, for the rivers that flow down from the mountains to the plains, for the trees and forests that provide you with the fuel for your holy, magical, and ritual fire. These are the elements of nature that sustain your very existence. These are your gods, or at the very least, gifts from a supreme creator.

Consider this beautiful hymn from the Rig Veda in honor of Ushas, the goddess of dawn.

> This light hath come, of all the lights the fairest,
> The brilliant brightness hath been born, far-shining,
> Urged on to prompt the sun God's shining power.
> Night now hath yielded up her place to morning.
>
> The sister's path is the same unending,
> Taught by the Gods, alternately they tread it.
> Fair-shaped, of different forms, and yet one-minded,
> Night and Morning clash not, nor yet do linger.
>
> 'Tis heaven's daughter hath appeared before us,
> The maiden dazzling in her brilliant garments.
> Thou sovereign mistress of all earthly treasure,
> Auspicious Dawn, flash thou today upon us!
>
> Arise! The breath of life again hath reached us!
> Dread darkness slinks away and light is coming!
> She hath blazed a pathway for the sun to travel,
> we have found the place where men prolong existence.[1]

The poetry is inspired, and the sense of wonder, awe, and reverence for the majesty of nature is evident in every syllable of the verses. There are many hymns like this in these ancient texts, each one resplendent in its own way and devoted to the elements of nature. Before the written word or ways to distribute them on a mass scale, the prayer hymns, chants, and shlokas were passed down orally from generation to generation.

This belief system was certainly not unique to the ancient Aryans. Similar hymns find a home in the older texts of the Sumerians, the Hittites, and the Egyptians, as well as the ancient Zoroastrians. The Aztecs, the Mayans, and tribes in Africa invented gods for every aspect of their lives. There were gods for birth and death, war and peace, the sun and the moon, the earth and the seas. Every natural phenomenon was explained by the will of gods. The eruption of a volcano or the tremors of an earthquake were sure signs that the earth god was unhappy. Famines and droughts laid waste to large cities or entire civilizations, and the people had no hope of a logical explanation. The underlying explanation was always the wrath of a supernatural being beyond human comprehension—the BGITS.

This is the spirit of the age of wonder—an age where humanity has no sense of its place in the universe, an age of innocence and simplicity. Animal sacrifices and elaborate ritual offerings to a BGITS god by those skilled in the art were performed with the necessary degree of precision and propriety. Only the priests had the knowledge and skill to perform them and, as such, could dictate terms to the most powerful of kings.

Rational explanations of natural phenomena were neither sought nor available. Human understanding was so limited that even everyday occurrences, such as the rising of the sun, were magical events that commanded a special place in the pantheon. Some, including myself, would argue that sunrises and sunsets are still magical, despite our ability to logically and scientifically explain them!

Rtá: The Underlying Order in the Universe

What is truly remarkable is that despite their lack of scientific knowledge, the ancient Aryans went a crucial step beyond their nature gods. They intuitively saw, in the beauty and wonder of nature, the consistent order that existed in everything in the universe. The rising and setting of the sun, the waxing and waning of the moon, and the coming and passing of the seasons were all predictable and orderly. The Rtá, this order in all aspects of nature—in any activity in the universe, including social and religious matters—was ascribed the highest status. All creation, animate and inanimate, even the gods, must obey the Rtá.

In the Vedic tradition, this recognition of a universal cosmic order was the ultimate reality. The Rtá represented a transcendental God, one that was rather remote and difficult to comprehend (the Brahman in later Vedic tradition). A more accessible and personal pantheon (Ishvar) was available, and in fact essential, to satisfy our emotional need for solace and comfort. These personalized gods formed a part of our everyday prayer and ritual. The Upanishads make this distinction clearly. The supreme consciousness—Rtá or Brahman—coexists with a multitude of personal gods and deities. Both were recognized as essential.

Finally, as we saw in previous chapters, a unique characteristic of many of these ancient traditions, including the Vedic, Greek, and Chinese religions, was their openness to discussion and debate about the nature of God and reality. There was no single scripture that had the corner on the truth and that must be obeyed. There was no revealed word of God that laid out the final and irrevocable truth about the universe. Philosophical and religious debate, whether they be Brahmodyas in the Vedic tradition or Socratic in the Greek tradition, were part of the religious experience. Everyone was free to question, debate, and ultimately choose a philosophy and a god (or gods) that appealed to them.

These characteristics led to a rich diversity of philosophical and religious beliefs and gods, which ranged from people of deep faith to the pure rationalists and the atomists. An incredibly wide range of personal gods and deities dominated everyday life and worship. They were the BGITS gods who influenced the lives of people every day. The distinction between the transcendental God (Brahman) and the gods of everyday worship was so much a part of the tradition that it was (and still is) an unstated and obvious given.

God in the Age of Belief: The Monotheists

The Abrahamic religions took an entirely different approach to God. For them, belief in the revealed word of God as documented in very specific scriptures was a first step in acceptance into the faith. Gone were the many gods and the wondrous praise of nature, the acceptance of many forms of worship, and the many manifestations of the one Supreme Being. The great monotheistic religions emanating from Jerusalem and Mecca instead asked their followers to believe in the revealed word of God as written in the Old Testament, the New Testament, and the Koran. These revelations were, for the believers, infallible and constituted the ultimate truth. Over time, as these religions expanded and became better organized, the acceptance of the particular word of God prescribed and interpreted by the clergy came to be regarded as the ultimate truth, and many followers became much more dogmatic.

Each of these scriptures preached monotheism. Perhaps more important, they required all believers to accept one—and only one—set of scriptures as the true word of God. Some interpreted their scriptures as preaching belief in a jealous God, one who did not look kindly on competition. As we saw in chapter 2, belief in any God other than Yahweh or Allah brought death and destruction. Some interpreted the scriptures as directing them to convert or kill all nonbelievers. Others believed that any such language in scripture should not be taken literally. Regardless of the specific interpretation, each of the Abrahamic religions required from its followers complete and unquestioning belief in a revealed scripture.

This form of uncompromising monotheism was new to the tribal cultures of both Arabia and Canaan. It had an important political consequence in both regions: It unified the tribes who accepted the supremacy of the one true God under a single banner and provided a distinct military advantage to this group of tribes. Over time, this advantage was to prove decisive in the spread of both Christianity and Islam.

Christianity during the Dark Ages

As each of the Abrahamic religions became better organized, it was clear that writing, speaking, or preaching any ideas that were viewed by the clergy as contrary to their interpretation of scripture was blasphemous and punishable by death. This had a chilling effect on the expression of ideas in Europe and the Middle East. The Old Testament has many stories of the fate that would befall anyone that went astray and pursued belief in a different God. The message in these stories is clear: Believe in the one true God, or be punished.

Indeed, Europe went into the Dark Ages for a period of about 1000 years. We do not know much about the development of ideas during this period of European history. What we do know is from the writings of church scholars and priests, who were some of the few people who were educated and had access to books (a rarity in those days) and had the luxury of time to read, contemplate, and write. Every word spoken or written was vetted by the Church and had to be in accordance with Church doctrine. There were numerous interpretations of the gospels and books on religious doctrine that were sanctioned by the church during this time. Very little else emerged from Europe during this age of belief.

The first signs of reform and deviation from strict church doctrine came in about 1250 CE, when Thomas Aquinas, a Dominican monk, began to introduce old Aristotelian logic into discussions about church doctrine. The Greek philosophers had been anathema to Church doctrine for over a thousand years, since they did not regard the revealed word of God as the highest authority and the source of all truth. In 1270 and again in 1277, the Bishop of Paris issued a condemnation of Aquinas, stating that Aquinas had placed the principles of Aristotelian logic above God's absolute power. This was a serious charge for the time and could have ended Aquinas's career quickly, had it not been for his status as a scholar and devoted theologian of some repute. In later writings, Aquinas denied the charge vehemently.

Aquinas exemplifies the conflict between reason and faith during the thirteenth century perfectly. His primary loyalty was to the truth as revealed in scripture. However, as one educated in the classics, he was also a great admirer of the Greek philosophers and fully appreciated their methodical techniques of logical deduction. However, whenever there was a conflict between the two, he abandoned logic and justified his conclusion by referring back to scripture as the highest authority, which, according to him, axiomatically must be true. This is best described by Bertrand Russell:

> [Aquinas] does not, like the Platonic Socrates, set out to follow wherever the argument may lead. He is not engaged in an

inquiry, the result of which it is impossible to know in advance. Before he begins to philosophize, he already knows the truth; it is declared in the Catholic faith. If he can find apparently rational arguments for some parts of the faith, so much the better; if he cannot, he need only fall back on revelation. The finding of arguments for a conclusion given in advance is not philosophy, but special pleading. I cannot, therefore, feel that he deserves to be put on a level with the best philosophers either of Greece or of modern times.[2]

Even a reform-minded scholar such as Thomas Aquinas saw the need for capital punishment for heretics. He writes in his well-known treatise *Summa Theologiæ*:

> With regard to heretics . . . they deserve not only to be separated from the Church by excommunication, but also to be severed from the world by death.[3]

Transition to the Age of Reason

In the two hundred years that passed between Aquinas in the thirteenth century and Bacon in the fifteenth, the tone of philosophical writing was slowly transitioning from one of faith and belief to one of reason and logic. The age of belief was giving way to the age of reason.

By the time the Renaissance had matured in seventeenth-century Italy and England, philosophers were writing and publishing books that openly questioned the validity of Biblical revelations. The incredible flowering of ideas during this age of reason and the changes it brought were discussed in detail in chapter 6. It was these Renaissance ideas that led directly to the modern scientific age and democratic institutions we cherish today.

The Golden Age of Islam

The development of Islam during this period followed a different course. In the two centuries following the death of the Prophet Muḥammad, Islam spread aggressively east into Iraq, Turkey, and Persia, and to the west all the way to Spain and northern Africa. Military campaigns helped spread its political and religious influence and established powerful and prosperous caliphates in Baghdad and Cairo. Two of these caliphates, the Rashidun (632–661CE) and the Umayyad (661–750 CE) are particularly noteworthy for their expansion of Islamic influence through conquest. After a series of assassinations, the last Umayyad caliph was deposed in 750 CE by the descendants of Muḥammad's great-uncle Abdul-Muttalib, of the Banū Hāshim clan, to establish the Abbasid dynasty.

The period between 750 CE and 1250 CE has sometimes been referred to as the Golden Age of Islam. The Abbasid caliphs moved their capital from Damascus to Baghdad to be closer to some of the more influential Persian politicians and scholars in the court. The Abbasid Caliphate is, without question, one of the most successful dynasties in the Muslim world. A continuous string of fifty-seven caliphs ruled most of the Muslim world for about 500 years. It started out as a rebellion by non-Muslim Arabs affiliated with one of the Arab generals. Over time, it was dominated by Arab Islamic traditions.

Unlike their predecessors, the Abbasids used this period of relative calm and stability to encourage the free discourse of ideas and to promote the development of science and critical thinking. The Abbasids established the House of Wisdom in Baghdad. Both Muslim and non-Muslim scholars were invited to gather there and translate into Arabic many of the classic works from places that they had either conquered or traded with. Ancient texts from Greece, Rome, India, China, and Persia were translated for the community of Muslims that had, by this point, adopted Arabic as a common language. The translations included the works of Aristotle and Plato; Indian texts on mathematics, astronomy, medicine, and philosophy; and Chinese and Egyptian texts on governance and papermaking. The resulting amalgam of knowledge was a unique blend of Hellenic, Islamic, Indian, and Chinese cultures and know-how. Much later, these Arabic translations would be translated into Persian, Turkish, and finally into Hebrew and Latin. They allowed important knowledge to be transferred from India and China to the West through a pan-Arabic conduit.

The Abbasids helped nurture their caliphate to the leading edge of medicine, mathematics, and science by being open to the ideas of other ancient civilizations and by assimilating and building on them. The decimal system and the concept of zero used in India for many millennia was introduced to the Arabs and the West through these translations. The mathematical and astronomical texts of Aryabhata (920–1000 CE), which enunciated the basic concepts of what we now know as algebra, were translated and compiled by the Arabs. The science of papermaking, perfected by the Chinese, was adopted by the Arabs to reproduce copies of the translations and make them more accessible to a wider audience.

Ibn Rushd and Avicenna wrote extensive commentaries on the works of Aristotle and Plato. These Hellenic ideas were not in line with Islamic theology but were accepted as such—not banned or restricted. Instead, these foreign ideas strongly influenced the religious and social dialogue among intellectuals of the day. Well-known Islamic scholars, such as Al-Kindi and Al-Farabi, used Aristotelianism and Neoplatonism to justify Islamic teachings, just as Thomas Aquinas did for Christian scripture in Europe. Central to Al-Kindi's philosophy was God's absolute oneness, which is also the central message of Islam. Al-Kindi conceived of God as an active participant in human affairs, through agents or intermediaries who execute his will. Al-Kindi viewed this concept as being consistent with the Hellenic ideas of God being the first cause or *unmoved mover*.

How did he reconcile the revealed word of God—the Koran—with Aristotelian logic? He claimed that prophecy and philosophy are two different routes that arrive at the same universal truth. Although God simply speaks his mind and reveals the truth to a chosen prophet, philosophers can arrive at the same revealed truth by many years of study and contemplation. Al-Kindi saw the prophet as being better at communicating the truth to the people around him. By establishing the oneness of the theologians and the philosopher's quest, Al-Kindi tried to reconcile the Koran with the Hellenic tradition.

Most modern philosophers would disagree with the basic assumption that philosophical discourse or logic will lead to the same point as the revealed word of God. Although one may disagree with his axioms and logic, Al-Kindi's main contribution was to introduce a new way of thinking about religious writings and to establish the groundwork for future Muslim philosophers to debate the meaning of the Holy Koran.

Abū ʿAlī al-Ḥasan ibn al-Ḥasan ibn al-Haytham, or Alhazen in the West, was an Arab scholar of particular repute for his contributions to science is. He was born in 965 CE in Basra and spent his entire productive life in Cairo, working in diverse fields ranging from optics to astronomy to mathematics. He wrote over 200 books and essays on a wide range of topics. In his most famous book, *Kitāb al-Manāẓir* (*Book of Optics*), he described how experimental observations could be used to explain certain optical phenomena. He used mechanical analogies to explain concepts such as the reflection and refraction of light from surfaces. Some modern scholars regard his work as an early effort to explain the workings of the physical universe by conducting deliberate experiments and proposing theories to explain his results. Among all the Muslim philosophers of that era, his approach to addressing questions about natural phenomena came closest to the Hellenic tradition of providing logical human explanations, backed up with experimental observations, rather than invoking God or the supernatural.

In medicine, Muhammad ibn Zakariyyā al-Rāzī (854–925 CE), a Persian physician and philosopher, best exemplifies the spirit of the time. Razi wrote over 200 manuscripts, and is best remembered for his careful and systematic observations about the diseases that he attempted to treat. His observations allowed him to make a distinction between smallpox and measles and to provide clinical symptoms of each disease. His medical ideas were later picked up by medieval European physicians who built upon this knowledge base many centuries later. His books on surgery and therapeutic medicine were translated and used in the West.

This golden era of Islamic culture and philosophy ended quite suddenly in 1258 CE when the Mongols, under Hulagu Khan, sacked Baghdad and laid waste to its cultural heritage. The Abbasid caliphs would never again wield the same influence and power they had enjoyed for over 400 years. The center of Muslim culture shifted to Cairo and would remain so until the Ottoman Turks conquered Egypt in 1517. The Christian crusades and the relentless attacks on Islamic institutions from the west further weakened the caliphates.

Philosophers like Al-Ghazālī (1058–1111 CE), one of the most prominent and influential theologians of Sunni Islam, were instrumental in pulling Islamic theology back to a more conservative interpretation. The tug-of-war between revealed scripture and Aristotelian logic (*falsafa*) is evident in all his writings. Al-Ghazālī had studied the Greek philosophers and was convinced that many of their conclusions were not in accordance with the Koran or the Hadith, which he regarded, without question, as the word of God and the ultimate source of truth. He wrote his critique of the Hellenic approach in his book, *Tahāfut al-Tahāfut* (*The Incoherence of the Philosophers*). Al-Ghazālī's thesis used Aristotelian logic to show that all issues, including those relating to God and religion, could only be resolved by a strict adherence to the Koran and not by philosophical reasoning. Al-Ghazālī's approach to resolving the contradictions between reason and revelation was accepted by most later Muslim theologians and led to an almost complete cessation of debate.

Islam in the Middle Ages

With the dominance of this conservative Islamic philosophical view and the lack of a strong caliphate, Islam entered a period that can be referred to as the *Dark Ages of Islam*. This was about 200 years before Europe and Christianity would emerge from their own Dark Ages.

The impact of a conservative and militant Islam bent on spreading the word of the Prophet was felt not only in Islamic countries, but also as far east as India and Indochina and as far west as Vienna, where many of the rulers of Western Europe, such as the Habsburg dynasty, fought to stop the spread of Islam into Europe. As the faithful from both Islam and Christianity locked horns, large armies were established, and for many centuries, religious crusades were conducted by both sides to spread their faith. Estimates place the number of people killed in the tens of millions.

Waves of Islamic conquerors swept through the relatively peaceful plains of the Indus and Ganges rivers. Most of these marauding armies were Turkish, Persian, and Afghan, probably driven as much by the spoils of victory as any religious zeal. Temples and churches alike were destroyed, and any idols they could find were desecrated, if not completely destroyed, since they violated the principle of Islam that does not allow for the representation of God in any physical form.

The impact on the religious and architectural heritage of the Indian subcontinent was catastrophic. Not a single major temple or cultural icon was left standing. In their place, and often using the same materials, mosques and symbols of Islamic culture, such as the Qutb Minar in New Delhi, were erected. The great university at Nalanda, which had stood as a center of Hindu and Buddhist learning for more than a thousand years, was burned to the ground. The contents of its great library were lost to humanity forever.

The spirit of tolerance and acceptance of ideas outside the Koran was gone. What replaced it was a fundamentalist Islam that saw no room for compromise. Lands and people were conquered in the name of Allah. Those who converted to Islam were spared, and those that did not were put to the sword, enslaved, or repressed.

God in the Age of Reason: The Renaissance

The struggle between rationality and faith began in earnest after Thomas Aquinas began his integration of Aristotelian logic with Biblical writings.

The fifteenth century saw a turning point in the development of ideas and philosophies related to God, religion, and our place in the world. The Renaissance began in earnest in the port cities of Italy. These cities were prosperous, bustling metropolises connected with the far corners of the known world through trade. Traders brought in not only fresh products, but also fresh ideas and cultures that were unknown to the rest of Europe.

The families who ran the trading businesses were wealthy, well educated, and pragmatic. They supported artists, philosophers and scientists, educators and artisans. Some of the finest Renaissance art and architecture emerged from the dynamism of these thriving Italian cities. These factors also made these cities the source of radical new ideas that dared to question the authority of scripture and the Pope that had dominated Europe for over fourteen centuries. Questioning and creative geniuses from Leonardo da Vinci to Galileo began to show that mankind was capable of building fantastic machines and explaining—even predicting—the heavens. With the arrival of the printing press and the rise of literacy, these ideas would ultimately spread over all of Europe.

The new rationalists were less constrained by scripture and more concerned with bettering humanity through an exploration of the natural world. A series of European philosophers and scientists—John Locke, René Descartes, Charles Darwin—struggled with reconciling their faith with empirical observation and inductive reasoning. The Hellenic traditions were resurrected but then abandoned or modified to include empiricism at the core of understanding and knowledge. It was no longer sufficient to hypothesize and propose general principles without the benefit of direct and reproducible empirical evidence to support the assertions.

Descartes explicitly used the term *laws of nature* and began to give them some form. He defined physical observations in terms of collisions between objects and said that the laws that govern these collisions apply without exception. Newton believed that God could alter the laws of nature. Laplace believed in scientific determinism (no miracles, no exceptions). God had no power to alter the laws, since they were his nature. The development of ideas in the age of reason thus progressed in small, unsure steps, proposed and perfected by some of the great thinkers of the time.

In addition to the advent of science, the fifteenth century saw transformative changes in Christian theology. Martin Luther launched the Protestant Reformation in 1517, which would forever transform Christianity. Over the course of the previous 1400 years, the Catholic Church had bestowed upon its clergy the role of intermediary between God and his people. This meant that a Christian could attain God's grace only through ordained Christian clergy. It was common Christian belief at the time that a person would enter the gates of heaven if God's grace had been bestowed upon them and they had been absolved of their sins. Both of these required the intervention of the Catholic clergy. Over the years, the clergy had misused this authority and become corrupt. In an attempt to raise money for themselves and for the Church, the clergy allowed the rich noblemen of Europe to contribute money and, in essence, buy God's grace or absolution for their sins. Martin Luther regarded the sale of indulgences (the Church's term for forgiveness of sins in return for money) as an abomination and spoke out against it, calling it a direct contradiction of the teachings of Jesus Christ. Luther believed that salvation and entry into heaven was a gift of God's grace received only through faith in Jesus Christ. For Luther, faith alone provided the keys to heaven.

This belief was a direct threat to the authority of the Catholic Church, the Pope, and the clergy. In 1520, the Pope warned Luther that he would be excommunicated unless he recanted forty-one specific sentences from his writings. Luther refused to recant and was declared an outlaw. His writings were banned, and he was warned that he would be punished as a heretic should he continue to preach his message. For most of the rest of his life, Luther preached his message to a modest group of German peasants who had grown equally weary of the clergy's abuse.

Martin Luther's influence on Christianity was profound and the power of the clergy would, over time, be severely curtailed by Protestantism. However, his insistence on absolute faith and belief in scripture would lead many generations of Protestants to struggle with reconciling modern scientific methods with their religious convictions. Later denominations, such as the Calvinists and Puritans, would adopt his underlying philosophy of *sola scriptura*—scripture alone—as an integral part of their religious doctrine.

Perhaps no religion has been subjected to the rigor of commentary, critique, and investigation as Christianity has, and modern Christianity is so much the better for it. With the dawn of the scientific age, it became clear that there was an urgent need to reconcile faith in scripture with rationality. Although faith may have been enough for Martin Luther, it certainly was not going to convince the rationalists and skeptics, who had spent a lifetime exploring the world with the well-honed tools of the scientific method. They required evidence of the existence of God, the claims of Christ's divinity, and the supernatural gifts ascribed to the messiahs.

In modern times, the debate has continued unabated. Contemporary Jewish philosophers, such as Emmanuel Levinas (1906–1995) and Jacques Derrida (1930–2004), along with some prominent theologians, have claimed that the supernatural events described in the Bible were not meant to be interpreted literally but were instead meant as allegory, to make a point, and to hold the attention of the reader. Derrida's deconstruction of language and its relationship to meaning (as a way of interpreting scripture) was later criticized by more analytical philosophers such as Noam Chomsky, who questioned Derrida's methods and logic.

Levinas, a French philosopher of Lithuanian Jewish ancestry, is also well known for his statement that God could be found in the "face of the Other." What he was implying was that the search for God began with service to humanity. According to his interpretation of Jewish scripture, the covenant that Abraham made with God was to serve humanity and make the world a better place in the process. This message was well received from a world reeling from the Great War.

Similarly, many hundreds of Christian theologians, philosophers, and commentators on the Bible have addressed this issue. The Society of Christian Philosophers, founded in 1978, has over 1,100 members from a wide range of denominations—the largest membership among the different groups belonging to the American Philosophical Association. It would be impossible for me to accurately reflect the opinions and ideas of such a large and diverse group here.

Some religious scholars make the point that the burden of logic and proof that is commonly applied to the natural world cannot and should not be applied to questions relating to religion or God, since they sit outside the purview of such tools. They reason that naturalistic (logical) explanations cannot be provided for concepts such as free will, consciousness, and intentionality. Similarly, the existence of God does not require proof and does not emerge from a logical explanation or observations.

However, the foundations of philosophy do rely on such logic and proof. Without them, it would be impossible to conduct a coherent discussion. Abandoning or relaxing the rules of logic when they are applied to God, as some have suggested, would not make a very convincing case and is not a line of thinking we will pursue in this book.

Judaism and Christianity have benefited immensely from the intense scholarly debate on issues of scripture and its relation to modern scientific developments. Over the past 200 years, both of these religions have developed a modern interpretation of scripture that provides a bridge between widely accepted secular democratic ideals and religious doctrine.

Tolerance and respect for other faiths, as well as acceptance of the rational and scientific explanations of natural phenomena, are now widespread in the West, completing the circle that started before the Dark Ages—from reason to belief and back to reason.

The Islamic world is just beginning to circle back to the rational worldview they had before their own Dark Ages, and it may take several decades for it to fully take hold in societies that have historically been religiously conservative and rooted in a literal interpretation of scripture.

I think it would be fair to say that despite the many hundreds of volumes written on the subject, there is near universal agreement among philosophers and scientists alike that religious doctrine must be accepted at face value—as an act of faith. There can be no expectation that such beliefs can be rationalized in the same way that a scientist would logically reach a conclusion based on evidence. The chasm between belief and rationality remains. This is the primary reason I have chosen to separate them in our redefinition of God. One part of what we know, our knowledge base of verifiable facts, leads to a transcendental definition of God, and the other, blind faith, leads to a God that will always remain subjective. Separating these constructs is the only way to reconcile the two powerful mental drivers within us: rationality and emotional instinct.

Coming Full Circle: From the Age of Wonder to the Scientific Age

When Albert Einstein, who epitomizes the age of science, was asked by Rabbi Herbert Goldstein in 1929 if he believed in God, he replied,

> I believe in Spinoza's God, who reveals himself in the lawful harmony of all that exists, not in a God who concerns himself with the fate and doings of human beings.[4]

This view of God bears a striking similarity to that of the early Aryans. The Aryans marveled at the universe around them and recognized that some immutable set of laws controlled the motion of the stars, the rising and the setting of the sun, the coming of the seasons, the raising of crops, and the behavior of all living things. Even in those ancient times, when mankind's knowledge of these universal laws was in its most primitive form, our ancestors recognized the importance of these laws and placed them above all else as the ultimate power and origin of all creation, the Rtá.

They were not satisfied with an arbitrary, God-wanted-it-so explanation of events in a world they saw as being remarkably orderly and elegant. Although they had no logical explanations for the events they witnessed, they recognized that there was something beyond the BGITS conception of God and postulated that there was indeed a higher order that even the gods must obey. This concept of a transcendent and universal set of laws is no different from Spinoza's God: As described by Einstein, Spinoza's God "reveals himself in the lawful harmony of all that exists."

Below, I compare Spinoza's *Treatise on Religion and the State*, taken from Will Durant's interpretation of the original, with Bloomfield's translation of the Rig Veda and its description of the Rtá alongside. The similarities are striking, and if we look beyond the styles of expression and the choice of words, the essence is the same.

| By *the help of God* I mean the fixed and unchangeable order of nature, or the chain of natural events; the universal laws of nature and eternal decrees of God are one and the same thing. . . . What the laws of the circle are to all circles, God is to the world. Like substance, God is the causal chain or process, the underlying condition of all things, the law and structure of the world. This concrete universe of modes and things is to God as a bridge is to its design, its structure, and the laws of mathematics and mechanics according to which it is built; these are the sustaining basis, the underlying condition, the substance, of the bridge; without them it would fall. And like the bridge, the world itself is sustained by its structure and its laws; it is upheld in the hand of God.[5] | As the basis of cosmic order, the Rtá rules the world and nature. The established facts of the visible world but specially the events of nature that recur periodically are fixed or regulated by Rtá. Those daughters of heaven, the Maidens of Dawn, shine upon the morning sky in harmony with Rtá, or when they wake up in the morning they rise from the seat of Rtá. The sun is placed upon the sky in obedience to the Rtá. He is called the wheel of Rtá with 12 spokes. This means that he courses across the sky as the year of 12 months. Even the shallow mystery that the red, raw cow yields white cooked milk is the Rtá of the cow guided by the Rtá. The gods themselves are born of the Rtá or in the Rtá (rtajata); they show by their acts that they know the Rtá, observe the Rtá and love the Rtá.[6] |

Spinoza and the Rig Veda say unequivocally that there is one infinite, necessary, and uncaused set of laws, an underlying consciousness or substance, that determines everything—we can call this essence *God*.

Everything is in God, and God is in everything. This infinite being is not one who acts to interfere with human lives to reward or punish us but, instead, is the necessary and logical outcome of the laws of nature. In fact, the laws of nature are, in essence, God.

This essential being or consciousness, therefore, is not to be worshipped or prayed to for favors. Instead, we should attempt to comprehend it through empirical observation and reasoning. This logically deterministic view of the world defines this shared concept of God. The ideas of a creator and of some act of creation that lies beyond the predetermined laws of nature are rejected outright. In their place is the idea that we and everything we see around us are the logical and inescapable result of the laws of nature.

Once again, I have chosen two passages, one describing Spinoza's concept of God (from Durant) and the other from Rao's description of the Rtá, interpreted from the Rig Veda. The concepts are remarkably similar and lead us to the same conclusions about God and his relationship with nature and with the physical world around us.

The will of God and the laws of nature being one and the same reality diversely phrased, it follows that all events are the mechanical operation of invariable laws and not the whim of an irresponsible autocrat seated in the stars. The mechanism which Descartes saw in matter and body alone, Spinoza sees in God and mind as well. It is a world of determinism, not design. Because we act for conscious ends we suppose that all processes have such ends in view; and because we are human we suppose that all events lead up to man and are designed to subserve his needs. But this is an anthropocentric delusion, like so much of our thinking. The root of the greatest errors in philosophy lies in projecting our human purposes, criteria and preferences into the objective universe. Hence our "problem of evil"; we strive to reconcile the ills of life with the goodness of God, forgetting the lesson taught by Job, that God is beyond our little good and evil.[7]

Rtá is described as the firm, fundamental and inherent law of nature (RV.4.24.8–9). It is the controlling and the sustaining power in nature. Rtá ordains the laws of the physical word; regulates the laws of birth, growth and decay in nature (RV 2.28.4); controls and balances all natural forces in [our] environment.... By the laws of Varuna heaven and earth are held apart; the planets rotate in their fixed orbits (RV 5.62.1). By Rtá the sun shines in heaven; the paths are set out for the Sun; the seasons (*Ritu*) change (RV 1.25.8); the hours are bound together; day and night alternate regularly. By the laws of Rtá the moon shining brightly moves at night, and the stars placed up high are seen at night but disappear by day. Rtá causes the rivers to flow into the ocean without overfilling it. Varuna the lord of Rtá is the binder. He binds together the deep-space, the space between the earth and yonder, the winds, the clouds and the rays of light.[8]

Einstein's concept of God—and, indeed, the definition of God that most modern scientists would provide—is completely consistent with the conception of Rtá, the ancient Aryan definition of God. Remarkably, we have come full circle in our definition of God.

For all intents and purposes, Spinoza's God and the concept of the Rtá are identical. According to both Spinoza and the ancient Rig Vedic priests, all creation, including the gods, are but mere puppets that are required to live by the universal laws of nature, the Rtá. These laws control not only everyday events but the fate and destiny of man, animals, inanimate objects, and the gods. Nothing and no one is exempt.

> That eternal and infinite being we call God, or Nature, acts from the same necessity from which he exists.[9]

Indeed, the Rtá is not the physical embodiment of nature (the trees, the rivers and the oceans, etc.) but instead the underlying essence of nature, the laws that govern the universe. It is not the forests and the clouds but the rules that govern the formation and movement of the clouds and the growth of the trees. It is this unchanging essence that pervades and controls all, and we are all a part of this supreme consciousness. There can be no other way.

The concept of the Indo-Aryan Rtá has a direct parallel in the Avestan, or Zoroastrian, faith of the early Persians and was clearly adopted by the Hittites and the Sumerians. This universal order is called Asha, and in cuneiform, Persian Arta. After 5000 years of philosophical introspection, we have indeed come full circle.

Substance, Form, and Brahman

The convergence of the definition of God proposed by the Renaissance thinkers and the concept of the ultimate reality embodied in the Rtá, proposed so long ago by the philosophers of the ancient Aryans, is truly remarkable. However, the convergence does not end there; it goes well beyond the concept of the Rtá. The following writings were separated by more than 2,000 years of human history and more than 2,000 miles of geography.

In the Kena Upanishad,[10] a student asks his teacher,

> "Who sends the mind to wander afar! Who first drives life to

start on its journey? Who impels us to utter these words? Who is the spirit behind the eye and ear?"

In response, the teacher describes this impelling force:

"It is the ear of the ear, the eye of the eye, the word of the words, the mind of the mind, and the life of the life."

And he goes on to say,

"What cannot be spoken with words, but that whereby words are spoken: Know that alone to be Brahman, the Spirit; and not what people here adore.

"What cannot be thought with the mind, but whereby the mind can think, know that alone to be Brahman, the Spirit; and not what people here adore.

"What cannot be seen with the eye, but whereby the eye can see, know that alone to be Brahman, the Spirit; and not what people here adore.

"What cannot be heard with the ear, but whereby the ear can hear, know that alone to be Brahman, the Spirit; and not what people here adore."

Compare this now with Will Durant's description of Plato's *forms* or Spinoza's *substance*:

Behind the surface phenomena and particulars which greet our senses, are generalizations, regularities, and directions of development, unperceived by sensation but conceived by reason and thought. These ideas, laws and ideals are more permanent—and therefore more "real"—than the sense-perceived particular things through which we conceive and deduce them. . . . This tree stands, and that falls; but the laws which determine what bodies shall fall, and when, and how, were without beginning, are now, and shall be, without end. There is, as the gentle Spinoza would say, a world of things perceived by sense, and a world of laws inferred by thought; we do not see the law of inverse squares but it is there, and everywhere; it was before anything began, and will survive when all the world of things is a finished tale.... Aristotle hints something of this when he says that by Ideas Plato meant what Pythagoras meant by "number" when he taught that this is a world of numbers (meaning presumably that the world is ruled by mathematical constancies and regularities). Plutarch tells us that according to Plato "God always geometrizes"; or, as Spinoza puts the same thought, God and the universal laws of structure and operation are one and the same reality. To Plato, as Bertrand Russell, mathematics is, therefore, indispensable prelude to philosophy, and its highest form; over the doors of his Academy Plato placed, Dantesquely, these words, "Let no man ignorant of geometry enter here."

Without these Ideas—these generalizations, regularities and ideals—the world would be to us as it must seem for the first-opened eyes of the child, a mass of unclassified and unmeaning particulars of sensation; for meaning can be given to things only by classifying and generalizing them, by finding the laws of their beings, and the purposes and goals of their activity.... We must classify and coordinate our sense experience in terms of law and purpose; only for lack of this does the mind of the imbecile differ from the mind of Caesar.[11]

Plato's *forms* and Spinoza's *substance* are concepts that are very similar to the Brahman in the Upanishads. They all possess the same essential qualities of permanence, infiniteness, universality, and omnipresence. Although material objects will ultimately decay and change, the essence of all reality remains unchanged. It is this unchanging reality that the sages of the Upanishads, Plato, Spinoza, and Einstein see as the ultimate reality.

The nature of this essence and how one might understand it is again described in the Upanishads.

> Brahman cannot be seen by the eye, and words cannot reveal it. It cannot be reached by the senses, or by austerity or by good actions. By the grace and wisdom and purity of mind, it can be seen, indivisible in the silence of non-distraction ...[12]

> By means of the higher knowledge the wise behold everywhere Brahman, which otherwise cannot be seen or grasped, which has no root or attribute, no eyes or ears, no hands or feet, which is eternal and omnipresent, all pervading and extremely subtle, which is imperishable and the source of all beings.[13]

These ancient philosophers have a consistent message: To understand the world around us, we must understand its substance, its underlying essence. For the authors of the Upanishads, as for Plato and Spinoza, this underlying essence is universal.

Spinoza's distinction between *Natura naturans* and *Natura naturata* allowed him to distinguish between the essential components of nature, such as the laws of nature, and the rest of creation, which essentially must follow as a consequence of these laws and the way they interplay and act on matter and energy. The underlying laws of nature are a part of this essence, and they—not the commonly observable manifestations of nature—define God.

Everything is a part of this essence and is one with it. The discovery of this Rtá, Brahman, or mind of God should be the ultimate goal of human existence. This transcendent essence forms the bedrock of the transient dance of creation. The Upanishad sages urge us to pursue this highest noble goal:

> That which is radiant, subtler than the subtle, that by which all the words and their inhabitants are supported—that there really is the indestructible Brahman. That alone is to be struck. Strike it, my good friend.[14]

From the ancient Aryans in India (2000 BCE) in the Axial Age (400 BCE) to Spinoza in the Age of Enlightenment (1600s) to Albert Einstein, who epitomizes the scientific age (1900s), we have come full circle in our quest for a definition of God. The ideals and aspirations of the first humans in the age of wonder (expressed in the hymns of the Rig Veda) had the same lofty goals as the great philosophical traditions that followed. Their spirit of intense inquisitiveness and wonder is best expressed in Einstein's own carefully chosen words:

The most beautiful and deepest experience a man can have is the sense of the mysterious. It is the underlying principle of religion as well as all serious endeavor in art and science. He who never had this experience seems to me, if not dead, then at least blind. To sense that behind anything that can be experienced there is a something that our mind cannot grasp and whose beauty and sublimity reaches us only indirectly and as a feeble reflection, this is religiousness. In this sense I am religious. To me it suffices to wonder at these secrets and to attempt humbly to grasp with my mind a mere image of the lofty structure of all that there is.[15]

I am satisfied with the mystery of life's eternity and with a knowledge, a sense, of the marvelous structure of existence—as well as the humble attempt to understand even a tiny portion of the Reason that manifests itself in nature.[16]

Tao and the Laws of Nature

The Confucian idea of order and harmony and the Taoist teachings, which came about more than a thousand years after the Rig Veda, were similar in the way they viewed the transcendental life force behind all beings. There is no mistaking the common sentiment expressed in the Vedas and in Chinese philosophy. The Tao is considered the essence of all reality and the source of order in nature.

> There was something formless and perfect
> before the universe was born.
> It is serene. Empty.
> Solitary. Unchanging.
> Infinite. Eternally present.
> It is the mother of the universe.
> For lack of a better name,
> I call it the Tao.[17]

In these two great intellectual traditions, the concept of an underlying consciousness that pervades everything is clearly evident. As with the Rtá, the gods obey the Tao, as does everything else—animate and inanimate.

> Man follows the earth.
> Earth follows the universe.
> The universe follows the Tao.
> The Tao follows only itself.[18]

The Rtá, as it was originally defined in the Rig Veda, is the Tao in the *Tao Te Ching*, Plato's *forms*, and Spinoza's *Natura Naturans*. In the age of reason, what scientists today would define as their quest to "read the mind of God" is conceptually no different from our ancient ancestors' desire to better understand the Rtá or the Brahman. Although these ancient people were very poorly equipped to address these complex questions about the physical laws of the universe, their intent is unmistakable. Without the benefit of the scientific discoveries that have occurred in the past 200 years, humanity was completely unprepared for such a Herculean task.

It is truly incredible that after 5,000 years of philosophy and science we have come full circle and rediscovered the wisdom of the ancient Aryans. This dynamic and intelligent early group of people marveled at the beauty and structured complexity of the creation around them. This is the same sentiment that many scientists express today. God can, therefore, be defined as the order in the universe or the laws of nature. If this is too abstract a concept, we can define God as the source of these laws, although no source is necessary.

Spinoza's God versus Scripture: Rationality versus Belief

This abstract definition of God, as embodied in the ancient Aryan concept of Rtá, has historically found favor with those who are more philosophically inclined: the rationalists, or the jnana yogis. However, for a vast majority of individuals, the practice of religion has been dominated by much more personal gods, instead of such abstract ideas.

The Abrahamic religions have traditionally been focused on the revealed word of God as stated in their scripture. Despite many attempts to reinterpret the scriptures and to explain the claims made in them on a rational basis, they remain primarily based on faith—the Holy Scriptures, as revealed by the prophets, are the only true word of God. Since this is a matter of belief, there needs to be no rational basis for it, and none is provided.

The tension between scripture and rationality is particularly acute in the Abrahamic religions, perhaps because of the insistence on strict adherence to scripture. The Greeks, the Hindus, the Confucians, the Taoists, and the Buddhists deal with much less of a dichotomy, because they regard their holy texts as philosophical guideposts, not the literal word of God. They encourage their followers to discover the path to God that is best suited to their individual capacities, needs, and experiences.

Because of this multitude of paths, it is much easier to reconcile these scriptures with rationality. Even though the Brahman reflects the inherent monotheism in Hinduism, it is entirely acceptable to worship a personal god, who is no more than a personal representation of the one Supreme Being. This also holds true of the ancient Chinese, pre-Islamic Arabs, and the Canaanites. We can view this as a form of pluralistic monotheism—monotheism in principle but monotheism that recognizes the need for personal gods.

What we then find in the practice of most Asian religions (Hinduism and, to some extent, Buddhism and Confucianism) is that even though they remain philosophically monotheistic (or agnostic, as is the case in Buddhism), in practice they offer adherents the freedom to choose more accessible—and, in many cases, anthropomorphic—gods or goddesses, which can be much more emotionally satisfying. Both rationality and belief can therefore find a home and live side by side.

This accomplishes two very important things. First, it allows people to respect—not just tolerate—gods in other traditions, since they are, after all, different manifestations of the same Supreme Being. There are no jealous gods, and belief in one does not preclude belief in another. Second, it satisfies both our rational and our emotional needs as human beings.

Summary

I have made the case that over the course of the past 5000 years, we have come full circle in our understanding of God. This is an amazing journey from man's earliest utterances about his concept of God to our modern ideas, molded by the immense strides we have made in science and technology. Over the course of our history, we have gone down many blind alleys and explored many avenues; however, they have always led back to the same central theme.

The early Aryans were remarkably astute in observing that while the gods were incredibly important in their own right, these gods were obligated to follow the rules set out in the universal, unchanging code, the Rtá. The sense of wonder at the consistent and underlying order in the universe has persisted in many forms over the course of human history—in the Rtá in the Rig Veda, the Tao in Chinese religions, the Brahman in the Upanishads, the Maat in Egyptian religions, the forms in Plato's *Republic*, the *Natura Naturans* in Spinoza's philosophy, and the laws of nature in modern science.

Belief in a supernatural being who directly interferes in the lives of human beings is being replaced with a definition of God that is consistent with our modern rational view of the world and is in line with our most ancient philosophical concept of God, the Aryan Rtá. We have returned to where we began in our quest for defining God.

It's All in the Mind: Rational versus Emotional Definitions of God

"Instead of uselessly opposing reason to passion—a contest in which the more deeply rooted ancestral element usually wins—[Spinoza] opposes reasonless passions to passions coordinated by reason, put into place by the total perspective of the situation. Thought should not lack the heat of desire nor desire the light of thought."

—Will Durant

We have thus far traced the historical evolution of our ideas about god and discovered that we have come full circle. We have made the point that it is not possible to prove the existence of god on a rational basis. Humans, however, are not just rational beings. Rationality is an important but small component of our intellect. There are other deeply rooted aspects of our mind, some of which have evolved to drive us, often irrationally, to action. For many of us, satisfying our emotional needs can be far more important than satisfying our rational mind. This implies that the concept of god that satisfies our emotional needs may be essential, even if it is not justified by rationality alone. We will explore these emotional dimensions in this chapter and see how they lead us to into the mind of a believer and how this brings us full circle again.

The Pragmatic Limits of Rationality

There is no doubt that a vast majority of people in the world believe firmly in the existence of a supernatural power that regulates our lives, punishes the bad, and rewards the good. This enlightened being looks over us and ensures that moral order is maintained and that humanity does not slip into immoral chaos. Recall the survey we discussed in chapter 1: Well over 90 percent of the respondents believe in God. This is true even though there is absolutely no evidence or rational argument for it.

Mark Stevens, in his book *God Is a Salesman*, puts it this way:

> Consider the power of it all: God, or the religions that explain and celebrate Him, prompt us to believe that He—
>
> - Exists
> - Created the world
> - Is all goodness
> - Is all knowing
> - Loves us
>
> Without a shard of proof or a scintilla of traditional CSI-type evidence that all of this is true, we embrace Him, adore Him, and worship Him. What force is responsible for this phenomenon?[1]

If the logic of the Big Guy in the Sky conception of God is so clearly flawed, we must ask ourselves why it has been so widely accepted throughout human history. How can it be that all ancient civilizations and most people, even in this age of scientific discovery, have bought into this idea of an all-powerful and interfering God? What is so appealing about this idea that millions have sacrificed life and limb for it? Let's explore the reasons, the idea's pluses and minuses, and why the time may be right to modify it and move toward a broader definition of God. This may lead, paradoxically, to a more profoundly religious society, with a definition of God proposed by our earliest ancestors and modified substantially by modern scientific advances. We are coming full circle in more ways than one.

Our quest to explain the success of the BGITS God, therefore, leads us inexorably to an exploration of why we behave the way we do as human beings. This is the domain of behavioral psychologists, who for decades have been puzzling over such questions. What drives us, what motivates us, and what ultimately satisfies us? Surely, our belief system—particularly as it relates to the larger, inexplicable questions—must have some psychological basis. This is a large, well-researched, and well-documented subject, but we will limit our discussion to what behavioral psychology can teach us about how we each deal with questions of God, religion, and faith, in our own way.

Before we explore the possibility of broadening our definition of God, we must address three very important questions:
- What is the universal appeal of a BGITS God?
- What is wrong with holding on to this concept of God? After all, it has been the de facto model of God for a vast majority of humanity for thousands of years.
- In this age of scientific enlightenment, can we do better?

The Rationalist that Never Was

A definition of God that satisfies our rational mind may be sufficient for those of us with a scientific bent, but for most of us, it is incomplete. This feeling of incompleteness stems from the fact that rationality does little to address the emotional component of our intellect. Although defining God in the abstract as the underlying order in the universe may be immensely intellectually satisfying, it does nothing to soothe us emotionally. The connection between our daily lives and the set of immutable and complex natural laws is difficult to accept at all levels of the intellect, even for the most scientific minds. In times of crisis and emotional need, we reach out to simpler, more accessible gods that do not require such intellectual effort. Those who have experienced the prolonged and terminal illness of a loved one or the untimely passing of close relative often find emotional comfort in God, religious services, meditation, and prayer. We do not much care about the logical sequence that brought us to our acceptance of an image we ascribe godly attributes to. This is perfectly understandable and, to a point, even healthy. After all, many of us may not be able manage the mental equanimity to relate to an abstract God at times of emotional and intellectual distress.

We need not look very far to see evidence that emotions rule our daily lives. More often than not, emotion trumps rationality, although we may not always be able to determine why. We see people driven to emotional ecstasy at the sound of their favorite hymn or sports fans driven to rage or even suicide by a critical loss by their favorite team. We see the unfathomable action of suicide bombings by individuals driven to the inexplicable by the teachings of misguided clerics. These are not the acts of a rational mind. Whether it is everyday random acts of kindness or unspeakable cruelty, human emotions hold incredible sway over what we think and do.

To truly understand the deep-rooted importance of our emotional being, we need to delve into the world of human psychology and the subconscious. As we shall see in this chapter, psychological profiles created over many decades show how differences between individuals and societies can lead to entirely different methods of intellectual and emotional satisfaction. These different motivations and desires lead to psychological complexities that are at the underlying core of religious beliefs. As different as we are from each other, we must—each one of us—find our own path to discovering God.

Snap Decisions: When Emotion Trumps Rationality

Ask any candidate running for office how important first impressions and visual cues are in determining a voter's decision, and they will tell you that they are of utmost importance. This fact is independent of the position a candidate takes on issues. Why should a better-looking candidate fare better than an average-looking one (as they often do)? Their ability to do their job is in no way affected by their physical appearance. Yet appearances do matter. We make decisions about people based on gut instinct—on impressions and biases we have accumulated over our lifetime.

We have a propensity to make quick emotional decisions and stick with them, despite compelling evidence that we are often wrong. In his book *Blink*, Malcolm Gladwell discusses a study of college students who rated their professors on their ability to teach effectively simply by watching a short video of them teaching, with no audio. The rating of the professor after a semester of teaching was virtually the same as the rating based on the short silent video viewed by the students. In fact, the rating had very little to do with teaching ability but rather seemed to depend on how likable the professor appeared. Having taught in a classroom for over thirty years, I found these results surprising and a bit distressing. I clearly should have focused more on my personality and looks than on my mastery of the subject I was teaching!

The Conscious versus the Unconscious Mind

Leonard Mlodinow, in his recent book *Subliminal: How Your Unconscious Mind Rules Your Behavior*, offered a fascinating look at the psychological basis of our actions:

> We are not like computers that crunch data in a relatively straightforward manner and calculate results. Instead, our brains are made up of a collection of many modules that work in parallel, with complex interactions, most of which operate outside of our consciousness. As a consequence, the real reasons behind our judgments, feelings, and behavior can surprise us.[2]

When confronted with a bewildering array of choices and limited time to reach a decision, our instincts kick in, and we decide on the basis of a combination of rational arguments, emotions, and beliefs—that is, preconceived notions based on our personal experiences. Imagine yourself standing in the laundry detergent aisle in the grocery store trying to pick from a dozen or so choices. You have a few seconds to make a snap decision. Your decision is unlikely to be made based on an analysis of the pros and cons of the cleaning ability or chemical constituents of each type of detergent but rather on how familiar you are with and how you feel about a particular detergent. In fact, if any of us were asked why we chose a particular laundry detergent or cereal, we would be hard-pressed to provide a logical answer.

Feeling good about a laundry detergent or a breakfast cereal may seem like an odd concept, but the goal of advertising is to make us do precisely that. Subliminal messages in advertising appeal to our inner being, our subconscious mind, without leaving a trace in our conscious thoughts.

Here again, Mr. Mlodinow provides an excellent example of buyers choosing between French or German wines in a store where they were made equally available. On days when French music was played in the background, 77 percent of the customers chose French wine. When German music was being played, 73 percent chose German wine. Almost all of the shoppers denied that the music had anything to do with their choice.[3]

This illustrates how little attention we pay to actual data and how much we rely on our mental image of the world around us—in other words, our instincts.

Mr. Mlodinow provides another illustration of the importance of our unconscious mind when he compares energy consumption by the brain during periods of intense mental activity with that used during periods of relative inactivity.

> Deep concentration causes the energy consumption in your brain to go up by only about 1 percent. No matter what you are doing with your conscious mind, it is your unconscious that dominates your mental activity—and therefore uses up most of the energy consumed by the brain. Regardless of whether your conscious mind is idle or engaged, your unconscious mind is hard at work doing the mental equivalent of push-ups, squats, and wind sprints.[4]

Combining the conscious and unconscious parts of our intellect is a wonderful skill that is essential to our survival. In fact, it is a good thing that we can make these snap decisions without the burden of a long, logical process; otherwise, we would never leave the grocery store!

We can all usually make logical decisions when presented with all the facts and a simple logical path to a decision, but many choices in our daily lives do not fall into this category. The information presented to us is almost always incomplete. The path to a logical conclusion is almost always convoluted, the time to collect our thoughts is limited, and sometimes the range of outcomes is uncertain. This applies to the decision we make in the grocery store and also to every other decision, including our belief in God.

The ability to make quick decisions is likely the product of an evolutionary process that rewarded rapid decision-making. In competition for survival, such ability made the difference between life and death. Careful, analytical, logical thinkers were not and are not favored in the survival of the fittest.

The most surprising aspect of these decisions is not that we make them, but that we stick with them—even justify them and reinforce them—when we have time to analyze the evidence afterward. In fact, once we have reached a conclusion, we selectively ignore data that contradicts it and actively look for information that supports it.

Our unconscious mind plays a central role in controlling our decisions and drawing our conclusions—and therefore our beliefs. Could it be that this unconscious component of our intellect is the primary reason for our belief in the traditional BGITS? To answer this question, we must better understand this unconscious bedrock of our intellect. What constitutes the unconscious force that dominates our behavior, including belief in God?

Belief versus Knowledge

Note that the key word in the discussion above is *belief*. *Belief* is subjective. "I believe in God" is a statement that is not open to logical discussion, much like the statement, "I believe in ghosts." It does not say anything about the logical validity of God's existence; in fact, the broader question of whether the belief is in any way rational becomes, in some sense, meaningless for the believer.

Knowledge, on the other hand, is a body of ideas that is verifiably and universally true. That the sun rises in the east and sets in the west is something that everyone can agree on. It's indisputable because we can all observe it, and its validity is independent of the observer.

Some aspects of our knowledge are not so obviously true. The existence of elementary particles, such as quarks or even electrons and protons, is not obvious. They are not directly observable, even with the most sophisticated scientific instruments. How, then, can we be so sure of their existence? No one has ever seen a dinosaur. How can we be so sure about their existence millions of years before the appearance of the first humans? Should these inferences be considered a part of our knowledge base? Should they be accepted even without direct human observation?

Fortunately for us, the scientific method provides a way to build a body of knowledge, even for phenomena we cannot directly observe. As we discussed in chapter 5, the scientific method ensures that all entries in our collective knowledge base meet certain basic standards:

- All theories must be based on independently verifiable, empirical data. In other words, if you or I or anyone else repeats an experiment, we should all obtain the same results.
- Theories are accepted if they are consistent with empirical observations.
- Hypotheses that are not verified empirically must remain hypotheses or be replaced by new ones.
- Logical deductions and inferences derived from past knowledge must also meet this stringent test of consistency with independently verifiable empirical observations.
- If new empirical evidence comes to light, it can invalidate long-established scientific rules, laws, and theories. This self-correcting mechanism is vital to the growth, quality, and consistency of our knowledge base.

A system built on this method yields a knowledge base that is not subjective but can be universally applied and verified, regardless of personal biases or beliefs. It is no surprise, that there is, by and large, a consistent set of scientific laws that are widely accepted by all scientists. There is no room for belief—only for a logical progression to conclusions based on empirical, independently verifiable, reproducible data and theory.

By contrast, beliefs are personal. They need not be based on empirical observations (and are frequently not) or on a logical thought process. It is likely that our personal belief systems are based on personal experiences and unconscious psychological factors that we are just beginning to understand.

What Controls Our Belief System?

Both a well-established knowledge base and a belief system are important to our intellectual and emotional well-being. As human beings, we need both—one tempered by the other. We understand the basis of our knowledge base quite well, and much has been written about it. Much less is understood about how we develop our belief system. What makes us believe something is true?

As we have discussed in earlier sections, rationality and logic play but a small part in our daily decisions. This is made evident by the fact that human beings have such varied belief systems. If these beliefs were the product of logic alone, we would all reach the same conclusion. The introduction of belief in the discussion about God often hinders any logical discussion. For some, the fact that they believe that God exists is sufficient to cut them off from the broader question of whether this belief is justified. Does it?

If we were to live as isolated human beings, differences in our belief systems would matter little, and any further discussion would only be of academic interest. Everyone could go on following their belief system, and everything would work out just fine. Fortunately or unfortunately, we live in a society where we interact with each other, and this means that our belief systems are often in conflict with someone else's. Over the course of human history, this has led to more violence and bloodshed than any other single reason. From the crusades to the holocaust, the burning of witches to human sacrifice, we can scarcely think of a time in our history when belief—indeed, religion—has not been used to justify murder, conflict, war, and genocide. In defense of religious beliefs, I should also add that our religious belief systems have also been the basis of incredible acts of human kindness and devotion to humanitarian causes.

It is vital then to understand what controls our belief system. Clearly, the answer to the universal appeal of the BGITS conception of God lies not in the logical dissection of the concept but in emotional and psychological factors that control our beliefs.

Our Evolutionary Predisposition to a Belief in God

We are a product of our evolution. Although we can debate this point with our creationist friends, there is overwhelming scientific evidence to prove that we are—as are all animals on this planet—a product of a Darwinian evolutionary process. This is not a matter of belief; it is an extensively verified part of our knowledge base. Does the evolutionary process predispose us to a belief in God?

The current state of the human brain is a product of natural selection that very specifically selected and rewarded certain behavioral patterns. Buried deep in our brain are evolutionary instincts that make up a vast unconscious intellect honed by millions of years of development. Does this vast storehouse of evolutionary intellect predispose us to a belief in God?

Michael Shermer, in his book *The Believing Brain*, points to psychological evidence for the innate tendency among all animals, including human beings, to infer cause-and-effect relationships between events where no such relationship exists. Shermer describes an experiment in which the well-known psychologist B. F. Skinner fed caged pigeons at random and irregular intervals. Between feedings, the pigeons would indulge in a series of random actions. When the food appeared, the pigeons would associate the appearance of the food with the actions they had just completed—even though there was no connection between the two—and would repeat the sequence of actions with the expectation of getting more food. The dance they had performed prior to the appearance of the food was repeated over and over again. Shermer terms this tendency to associate a pattern between a result and their actions *patternicity*. Experiments conducted later with human subjects showed similar behavior.

Indeed, humans go one step further. We not only establish patterns; we "infuse patterns with meaning, intention, and agency."[5] In other words, we invent an entity, an agent, that is responsible for the pattern, and this agent is assigned a deliberate intent, whether such agent or intent exists or not. As Shermer puts it,

> We often impart the patterns we find with agency and intention, and believe that these intentional agents control the world,

sometimes invisibly from the top down, instead of bottom-up causal laws and randomness that makes up much of our world. Souls, spirits, ghosts, gods, demons, angels, aliens, intelligent designers, government conspiracists, and all manner of invisible agents with power and intention are believed to haunt our world and control our lives.[6]

This strong tendency to believe cause-and-effect relationships and to imbue them with intent forms the basis for our belief in God. Again, as Shermer puts it,

> God is the ultimate pattern that explains everything that happens, from the beginning of the universe to the end of time and everything in between, including and especially the fates of human lives. God is the ultimate intention of the agent who gives the universe meaning and our lives purpose. As an ultimate amalgam, patternicity and agenticity form the cognitive basis of shamanism, paganism, animism, polytheism, monotheism, and all other forms of theisms and spiritualisms devised by humans.[7]

In Search of a God Gene

Some have made the case that our DNA predisposes us to a belief in God. The thesis is that the incredible success of religion in our society must stem from our fundamental biological makeup or some part of our DNA that we should be able to identify. As human beings, we are biologically defined by our genes. Our genes define the color of our skin, how many arms, legs, and fingers we have—in other words, our physical appearance and cell biology. However, the connection between specific genes and human behavior is far from resolved.

For this reason, I can only agree with this thesis in part. Religion, or a belief in God, is not a physiological condition. Therefore, unlike other physiological conditions, such as Parkinson's disease, there is no single identifiable strand of gene that leads to a belief in God.

One way to isolate genetic influences from cultural and environmental influences is to eliminate the effect of genetics by studying identical twins. In a study of over 3,000 twins, psychologists have shown that "religious affiliation is (as might be expected) a cultural phenomenon, but genetic factors manifest a moderate degree of influence on religious devotion and conservatism."[8] Using the same data, Waller[9] showed that there was an equal influence of genetic and environmental factors in determining the religious inclinations of identical and fraternal twins. These studies clearly suggest a correlation between genetic factors and religious inclinations.

However, a correlation between two variables in a study does not imply a cause-and-effect relationship. In fact, it is likely that the correlation between religious inclination and genetics is mediated by several intermediate cause-and-effect relationships that we do not completely understand. As Spilka put it, "Genetic factors are most likely expressed through cognitive, motivational and social avenues, which are involved in personal religious expressions."[10]

It is more likely that the human genome leads to the development of a brain that is predisposed to thinking about abstract matters, such as God, in a certain way—to reconcile illogical matters in a way that leads to the concept of a power greater than our own who ultimately controls our destiny. This higher authority appears to be the solution every major religion in the world has converged on from the early days of human civilization, which suggests that the human brain is predisposed to this concept of God.

What we can say, then, is that although there is no direct link between our DNA and our concept of God, our DNA leads to a human mind that finds the Big Guy in the Sky concept of God entirely acceptable for many practical purposes. It is a common denominator that appears to explain the inexplicable need for a soothe-the-senses and calm-the-emotions kind of God. This concept leads to emotional satisfaction and provides meaning to our lives. Most important, it keeps us happy and satisfied that a reasonable—if not entirely satisfactory—explanation has been provided for the questions that only humans tend to contemplate: *Why are we here? Who created us? Who guides the universe?* These are questions that the scientific method has a difficult time providing emotionally satisfactory answers to.

Basic or Unconscious Desires and Motivations

Psychologists have postulated that our behavior is driven by unconscious instincts and by our innermost desires and motivations. For Sigmund Freud, our primary motivation—and perhaps our only motivation—was procreation. Subsequent generations of behaviorists have embraced the powerful idea of primary motivations but have disagreed about what these primary motivations are.

I have chosen to highlight the primary or instinctual desires that were proposed by a more recent popular psychologist, Steven Reiss. In his book *Who Am I?* Reiss[11] postulated a set of basic desires, which he took great pains to empirically establish through a systematic analysis of surveys conducted on a wide variety of subjects in the United States.

Table 8.1 shows Reiss's sixteen basic desires and their associated end goals. Individuals will have different dominant desires: For some, social contact may be the primary driver; for others, acceptance as a part of a group dominates. Regardless of the dominant basic desire, Reiss claims that some combination of these basic desires controls every person's emotions, beliefs, and behavior.

Table 8.1. Basic Human Desires[12]

Basic Desire	*End Goals*	*Quality Ascribed to Gods*
Power	Achievement, competence, leadership	Creator, omnipotent, almighty, BGITS Gods
Independence	Freedom, ego, integrity	Self-sufficient, self-contained, and distinct from this world
Curiosity	Knowledge, truth	Omniscient
Acceptance	Positive self-image, self-worth	Benevolent, forgiving, accepting of all beings
Order	Cleanliness, stability, organization	Maintains order in the universe, keeps chaos at bay
Saving	Collection, property	Rewards believers

Basic Desire	End Goals	Quality Ascribed to Gods
Honor	Morality, character, loyalty	Author, keeper, and enforcer of all moral laws
Idealism	Fairness, justice	Image of perfection in a human being
Social contact	Friendship, fun	Friend, father, companion
Family	Children	Creator of all living beings, father figure for all beings
Status	Wealth, titles, attention, awards	King maker, provider of ultimate authority to all rulers
Vengeance	Winning, admission	Punishes all non-believers
Romance	Beauty, sex	Symbol of ultimate beauty, source of fertility
Eating	Food, dining, hunting	Source of all food and nourishment
Physical exercise	Fitness	The source of all power in the universe
Tranquility	Relaxation, safety	Ensures harmony and peace on earth and in the universe

Reiss argues that each individual ascribes their God with attributes intended to satisfy each of these different basic desires, without recognizing that this is what they are doing, and religions tend to differ in the levels of importance their members attach to God. Each desire has a counterpart; in some instances, this antidesire can provide useful insights into human behavior as well.

Reiss points out that several prominent psychologists in the past have proposed different primary desires. Perhaps the most important contributions were made by William James and William McDougal in the early twentieth century and Abraham Maslow in the late. The adjectives *primary*, *basic*, and *instinctual* have been used interchangeably, as have the terms *desires* and *motivations*. Our discussion here is independent of any specific list of primary desires. What is important from our perspective is that each of these experts in behavioral psychology has established the strong connection between motivations and human behavior.

Indian and Chinese philosophers intuitively recognized the importance of these basic desires in all human beings. For the eastern philosophers in Hinduism, Buddhism, and Taoism, liberation from this world of desires was the path to ultimate happiness. This could be achieved by detaching our desires from our actions and recognizing our oneness with the supreme consciousness, the Brahman, or the Tao.

How the BGITS Satisfies Our Basic Desires

If our basic desires were met by a BGITS God, it would provide a reasonable explanation of the universal acceptance of this concept. In fact, as we shall see, our basic desires are not only met, but they are satisfied in a way that no other concept can hope to match. It is no wonder that human beings all over the world have independently developed this concept of God and that it has persisted for millennia.

The essential concept of BGITS gods in different civilizations is remarkably similar. Each one of these gods is omnipotent and omniscient. Some are based on our innate feelings of fear, revenge, and retribution, whereas others evoke awe and admiration; a few are focused on redemption and forgiveness. The common thread in each of these concepts is a God who rewards the good and punishes the bad, a God who interferes directly in our lives. Let us explore the question of whether the BGITS concept of God satisfies our basic instinctual desires in such a powerful manner that all cultures and traditions are irresistibly drawn to it, regardless of logic.

Satisfying Our Basic Desire for Acceptance

Our desire for acceptance is remarkably powerful, and to avoid standing out from the group, we often turn into conformists. Children, for example, will go to extraordinary lengths to be accepted by their peers, and this desire is an important if not the dominant influence on their behavior. I am not sure we ever grow out of this. Acceptance by our parents, our friends, our teachers, and our bosses—even the hotel clerk—is a basic desire rooted in evolutionary conflict resolution.

In God, we find the ultimate accepter. He loves us for who we are, no questions asked. He accepts all our failings and asks nothing in return, except belief. Our parents may express some minor irritation or measure of criticism, but not God. This can be immensely satisfying but is particularly important for those who crave acceptance and are mortified by rejection and criticism.

How God Satisfies Our Basic Desire for Order

Organized religion and its associated rituals and teachings provide a measure of satisfaction for those of us who desire order. Although our own lives may not be as orderly, we can count on the weekly service to provide the measure of order we are lacking. Whether the somber *ding-dong* of church bells, the clanging of holy Hindu temple bells in the early hours of the morning, or the voice of the muezzin calling devout Muslims to prayer, these religious metronomes provide order in the lives of hundreds of millions of people all over the world. Faith defines an orderly and disciplined lifestyle amid the chaos around us.

The desire for order can lead to some interesting lapses in logic. We often ascribe cause-and-effect relationships where none exist. For example, there is nothing to support the common religious belief that bad things happen to people who defy the will of God. Although fear may be a good motivation for many among us to behave in a moral and ethical manner, there is no evidence of divine retribution.

Many of us seek order through a logical explanation for the world around us. We often ascribe reasons for inexplicable events to God's grand plan. However, when bad things happen to good people, the BGITS concept of God does not provide an adequate explanation. Some religions overcome this gap in logic by postulating reincarnation. The logic goes as follows: If bad things happen to good people in this life, they must have done something bad in a previous life. Although this is a valiant attempt to regain logic, reincarnation is impossible to verify and must be accepted as an act of faith.

This basic desire to look for logical explanations is so compelling and the explanation of a merciful God is so inadequate that we may resort to any belief system that provides some semblance of comfort.

Satisfying Our Desire for Community and Social Contact

Man is a social animal, and social contact is a powerful primary desire. In today's busy world, where everyone has work to do and places to go, it is no wonder that social interaction is becoming more and more difficult. There is less interaction among neighbors, and families now tend to live so far from each other that it is increasingly difficult for them to have the sense of a close-knit community. Religious institutions have replaced family and neighborhoods as the social fabric of our modern society. When I asked one of my neighbors the main reasons she attends church, her response was immediate and pragmatic: "I enjoy the social interaction and the camaraderie." A church service can be some people's only social interaction for the week.

Social cooperation has been the cornerstone of human survival. Groups that are socially cohesive are much more likely to survive. Religion provides a perfect rallying point for people to both socialize and collaborate. Belief in a common God brought people together in large numbers and formed the basis for most early civilizations, and nonbelievers were at a distinct evolutionary disadvantage because dissent was usually not tolerated.

Social behaviors such as affiliation and attachment have well-known biological foundations[13] that involve hormones that constitute the substrate of much social behavior.

Social cooperation may be similarly innate. Over a half a century ago, Ashley Montagu articulated the radical assertion that cooperation is the "most important factor in the survival of animal groups."[14] Cooperation is allied with evolution in general and natural selection in particular, especially when an individual's self-interests, such as safety, procreation, and food, are best protected by a social group—which is almost always the case with humans.[15]

In early human civilizations, all-powerful gods were the focal point for social cohesion. For example, the worship of the one true God, Yahweh, by the many tribes of the Canaanites (chapter 3) united these disparate groups. The odds of survival were bleak outside of this sort of community. Any tribe that did not believe in Yahweh was unlikely to survive the pressures imposed on them by the tribes who did believe in this jealous God. With this prerequisite, it's no wonder that evolutionary forces shaped our basic instincts to favor organized religions.

Great temples, churches, and mosques were constructed to honor the gods and served as central meeting places for the community of believers. Religious ceremonies, festivals, and community rituals were usually mandatory. Social bodies such as organized religion need order, rules, and laws that govern the behavior of their members. To give these laws teeth, punishments and rewards were defined, and to implement them, there was a hierarchy of enforcers and preachers—underlying the importance of clergy in nearly all religions. They controlled the rituals and were the channel of all communication with the gods. This is still the case with many religions.

Belief in God is no longer a prerequisite for attending "religious" services. Many humanist and atheist organizations have regular meetings to meditate and congregate—primarily to provide their members with a sense of community and belonging. This basic human desire is so persistent that it alone can drive individuals to organized religion.

Does God Satisfy Our Basic Desire for Vengeance?

This is an odd one, but for anyone who has read the gory details of the animal and human sacrifices of the Incas, the Mayans, the Egyptians, or the Chinese, there should be no doubt that many ancient civilizations conceived of gods that would not think twice about exacting vengeance on anyone who dared question their authority or who harmed their chosen people. Why did civilizations across the globe conjure up gods that would ask such heinous acts of their followers? Why would we want such an unforgiving deity? This too must stem from some instinctual human desire. Reiss argued that these gods stem from our basic desire for vengeance, and Russell put it this way:

> Religion is based, I think, primarily and mainly upon fear. It is partly the terror of the unknown and partly, as I have said, the wish to feel that you have a kind of elder brother who will stand by you in all your troubles and disputes.[16]

The concept of a vengeful God is not limited to primitive societies. All modern religions are replete with stories of vengeful gods who protect their followers and punish nonbelievers. The desire for vengeance also leads to the opposite desire, compassion and forgiveness. Gods are vengeful and merciless in their pursuit of the nonbelievers and merciful and kind toward their followers. This dichotomy is essential to ensuring a devoted and loyal following. In this vision of God, we worship someone who is capable of the ultimate revenge and of sublime forgiveness. That's a powerful combination that is hard to resist, even if it is attributed to an entity that may be a figment of our imagination.

God and Our Basic Desire for Love

The tradition of associating an image of God with our intense romantic desires goes back millennia. Our desire to love and to be loved is fulfilled by a flawless divine being. For many Christian denominations, Christ's love knows no bounds. He even sacrificed himself for us so we could be saved. What more could a person ask for? The believer or devotee fulfills his or her deepest desire for unconditional love, and God asks nothing in return except the devotee's faith and acceptance of his divine reality.

God Satisfies Our Basic Desire for Peace and Tranquility

The desire for mental peace and tranquility is one that has been emphasized in Eastern and Abrahamic religions. Meditation and contemplative prayer are at the heart of Hinduism, Buddhism, and Taoism. God can best be understood when the soul is at peace and the heart and mind at rest. Meditation halls, temples, and monasteries are designed to rest and focus the mind in search of God. The form of God that emerges when we put tranquility as the primary basic desire is one of a contemplative figure, deep in thought, like the familiar images of the contemplative Buddha. We see ourselves in this image and try to emulate his repose in an attempt to satisfy our desire to achieve peace. Prayer to and contemplation of a divine being provides a deeply satisfying emotional experience to the contemplative believer.

We could make similar cases for how God satisfies our other basic desires, but it's sufficient to summarize by saying that our belief in God is driven by deep-seated basic desires that must be satisfied to provide us with the emotional satisfaction we seek.

Our Instinctual Desires Determine Our God

We have seen in previous chapters that civilizations often developed concepts of God that were consistent with their dominant societal traits. Reiss claims[17] that within societies, every individual, if given the choice, migrates to a concept of God that most appeals to their dominant basic desire.

In the West, a compassionate, loving God emerged because it fits in with the current social ethos. In more culturally and economically diverse societies, such as India or Southeast Asia, the gods vary from the terrifying and vengeful goddess Kali to the meditative and peaceful Buddha, from the loving and divine Krishna to the goddess of wisdom and learning, Saraswati. These are clearly images of God that are designed to appeal to people with different instinctual desires.

As modern man emerged from the darkness of fear and superstition, dominant desires have evolved, and so has the preference for our image of God. There is no doubt that modern religions are less violent than ancient ones. Although most ancient civilizations—the Egyptians, the Minoans, the North American Indian tribes, the Aztecs, the Mayans, and the ancient Aryans—all showed a propensity for violent sacrifices and rituals, murder in the name of God has largely lost its ritual appeal. However, the violent struggle between believers of different faiths has continued. As our instinctual desires have changed as a society, so have our gods, or at least the particular ideals we like to ascribe to them.

My God! What More Could We Possibly Want?

The BGITS concept of God—an interventionist God who takes care of his believers and punishes nonbelievers—has emerged over millennia and across every continent, and as we've seen, this is no coincidence. The BGITS satisfies many, if not all, of our instinctual desires.

And what's wrong with that? The benefits of a BGITS conception of God are obvious:

- It satisfies us emotionally.
- It provides our lives a sense of purpose.
- It provides order in our lives.

- It is a source of comfort in times of emotional distress.

What more could we possibly want? God and organized religion offer this appealing idea that satisfies our deepest psychological needs. Is this not reason enough to continue on the same path as our ancestors?

We Can Do Better

Let's think for a moment about how well the BGITS definition of God has served us over time. Even a cursory review of human history shows that although it may satisfy our emotional needs, it leads to serious societal problems. If these beliefs breed unchecked, they lead to the false conclusion that one belief system is superior to another, which inevitably leads to conflict. Beliefs not tempered by rationality have led to some of the most destructive conflicts that humanity has ever seen, and this will continue unless we reassess how we deal our beliefs and the beliefs of others around us.

Religious intolerance (a simple disagreement about our belief systems) has resulted in unimaginable human suffering. There is no doubt that there has also been a tremendous amount of humanitarian work as a direct consequence of organized religion. Can we keep the good and throw out the bad?

Fortunately, I think we can. We have the opportunity to go a step further than the BGITS concept, much as the ancient Aryans did. This time, however, with all the advancements we have made in science and technology, in our understanding of the world, and of ourselves, we are much better equipped to both satisfy our instinctual desires and reconcile them completely with our rational view of the world. This will lead to a more peaceful, ethical, and tolerant world, if we consciously make an effort to recognize and seize the opportunity.

Summary

We started our journey in this book by poking holes in the reasons for the existence of God and reached the conclusion that, from a purely logical perspective, it was not possible to deduce the existence of a BGITS God. In this chapter we examined why despite the lack of evidence, an overwhelming majority of humanity believes in God and has done so for our entire known history. I reasoned that human beings are not just logical machines. Rather, our intellect is made up of an emotional (or instinctual) part and a logical part, and the instinctual component is just as important—if not more so—as the logical. The factors that control our beliefs go beyond the realm of rational thought and are embedded deep in our unconscious mind, under the sway of powerful psychological and physiological factors. These deep-seated influences work in conjunction with and often override rationality. The incredibly powerful human need to satisfy our basic emotional and instinctual desires lies at the root of our belief in God.

The need to satisfy both our rationality and our emotional instincts is equally important. Again, we come full circle with regard to the need for a concept of God. The lack of rational proof of the existence of a BGITS God is not reason enough to completely abandon the concept. We need a redefinition of the term God that is consistent with both logic and emotion. A supreme being that satisfies both our logical definition of a God and a more personalized God that appeals to our instinctive needs.

In redefining God in this manner, every individual must find a balance between both ends of the spectrum—rationality and logic on one hand, and emotions and instinct on the other. This definition of God would bridge the gap between knowledge and belief and would lead to what I call *reasoned faith*. It would offer us a spectrum of choices, depending on where we lie as individuals on the continuum between uncompromising rationality and unconditional belief and faith.

After rejecting arguments for the existence of a BGITS God, we can now accept the emotional and psychological need for such a God. On our journey of rejection and acceptance, we've come full circle and arrived at a much better understanding of our fundamental human needs. We now need to redefine God in a way that will satisfy both our rational and our emotional needs, as we'll discuss in the next chapter.

9

Satisfying Our Rational and Emotional Needs: Coming Full Circle Again

Both Reason and Faith must get our nod
As we all come together under God
For Faith without Reason is blind
And Reason without Faith unkind.

Reasoning or logic cannot prove, in the sense that a scientist can prove, the existence of a BGITS God. In the last chapter, I reasoned that man is not just a rational being but an emotional one as well. Our belief in the BGITS concept of God may be logically untenable, but it plays a very important role in satisfying our deep-seated instinctual desires. We all have unconscious mental faculties that we rely on to make quick, instinctual decisions and logical mental faculties that we use for reasoning and analysis. In fact, most everyday decisions are made by a combination of logic, emotion, and instinct. Our behavior is just as likely to be controlled by our emotions as by a logical progression of thoughts.

In the last chapter I also made the case for the following:

- The success of the BGITS concept of God is based on our need to satisfy our emotional needs or instinctual desires.
- Every person's vision of or path to God is dependent on their personal dominant instinctual desires.

What if we were to define God in a way that would satisfy both our rational minds and our emotional desires? How can this be accomplished? How would we as human beings benefit? In this chapter we explore the possibility and the immense value of remaining rational while satisfying our emotional desires. Doing so requires a redefinition of God that combines the oldest conceptions of God, put forth by our ancient ancestors, tempered by our modern understanding of nature and the world around us.

The Need for Redefining God

It is not a coincidence that a majority of the population in the United States and Europe—and probably over 90 percent of the rest of the world—believe in a BGITS God, a caretaker-God who looks over and influences what we do in our everyday lives. Since this concept of God is based on belief, rather than on rational explanations, it has led to divergent systems of faith (religions and religious denominations) that conflict with one another.

In most cases, we confuse opinions expressed in religious texts with universal truths and accept them as a part of our knowledge base because that is what we have been taught since childhood. Ajmal Kasab, the only Pakistani terrorist captured alive after the Mumbai massacre in 2008, was interrogated on videotape by the Mumbai police after his capture. The video was included in the HBO documentary *Terror in Mumbai*, and it offers a glimpse into the mind of a youth so completely brainwashed since childhood that he was unable to separate fact from fiction. Asked why he had shot forty-nine people in cold blood, his response was completely incomprehensible to a logical mind. He believed he was doing God's bidding and that, by being killed in this holy endeavor, he would go straight to heaven, where beautiful virgins would be waiting for him. His body would be radiant and fragrant, blessed by Allah.

Where did he get such crazy ideas? Religious fanatical clerics in Pakistan had brainwashed him. The young boy in the video completely believed this warped interpretation of the Koran. The personal opinions of some demented religious scholars, driven almost entirely by intense religious emotion and a belief unfettered by rationality, led to the murder of innocent people.

This is by no means an isolated incident. Thousands of people are killed by suicide bombers every year. The motivation for most suicide bombers is religious. This incredibly strong emotional response completely overwhelms any rational thinking and leads to acts of unspeakable brutality. The recent massacre of 162 children at a school in Peshawar, Pakistan, is one such gut-wrenching, heart-breaking event. What could possibly motivate people to commit acts of brutality against people of their own faith and in their own community? No religion or scripture condones murder. There can be no logical grounds for justifying an act like this. But incidents like this continue to dominate our news.

The justification for this violence almost always leads back to an interpretation of religious scripture by misguided and sometimes politically motivated religious scholars. Their sermons are opinions, formed by the gross misinterpretation of profound, well-intentioned scripture and by the blind faith that every believer is encouraged to practice. The only way to eliminate this religious madness is to temper the believer's religious emotions with the light of rationality, which leads to moderation and acceptance of the belief of others. We must redefine God in this manner if we are to stop ourselves from annihilating each other on the basis of strongly held yet irrational personal beliefs.

The Dangers of Unrestrained Belief

In the words of Albert Einstein,

> Nobody, certainly, will deny that the idea of the existence of an omnipotent, just, and omnibeneficient personal God is able to accord man solace, help, and guidance; also, by virtue of its simplicity it is accessible to the most undeveloped mind. But, on the other hand, there are decisive weaknesses attached to this idea in itself, which have been painfully felt since the beginning of history.[1]

If I believe in something—say, a Tortoise God that grants boons when I chant a hymn and rub his refulgent shell—must I also believe that this is the only valid belief system and that all others are wrong? Must someone of another faith either be converted or severely punished? This seems to be what many religions preach today. Even belief systems that are closely related, such as the predominant denominations of the Abrahamic religions, have transformed these differences into religious wars that have raged for centuries. They have shown over the past two millennia that differences in beliefs (that I would consider minor) are worth shedding the blood of many millions of people for. Whether it is the Crusades of the Dark Ages, the Shia versus Sunni conflicts in the Middle East, the persecution of Protestants by the Roman Catholic Church, or the Holocaust, it seems there is no limit to the horrors we are willing to inflict on our fellow human beings for seemingly minor differences in religious beliefs. The need to reframe our definition of God is quite evident. Let's discuss the inadequacies of the current BGITS concept of God, why a redefinition of this concept is necessary, and the benefits a new definition of God can bring.

Redefining God: Satisfying Both our Rational and Emotional Needs

In today's age of science, we have a unique opportunity to reframe the discussion around what it means to be religious and to believe in God. Although it may be tempting for some to abandon the notion of God completely for lack of logical proof, this would be a mistake. As we saw in the last chapter, the notion of a BGITS God fulfills deep human desires that cannot be fulfilled in any other way. Rather than abandoning such a helpful concept, we should adopt and modify it, using the best of what we have learned over the past few centuries.

To be compatible with human nature and, therefore, to be sustainable in the long run, our definition of God must achieve two basic goals:

- It must satisfy our emotional and instinctual desires.
- It must harmonize these unconscious emotional needs with rational, objective explanations of the world around us.

In the past, the vast majority of humanity has successfully satisfied the first objective with little regard for the second. As we saw in preceding chapters, meeting the former objective leads us inexorably toward belief in a BGITS God and toward long-standing religious doctrine. Although there are substantial variations among religious texts in the names and nature of God or in his son or messenger, the underlying concept of the BGITS is usually revealed in a religious text. The Holy Bible, the Holy Koran, and the Torah all fall into this category. They are each the revealed word of God and cannot be questioned by mere mortals. For some, this requires unquestioning faith in the authority of the holy text with no room for skepticism. As we saw in chapter 6, this was more than sufficient in many societies during much of human history.

The second objective requires us to reason our way into a concept of God that is logically consistent, but this path does not lead us to a God that concerns himself with everyday human affairs, a BGITS God. Instead, it leads us to a definition of a Supreme Being more akin to that of the ancient Aryans, the Renaissance philosophers such as Spinoza, and modern scientists: God is nothing more than the underlying essence of the material world that we experience every day. One aspect of this essence is represented by the all-pervading laws that govern our universe.

These two definitions of God can be complementary rather than contradictory. Merging the two points of view will lead us to the redefinition of God I am proposing in this book.

This new definition of God entails the existence of a universal, unchanging, and all-pervading supreme entity or consciousness that determines the dynamics of the universe, without attributing any supernatural powers to it. The nature of this underlying essence can be explored through the fundamental laws that govern our universe. These laws can, in turn, be explored though the application of the scientific method, which ensures that their acceptance is logically incontrovertible and universal, not a matter of personal belief. This definition presents a philosophically and logically satisfying definition—but is still rather distant and remote.

Accepting more personal and accessible gods that appeal to our instincts and emotions bridges the gap between our rational mind and our instinctual needs. Such personal gods are manifestations of or surrogates for the ultimate reality but are much more accessible than a remote universal essence. A very important distinction between these personal gods and a BGITS God is that they do not possess supernatural powers but have powers that are circumscribed by the universal laws of nature. Prayer and ritual to worship our personal gods brings us peace of mind, or strength of purpose, but there can be no expectation of miracles or supernatural interventions. Our process of redefining God, therefore, has three important steps.

Step 1: Define a Transcendent God

It is important to first establish what we can agree on without invoking belief. This is clearly a tall order! Over the course of human history, up until the nineteenth century, this would not have been remotely possible, since there was no agreed methodology that had been established to accomplish this. Ideas were a matter of belief, most of it derived from ancient scripture. Now, for the first time, we have a method—the scientific method—that allows us to establish universal, verifiable truths, which I have called our *knowledge base*. Anyone on the planet can check and verify whether a statement is indeed true.

Today, in most Western democracies, it is these independently verifiable facts and theories that we teach our children in school textbooks. This may seem like a given to us, but this certainly is not the historical norm. Only a few hundred years ago, children were almost exclusively taught according to the scriptures. Very few people actually went to a school, and literacy was mostly limited to royalty and the clergy. The beliefs embodied in the scriptures were passed on from generation to generation. Such teachings often violated logic but this did not matter. Any dissent was met with a ruler across the knuckles, prison, or burning at the stake. As we saw earlier, the writings of Thomas Aquinas provide classic examples of the power of enforced belief. Belief was synonymous with knowledge, and there was no effort to distinguish between them.

This, of course, has changed dramatically in most countries over the past 400 years. The Renaissance and the birth of scientific inquiry in the age of reason allow us to clearly identify universal truths and laws and to separate them from personal or societal beliefs. Today, in most developed and many developing countries, where literacy rates exceed 80 percent and universal education is a cherished goal, this distinction is maintained through a clear separation of religious scripture and school curricula. Unfortunately, in some theocracies, the ghosts of past religious doctrine are still the law of the land, and entire segments of the population are deprived of literacy and a basic education. Keeping the population ignorant makes them easier to control.

We should not let religious fanatics or clergy suppress and control our access to knowledge. It is this group that most often argues against the validity of the scientific method. We are already well on the path to universal literacy in many of the secular democracies of the world, and we should not waver.

We recognize that our knowledge base is by no means complete. It does not offer answers to many important questions. It does not adequately explain many observed phenomena. We do not know why the universe appears to be expanding or whether the hypothesis that the universe is in a constant cycle of expansion and contraction is entirely correct. We do not know precisely how the elements formed complex molecules that ultimately led to the formation of complex biological molecules and living organisms. But not knowing the exact mechanisms of a process in no way diminishes the importance—and certainly not the existence—of the process. This incomplete knowledge makes it even more important to adhere strictly to the scientific method and to be doubly careful not to contaminate our knowledge base with ideas that do not meet the strict criteria for inclusion.

This is precisely the strength of the scientific method: It provides us with a systematic way to weed out untruths and replace them with hypotheses that are in accordance with all currently known independent observations. This is a continuous and exciting process of discovery that is not subjective. Individual opinions and divine revelations count for very little. What we must commit ourselves to is not only the facts and theories that are in the knowledge base but, more importantly, to the process of establishing their validity. If we remain true to this process, as science has over the past two hundred years, we ensure that our knowledge of the world will grow, regardless of our personal beliefs.

Our transcendent God can now be defined as nothing other than this all-encompassing order of the universe, the universal set of natural laws, the underlying essence of all reality, or the universal consciousness represented by our knowledge base. This concept of God is universal and independent of religious beliefs because it does not require a set of unsubstantiated beliefs, religious faith, scripture, or doctrine—but does not preclude belief in them either. This definition of a transcendent supreme being is conceptually no different from the grand concept of the Rtá first proposed by the ancient Aryans in the Rig Veda (see chapter 2) as they gazed in amazement at the brilliance and beauty of our universe. As they so presciently reminded us, even the gods must obey the Rtá! It is also similar to the Maat of the ancient Egyptians and the Tao of the ancient Chinese (see chapter 3). It is Plato's form, Spinoza's substance, and Einstein's God (see chapters 4 and 5).

The big advantage we have today is that we have an accepted and proven method to establish the elements and laws that make up this underlying essence of all manifested reality. This now allows us to admire these universal laws as never before.

In summary, step one is to use the scientific method to filter out what is untrue for all matters in life, whether they be religious or otherwise. Be skeptical about all claims and statements. If the claims do not pass this filter, reject them as interesting but unsubstantiated myth.

This filter should also be applied to the scriptures. Doing so will allow us to view all scripture as I—and many clergy—think they were intended: as wonderful parables, lessons in morality authored by exceptionally wise men. Literal interpretations of scriptures do not pass the scientific filter and as such should not be part of our knowledge base. It is only when we apply this filter that we can separate fact from fiction, knowledge from personal belief, and reality from myth, legend, and superstition.

Step 2: Believe in a Personal God

As we saw in the previous chapter, our need to satisfy our emotional desires can in many instances completely overshadow our rationality. Trying to rationally understand the essence of reality through the immutable laws of nature is difficult even for scientists and ignores our deeper emotional needs. For many of us, belief in such a personal God (or gods) provides comfort and solace beyond measure.

So what distinguishes this idea from the BGITS God? There are two primary differences between the common conception of a BGITS God that most people believe in today and the personal God I am suggesting here:

1. The belief in a personal God must remain separate from but coexist and be consistent with the universal, transcendental God we defined in step 1 on the basis of our knowledge base. One satisfies our rational mind, and the other our instinctual desires.
2. The attributes of (and, therefore, the expectations of) a personal God must not violate any of the principles of the universally accepted knowledge base. Such differences will invariably lead to inconsistencies in belief and personal and social conflict.

A personal God could be a loving friend, a savior, an inspiration, a moral authority, a father figure, a loyal ally, a lawgiver, an arbiter of justice, one who exemplifies perfection and goodness and provides solace in times of emotional distress—or none or all of the above. The point is that a personal God can be whatever a person wants him to be. A personal God is exactly that: a subjective God that we can create from our own religious customs and traditions, philosophical biases, and psychological desires and needs.

However, there are certain attributes a personal God cannot have if we are to rise above religious conflict. In the spirit of the ancient Aryans, a personal God must abide by the Rtá, must obey the immutable laws of nature, must conform to our knowledge base. There can be no miracles and no supernatural occurrences, since these would violate the universal laws. As the ancient Aryans would put it, "Even the gods must obey the Rtá!" By embracing this ancient idea, we have come full circle both historically and philosophically.

For many religious traditions, such a personal God is indeed very different from our current view of a BGITS. Let's make this distinction clear: Historically, and even today, we expect a BGITS God to be one who listens to and answers our prayers, performs miracles rewards his followers, and punishes those who "whore after other Gods." These expectations arise from our deep-seated desire for security from and faith in a kind and benevolent God who intervenes in our daily lives.

Unfortunately, these expectations clearly violate our universally accepted knowledge base and, as such, should not be expected of any personal God. Such a definition would be inconsistent with the universal order that we have accepted as being true. As we shall see in the next chapter, ensuring that we stay within the confines of the rules prescribed by the Rtá ensures that we avoid the evils of superstition, belief in the supernatural, witchcraft, and bigotry that have haunted humanity for centuries.

What I am proposing here is simple: We must make a clear distinction between our personal gods, based on our subjective beliefs, and the objective and universal truths that constitute our knowledge base. This separation allows us to satisfy both our rational minds and our deepest emotional desires, both of which are an integral part of who we are as human beings. By doing this, we separate the objective from the subjective, our knowledge from our beliefs. This is such an important distinction that I will emphasize it again as step 3 in our process of redefining God.

The distinction between a personal God based on personal belief and a universal consciousness based on a universally accepted knowledge base is not recognized by the traditional interpretation of many religious scriptures, including the three Abrahamic religions. Modern interpretations, however, do make a serious effort to ensure that the scriptures are not interpreted literally and that portions of them that are inconsistent with well-established science are viewed as allegorical.

As we saw earlier, in Judaism and Islam the concept of God is beyond the realm of human understanding, a figure so remote that one may not even utter a name lest we minimize it by attempting to describe it. In Christianity the concept of God has varied from the Trinity of the Father, the Son, and the Holy Ghost to Jesus himself. In all three religions, a believer traditionally accepts the Holy Scripture without question; any other way is blasphemous and leads to excommunication. Although there may be slightly different interpretations of the scriptures among the various denominations of the religion, scripture-based faith overrules the knowledge base.

The current argument between intelligent design or creationism and the theory of evolution is a good example of this conflict between belief and our knowledge base. Literal interpretations of the Bible clearly lead many Christians to believe that the earth and the cosmos came into being about six thousand years ago, in a single act of creation by God. This literal interpretation of scripture is in direct conflict with all the evidence we have today, yet it remains the prevailing view of many millions of people for whom the revealed word of God trumps reason and the laws of nature. This belief then leads to social conflict with others who do not subscribe to such creationist beliefs. Our children are caught in the crossfire as a battle rages over what is taught in the classroom and what appears in textbooks.

It doesn't have to be this way. If we accept, as many modern religious scholars and clerics have suggested, that the Holy Scriptures offer deep and thoughtful insights into how to live our lives but do not constitute a common knowledge base for all religions. Recognizing this distinction, we allow for both knowledge and faith. Ignoring fact in favor of belief leads only to ignorance and conflict.

The world was not created six thousand years ago. There is indisputable and overwhelming empirical evidence from rock samples and the fossil record collected and analyzed by thousands of scientists. Whether we believe it or not, it's the truth. The story of creation told differently in different religious traditions and other stories such as parting of the sea in the Old Testament will remain wonderful legends meant to teach us important life lessons.

We must accept the fact that all religious scriptures offer a view of a personal God who may satisfy our emotional needs wonderfully but who does not offer universal truths that we can all agree on. Failure to accept this concept will continue to lead to persistent and devastating religious conflict, as it has for millennia.

Not all people need a personal God. For this group, the concept of God as a universal consciousness representing the essence of the universe is sufficient. These people include many scientists and philosophers today.

Some are agnostics, and a growing number of them are atheists, who reject outright the concept of a personal God. The rejection of a personal God is a perfectly acceptable alternative within our new definition. In the terminology of the Vedas, these people are the jnana yogis of the world. For them, the rational explanations of the world are sufficient. There is no need for any additional balm to soothe their emotional being.

Step 3: Constantly Differentiate Knowledge from Belief

The single most important element, and one that is important enough to establish as a critical and separate step to redefining God, is to clearly and consistently differentiate between *knowledge* and *belief*.

This third step may seem redundant, but it provides the basis for religious tolerance, which could be the key to ending much of the violence in our world. Distinguishing between knowledge and belief is the anchoring principle that prevents us from sliding back into the abyss of religious fanaticism and intolerance. It is, therefore, crucial that we be constantly vigilant in our own thoughts and actions (and that we advise others to do the same) to ensure that if our personal beliefs do not agree with those of our neighbor, we respect these differences rather than seeing them as a violation of our shared intellectual and moral code.

There are many examples throughout human history of belief—directed primarily by misinterpretations of religious scripture—being used as justification for torture and genocide. The burning of witches is a good example of how completely unsubstantiated belief resulted in the murder of tens of thousands of women. Women were accused of being witches or being possessed by the devil, without proof or just cause. These proclamations, based almost entirely on a warped interpretation of scriptures, were used to systematically abuse and torture women for two centuries. If the victims proclaimed their innocence, the "witches" were tortured until they confessed to their sins, real or imagined. Any rationalists who attempted to plead for their innocence with a rational explanation of the facts were themselves accused of heresy and subjected to the same torture and death. And death did not come easily; the accusers took a perverse pleasure in ensuring that those who had violated their belief system suffered as much as possible before their souls were sent to eternal damnation. Such are the horrors of uncontested belief. It is, therefore, essential to ensure that all beliefs, including those in a personal God, remain consistent with the universal knowledge base.

It will come as no surprise that while such extreme cases of murder and torture are rare today in the West, they are still commonplace in many theocracies, where apostasy is punishable by death. The *Charlie Hebdo* massacre in 2015, for instance, over a newspaper printing a cartoon of the Prophet Muḥammad, is a terrible reminder that blind—and violent—faith persists even in this modern day and age.

In nations that are essentially Islamic theocracies, any perceived disrespect of the Prophet or the Holy Koran is punishable by death or worse. There is no room for another belief system. If history has taught us one lesson, it is this: This sort of intolerance will inevitably result in conflict and bloodshed. This has certainly proved to be true in each of these countries. The cycle of intolerance has lead from one extreme interpretation of Holy Scripture to another, with violence inflicted on a religious community by its own believers in the warped ideology of the cleric du jour. The Islamic State and Boko Haram stand out as modern examples of the devastation that blind faith can incur on large segments of the world's population.

In addition to clearly distinguishing knowledge from belief, we should constantly ensure that our beliefs are consistent with the universal knowledge base. It is easy to begin to accept religious beliefs that lead us down the path of superstition and bigotry. I can remember instances in my life where well-educated, well-meaning relatives tried to convince me to use astrological charts to make decisions about when to start my job and when to get married. This is a rather common practice in India, and auspicious dates are often picked for every major event in one's life. Fortunately for me, my parents and my close relatives were just as skeptical as I was about the role astrology should play in our daily decision-making. Many people are not so fortunate. The parents of one of my relatives were convinced by a clergyman that it would somehow be unlucky for their older daughter to be married before she was thirty years of age. In a culture where marriages are arranged, the poor girl never got married at all. Her life was changed by belief in astrological predictions that have no basis in fact.

Here is the problem: In confusing personal belief with reasoned truth, we not only lose the ability to get along with others who may have a different belief system, but because religious belief is so tightly bound to our emotional needs, we find it confrontational and offensive at a personal level when those beliefs are questioned. We know what happens when this is repeated on a larger societal level, on the scale of communities and countries pitted against each other in religious wars. The problem here is not with believing something written in scripture. The problem lies in confusing personal beliefs with universal truths and believing things that are clearly in conflict with our knowledge base.

The problem is compounded by the fact that many religious scriptures contain specific language that can be interpreted as directing us to be intolerant of other faiths. Quite often, this language was written in a time and place where it might have been appropriate. But it certainly is not appropriate today.

A Transcendental God versus Personal Gods

Let me elaborate a bit about the important distinction I have made between the concept of a Supreme Being (or universal consciousness, as revealed in the universal laws of nature)—and personal Gods.

As we have seen, one way to view this separation very clearly is through our knowledge base and our personal set of beliefs. As we discussed in chapter 6, the scientific method acts as a perfect filter for what facts, data, and theories should constitute our knowledge base. Knowledge of the universe around us that meets the strict criteria set forth by the scientific method is accepted as true until it is falsified by later discoveries. This knowledge is not subjective; it does not matter whether it satisfies our emotional desires. This knowledge base forms the set of laws that all human beings can rationally agree on. This universal order completely determines the dynamics of the world around us, the cosmos, and even the gods.

Personal or religious beliefs have an important role to play in satisfying our deeply rooted instinctual needs, but they are not universal. They come from our personalities, our emotions, our upbringing, our family and social traditions, and even our evolutionary past. Every individual has their own set of beliefs, shaped by their own unique experiences. These beliefs serve an important purpose in providing emotional and mental support and stability to every human being. Identifying a personal God that satisfies these emotional needs can be a vital part of everyday living. This could be a loving and caring God that supports us in times of need or one that inspires and motivates us to do good deeds.

By recognizing the difference between knowledge and belief, we appreciate and reemphasize the fact that our belief in a God is exactly that—a personal belief. As such, it is subjective. Accepting the fact that our beliefs are subjective and that others may have different beliefs is vital to our new definition of God. It allows us to respect the beliefs of others. We are no longer blinded by the belief that ours is the only faith that is correct.

The Consequences of Redefining God

Redefining God in this manner, by combining transcendental and personal Gods, has two primary and very important consequences (as well as many others that are discussed in the next chapter):

1. It allows people with entirely different conceptions of God to find common ground, to respect the beliefs of others.
2. It satisfies people who are predominantly rational and people who are predominantly driven by instinct and emotion.

People of faith, for whom a belief in a God is essential to meet their instinctual desires, will now be able to relate to people for whom such a definition of God may be unnecessary. For those who are more rationally inclined, the need for satisfying emotional needs may not be as important, and they can personally abandon the notion of a personal God, but they should understand why others need to believe in such an entity.

Meeting the first objective without the moderation provided by the second leads inevitably to social and religious conflict. Is it possible to temper our emotional and instinctual desires with rationality? In my view, this is indeed possible and, in fact, is the only way we can live peacefully with each other as people of different faiths. Our religious beliefs need to be guided by our rational appreciation that the BGITS concept of God can have different flavors, one as good as the other, and that a singular, interventionist God has no place in today's world. As we will discuss in the next chapter, the effect of this simple recognition and the resulting broadening of our religious and social goals will have a dramatic influence on how we live our lives and how we define our belief system.

Is This Even Possible?

How can we best achieve this amalgam of personal religious beliefs, scripture, and rationality? Is it possible for a person to separate belief from universally accepted truths? If we believe in something, does that automatically mean that we think it to be universally true and that we must bring others to believe the same? Are there historical examples of this being done on a societal scale? It may seem like a difficult if not an impossible dream—but many millions of people have already taken this path. It was the path taken by some of the Founding Fathers of the United States over 250 years ago when they built a secular, democratic nation under God; by modern day scientists; and even by the ancient Aryans.

Clear distinctions between personal beliefs and universal truths are not restricted to religion. We readily accept that political and social opinions are exactly that: personal opinions. We spend a considerable amount of time, effort, and money trying to change other people's opinions, yet no one would claim that their personal choice of president, or political party, or their stand on the death penalty, or how the Fed should set monetary policy are universally accepted truths. We all recognize that these are opinions and open to debate. Why should religion and religious belief be different?

The laws of nature, which we have only begun to understand, have been tested and validated by multiple independent observations. This strict adherence to empirical reproducible evidence—removed from personal opinion—governs what we allow ourselves to call *true* and include in our universal knowledge base. The knowledge base allows us to build on prior knowledge, rather than starting from scratch or retesting every idea. If we had to re-prove Newton's laws every time we designed a rocket, it would take us a very long time indeed!

This is not to say that these laws are infallible. They have been revised or even disproved as new evidence became available. Continuously updating the knowledge base has allowed humanity to continually verify that it is as close to truth as we can get at the time. Scientists most certainly hold personal opinions on a variety of topics, from religion to societal matters, but those opinions have no place in the scientific domain. This distinction between personal opinion and universal truth is both explicitly and implicitly understood.

The point I'm making is that it is entirely conceivable to have a set of personal beliefs that one holds dear but that is also distinct from the universal knowledge base. What makes our situation unique today is that we have a method—science—that can be used to define this universal knowledge base with an unprecedented level of confidence.

Not Only Can It Be Done, It Has Been Done Before: Coming Full Circle

I was raised in a liberal Hindu tradition, where the separation of a personal God from the universal consciousness—the Brahman or the Rtá—was not only possible but a given. This distinction between the underlying order in the universe and personal gods has been hardwired into Hindu philosophy since ancient times. Hindus have millions of gods, which are all, in our terminology here, personal gods. Each one of them is seen as a manifestation of the Brahman, the ultimate reality or universal consciousness. In the Vedantic tradition, the acceptance and respect for many alternate personal gods as distinct from the universal Brahman is an integral part of the culture and religion. These gods take different forms and represent the one universal consciousness. This fairly basic precept is sometimes forgotten. The choice of one (or more) gods over another is, therefore, not a reason for conflict.

This is why, for over more than 3000 years of history, there have been very few religious wars driven by the desire to impose one Hindu god over another. The spread of Hinduism into Southeast Asia was not a religious conquest; it was conducted through teachers and scholars who were sent far and wide, from present day Afghanistan to Sri Lanka through most of Southeast Asia. Asian religious traditions have historically had a more accepting and peaceful approach to resolving differences in religious beliefs. The ideals of Hinduism and Buddhism, Taoism and Confucianism were spread throughout Asia not by the sword but by persuasion and goodwill. Although these cultures may have found other reasons to kill their fellow human beings, religious belief was not a major contributor.

It's easy for this distinction to be lost in the fray of daily living. For many modern Hindus, the many personal gods are all that remains of the ancient belief system, and the high philosophy of the Brahman has been forgotten. This has led the personal gods to become no different from a BGITS God. This is the intellectually easy way, the path of least resistance (as Galileo warned us). And it is clearly inconsistent with our knowledge base and has unfortunately led to superstition and belief in miracles and magic.

Similar traditions existed in other ancient societies, where a multitude of gods were worshipped, each serving their own well-defined purpose. In Greece, a person could worship Poseidon, the god of the sea; Gaia, the goddess of the earth; or, on certain occasions, Ares, the god of war. Above all, there remained Zeus, the god of sky and thunder. He occupied a special place among the complex and mythical pantheon of Greek gods. In the rich traditions of the ancient Egyptian gods—Amun, Atum, Bes, Ra, Isis, Hathor, Anabis, Nun, Osiris, Thoth, and a host of others—each served to satisfy basic human instinctual desires. These personal gods dominated the social and cultural fabric of Egypt. It was the nature god Amun-Ra and the god that ensured justice and order in the world, Maat, that occupied preeminent positions in this pantheon. Similarly, in pre-Islamic Arabia, the Kaaba was adorned with idols of many tribal gods, each with their own unique traditions and heritage. These tribal gods coexisted peacefully for many millennia. In all these diverse traditions, one thing is apparent:

Whenever a king or the clergy insisted on adherence to a single "true" deity, wars ensued.

Fortunately, historical precedents in ancient traditions show that the integration of logical reasoning with faith can be accomplished. Again, we learn from the great Asian and Greek philosophers of the past. In all of these ancient religions, there is a supreme entity that regulates the universe. The nature of this Supreme Being is often left ambiguous (as in the *Tao Te Ching* and the Rtá in the Rig Veda) or undefined (as in Buddhism). There is a clear recognition that it is very difficult, if not impossible, to comprehend the nature of this supreme reality and because of this, there are many acceptable paths to trying to comprehend its true nature. As the Vedas and the *Tao Te Ching* say on many occasions, each person must find his own unique path to the truth. The religious scriptures, the rituals, the priests, and the places of worship are simply aids in this journey.

It is indeed possible to accept differences in individual beliefs, as long as we can all agree on some universal truths. For example, in the Vedic tradition, these truths are defined by scriptures that are reputed to be penned by sages and rishis, learned men whose wisdom transcended space and time. The wonderful stories in post–Vedic texts such as the Ramayana and Mahabharata were meant to inspire and instill a feeling of devotion to personal gods but not to place them above all else.

Nowhere is this more obvious than in the divinely romantic stories of Lord Krishna and his beloved *gopis*. The devotee could immerse him- or herself in the sublime and blissful love of Krishna, far removed from the intellectual pinnacles of the Brahman and the Rtá, and could discover their own personal god. This way was likely to be followed by a bhakti yogi, a person much more inclined to satisfy their emotional desires than their rational needs. A rationalist's point of view does not preclude belief in Krishna or some other personal god; in fact, the Hindus invented several million gods to ensure that everyone could have their pick so no soul would go untouched by a personal god. The choice was a matter of personal belief and was recognized as such, so that there was no disagreement over one "true" God.

Integration of Transcendental and Personal Gods in the Upanishads

In redefining God in the manner proposed here, we are borrowing conceptions that are as old as our most ancient human traditions. The ancient Aryans recognized this inherent need in all humans to satisfy their rational and emotional needs when addressing the ultimate questions, and they provided alternate paths that conformed to these individual needs. In a detailed translation and commentary on the principal Upanishads, Dr. Radhakrishnan (a highly regarded philosopher and the second president of India) wrote about the clear distinction made in the Upanishads between the ultimate reality and personal gods:

> The most remarkable account of a superpersonal monism is to be found in the Hymn of Creation. It seeks to explain the universe as evolving out of One. But the One is no longer God like Indra or Varuna, Praja-pati or Vishva-karman. The hymn declares that all of these gods are of late or of secondary origin. They know nothing of the beginning of things. The first principle, that One, Tad Ekam, is uncharacterizable. It is without qualities or attributes, even negative ones. To apply to it any description is to limit and bind that which is limitless and boundless. "That One breathed breathless. There was nothing else."[2]

The creation hymn (quoted in chapter 2), one of the oldest recorded hymns composed by mankind, makes this profound distinction very clear. Again, in the words of Radhakrishnan,

> This hymn suggests the distinction between Absolute Reality and Personal God, Brahman and Isvara, the absolute beyond being and knowledge, the super-personal, super-essential godhead in its utter transcendence of all created beings and its categories and the Real manifested to man in terms of the highest categories of human experience. Personal Being is treated as a development or manifestation of the Absolute.[3]

This distinction between the Brahman and personal gods, which are manifestations of it, is central to the Upanishads and, in fact, to ancient Hinduism. It is this remarkable insight that the Vedantic philosophers provided that I have built our modern definition of God on. We have come full circle.

Integration of Transcendental and Personal Gods in the Bhagavad Gita

The *Bhagavad Gita* provides the essence of the philosophy laid out in the Upanishads. As we saw in chapter 2, it lays out many different paths to understanding God.

For the rationalists, a logical explanation of the world is sufficient, and there is no need for a personal god. These philosophers, scientists, engineers, and physicians among us are inclined to seek more rational explanations of the world. In the terminology of the Aryans, these are the jnana yogis, the knowledge seekers. *Jnana* literally translates to "knowledge." They are the Greek logicians and Sophists. They seek and are perfectly satisfied with purely rational explanations of the world. For them, the path to understanding God does not require a personal god; the abstract concepts of the Rtá are sufficient. These individuals, who find reason completely satisfying, have always been a relatively small proportion of the population.

For others, a personal god is far more meaningful and important. In the language of the *Gita* and the Upanishads, these are the bhakti yogis of this world, devotional worshippers. For them, establishing a personal and intimate relationship with their god is essential. This relationship takes the form of a personal bond with a father- or mother-like figure. Prayers are enhanced by the most sublime music and hymns, and by verses written, spoken, and sung in praise of this personal God. Some of the most moving music ever composed has been devotional music. It can so move the listener that it is said to be able to make believers out of staunch non-believers. Some mystics claim to find God in the emotional ecstasy induced by devotional songs and dances.

For others, neither the philosophically remote universal consciousness nor an emotionally satisfying personal god is particularly interesting, meaningful, or important. Doing their job well and being successful in the world is more important. These are the karma yogis and the men and women of action, for whom the answers to the ultimate questions lie not in philosophizing but in doing their job well and focusing on everyday actions.

As the Vedas clearly spelled out, these paths to achieving nirvana or seeking the ultimate truth are equally justified and valid; one is not superior to the other, nor are they mutually exclusive. A person can choose one or more of these paths that play to their strengths and that feel the most comfortable for their personality and the circumstances in their lives.

With the benefit of our modern understanding of human psychology, we are coming full circle to a point of view put forth by the ancient Aryan philosophers. Even though they believed in an overarching supreme being (the Rtá), they believed in different paths to knowing this ultimate transcendent reality. Indeed, every individual was encouraged to follow a different path, based on the individual's dominant unconscious desires and intellectual propensities.

The ideas in the *Upanishads,* put into a modern psychological context, are similar to the basic ideas put forth by modern psychologists that emphasize the importance of dominant motivations or desires in each one of us. The instinctual desires of the individual control the path that will suit them best. This preferred path is the one that will provide them with the most emotional and rational support, and it usually involves the integration of a transcendental God with a personal god. Every individual must choose which one of these gods satisfies them most at any point in their life. Although their paths may be different, their ultimate goal is the same: a better understanding of what they personally call God.

Integration of Transcendental and Personal Gods in the Greek Tradition

For the Greeks, the wisdom enshrined in their classics and the words of the great philosophers defined the universal truths. Individuals were free to choose their beliefs, whether in the Oracle at Delphi or in one of their many gods. Zeus and Poseidon were not jealous gods and one was free to choose a personal god or Gods. This choice was distinct from understanding the way the universe worked. For many Greeks, Logos ruled the universe; there was no need to invoke a supernatural being to explain the workings of the world. The belief that the workings of the world could be deciphered through human intellect was unique in ancient Western civilization. The philosophers and scientists of the day defined universal truths, as well as they could with their current understanding, whereas the gods held sway in the emotional arena through the folklore in a way that made life much more interesting.

Where Are We Now in This Process?

The process of redefining God in this manner is already well on its way in many Western countries, although it may not be recognized as strictly following the steps described earlier in this chapter.

As we discussed in chapter 1, the number of Americans who say they have no religious affiliation has doubled since 1990 to 16 percent of the population.[4] In a March 2012 *Time* magazine article by Amy Sullivan,[5] Erin Dunigan, an unofficial chaplain for the Not Church group, said, "My sense is that for most, they're not rejecting God. They're rejecting organized religion as being rigid and dogmatic." In many Western countries, organized religion is facing significant headwinds. An increasing number of people are turning to small, organized communities of like-minded people. These minichurches provide a sense of community for people who previously derived this sense of belonging from regularly attending religious services. The loss of social and community interaction can often result in a sense of loneliness and isolation that can be a primary motivator for many people to participate in organized groups.

In larger cities in the United States, there is a growing movement among the younger generation to seek their own path and to form communities that will allow them to pursue their religious road without the constraints of what they view as outdated theology. These people welcome the comfort that their personal relationship with their God brings them. They are not atheists in any sense of the word.

Organized religion often insists that a particular version of a personal god is the only acceptable one. There is a growing recognition that different personal gods are entirely compatible with each other and that this tolerance is essential for people to coexist peacefully.

Summary

We are at a unique juncture in our development as human beings, where the mysteries of the universe have begun to unravel before us, and we have, for the first time, developed a widely accepted method (the scientific method) for building a universally accepted knowledge base. If we can build agreement across religious divides based on this common knowledge base and we can recognize the subjectivity of our beliefs—while not entirely abandoning them—we can reduce religious and sectarian conflict substantially and can pass on this legacy to the coming generations.

Our redefinition of God proceeds in three steps:

1. Recognizing the universal order of the universe, defined by the scientific method, as the source and basis of a transcendental entity
2. Believing in a personal god to satisfy our emotional needs
3. Continually reinforcing the difference between universal knowledge and personal belief

Not only is it possible to define God in this manner, but it has been done before as we have learned. What is different this time around is our ability to much more precisely define the universal knowledge base that forms the basis of the definition of a transcendent God.

By following the steps listed above, people with very different customs, prayers, rituals, and gods based on their own personal beliefs can coexist peacefully and respect each other's beliefs. Since rationality cuts across all religions, it unites us as a human race while preserving our unique individual differences and keeps us away from superstition, witchcraft, and the supernatural. Rituals, prayer, faith, and the clergy are then looked upon with the proper perspective.

Following these steps is not easy, because it goes against well-established religious doctrine and dogma. However, the potential benefits make this difficult endeavor well worth the effort.

What Does It All Mean for Me?

"A man who is convinced of the truth of his religion is indeed never tolerant. At the least, he is to feel pity for the adherent of another religion but usually it does not stop there. The faithful adherent of a religion will try first of all to convince those that believe in another religion and usually he goes on to hatred if he is not successful. However, hatred then leads to persecution when the might of the majority is behind it."

—Albert Einstein

Most of us today believe in a God (mostly through organized religion) who fulfills our deep-rooted, unconscious, instinctual needs. In many instances, rationality and logic are set aside—if not abandoned completely—to justify some of our religious beliefs. Since every organized religion offers its own set of beliefs, it is not surprising that there are conflicts between them based on different interpretations of scriptures.

Our redefinition of God conforms to human nature and satisfies both our rationality and our deepest emotional needs. Our knowledge base of universally accepted facts, data, and theories—based on the scientific method—is not subjective. It does not aim to satisfy our emotional desires, nor does it need to satisfy religious scripture or some interpretation of scripture. It stands on its own, and any objective observer will arrive at the same conclusions.

Our belief in a God is exactly that, a belief. As such, it is subjective.

Accepting the fact that our beliefs are subjective and that others may believe differently, we should no longer be blinded by our faith. With the proposed hierarchy of the universal knowledge base over personal belief, rational arguments will temper belief with the voice of reason.

How does redefining God in this manner shape our social interactions, our ethics, and our everyday lives? More broadly, what societal, religious, and political impacts can it have? Below, I outline the important societal and personal implications of redefining God.

Reducing Religious Intolerance and Conflict

All religions, at their core, preach respect and empathy for all human beings and indeed all living creatures. However, a literal interpretation of scriptures can lead to intolerance of other faiths and, ultimately, to violence. How can such well-intentioned sources lead to such horrible results? Is the intolerance of others' religious beliefs consistent with scripture? And if it is, how far are we willing to go when dealing with other faiths? Some zealots are clearly willing to kill and maim in the name of their God and they justify it on the basis of their religious doctrine.

Human history is filled with the horrors of wars and persecution of minorities, where the primary driver has been differences in religious faiths. The Crusades (from about 1100 to 1300 CE), the Thirty Years' War (1618–1648), and the French Wars of Religion (1562–1598) resulted in the deaths of over 10 million Protestants, Catholics, and Muslims. If monotheism is interpreted in an intolerant and dogmatic manner, as was the case in medieval times, the result is devastating conflict.

We don't have to go back even that far to discover the dangers of religious intolerance. In the twentieth century, the systematic genocide of six million Jews in Europe is a stark and tragic reminder of the power of religious and social bigotry. For the first time in human history, we were able to see visual and documentary evidence—stark images of human savagery—from the concentration camps all across Europe. Germans who were otherwise perfectly kind and responsible human beings systematically killed millions of their fellow European citizens in an unprecedented act of genocide. How could this happen on the same continent that gave us the Renaissance? How could the religious majority target a relatively small religious minority in the most brutal way, over a period of many years, and not face the slightest resistance from its citizens?

Some would argue that this was not a religious crusade but rather a political, social, and economic one. Perhaps there is some truth in this. The fact remains that the genocide was conducted on a purely religious basis, whatever the motivations. When a group of people orchestrate the murder of millions of innocent countrymen for no other reason than their Jewish faith, we begin to understand the gravity of Einstein's quote.

The attacks on the World Trade Center and the Pentagon that took the lives of over 2,000 people in 2001 illustrate the level of passion and hatred that religious fundamentalists can harbor. One can only point to their religious upbringing and their fundamentalist training as the root cause. When suicide bombers shout "*Allahu Akbar*," or "God is great," before detonating their suicide vests, what God are they shouting about? Would any God condone such senseless killing?

In the last few years, these religious fanatics, trained as suicide bombers and suicide squads, have increasingly targeted their own communities and people of their own faith.

The ten-year war between the Shia-dominated Islamic Republic of Iran and Sunni-ruled Iraq again shows the incredible lengths people will go to in order to defend their beliefs. Here, religion and territorial ambition combined to ravage an entire generation of Persian and Arab youths who would have been much better served if their leaders accepted the differences in their beliefs. The fighting between Shias and Sunnis in Iraq itself has torn the country apart, leading to the rise of the so-called Islamic State, or ISIS, who follow an even more radical interpretation of Islam.

The historical evidence is indisputable: Religious intolerance leads to violence, war, and senseless killing.

The seemingly never-ending stream of suicide bombings we see today is a constant reminder of the power of "belief." It is hard to imagine what would drive a young person to "believe" so completely in something that they not only sacrifice their own life but are willing to kill others. This is clearly not a rational decision, nor a religious one, since all religions profess to be a peaceful.

Studies conducted on the recruitment and training of potential suicide bombers have shown that these individuals are almost always young, in financial distress, and poorly educated. Their education is usually limited to indoctrination in the scriptures in a religious school since early childhood by clergy who have undergone the same thorough indoctrination from an early age. The indoctrination leads to their absolute belief that their God wants them to perform these heinous acts. Rationality is never given a chance in this cycle of indoctrination, death, and mayhem.

Most fundamentalists believe that their scripture is the word of God—not an interpretation, but literally his actual words. Any variation, no matter how small, from this one true version of the word of God is unacceptable. Every orthodox believer is duty bound to defend the religion, and that means, for some, that persecuting and even killing people who do not believe in the same God is justified by scripture. This degeneration of monotheism to fundamentalist religious dogma leads down the very slippery slope of intolerance, first against people of different religions but then against people with a slightly different interpretation of the same scripture. This is magnified many times when politicians or a well-organized religious machine facilitates or encourages intolerance. As Mark Twain put it in his inimitable style,

> Man is a Religious Animal. He is the only Religious Animal. He is the only animal that has the True Religion—several of them. He is the only animal that loves his neighbor as himself and cuts his throat if his theology isn't straight. He has made a graveyard of the globe in trying his honest best to smooth his brother's path to happiness and heaven. . . . The higher animals have no religion. And we are told that they are going to be left out in the Hereafter. I wonder why? It seems questionable taste.[1]

In the west, the Renaissance, led by free-thinking philosophers such as Bacon, Locke, and Spinoza, jolted society out of the Dark Ages and inspired the scientific revolution. Scientists such as Galileo and Newton paved the way for a rational and empirical understanding of the universe. This transition to reasoned belief occurred despite the opposition of the Church, with its absolute hold on society. Many were excommunicated, imprisoned, or sentenced to death for questioning the veracity of scripture. Others were afraid to publish anything that violated the established religious norms of the time for fear of reprisal. Over the span of four hundred years, Christianity and Judaism gradually modernized into the tolerant faiths they are today.

The Protestant Reformation played an important role in redefining the role of the clergy. The power of the Church, which was absolute early in the Middle Ages, gradually began to wane with the invention of the printing press and the increased accessibility of books. Education, it turned out, was the magic bullet that ultimately led to the modern ideals of freedom, democracy, and religious tolerance that many of us enjoy today. It took the efforts of many hundreds of reformers, writers, philosophers, and scientists to reform the political and religious system in the West.

In the Muslim world, this effort began in earnest during the rule of the Caliphates in Turkey. The caliphs encouraged science and education, but this attempt at reformation was not allowed to flourish beyond its infancy. The power of the clerics proved to be too much. With the plunder of Constantinople by the Mongols, this Golden Age of Islam came to an end and literalist Islamic beliefs dominated society once again. This medieval religious tradition persists today in many parts of the Islamic world.

As a result, in many Islamic countries, the influence of clerics and religious schools has resulted in a system that can tolerate no dissent. Fundamentalists preach the killing of people for drawing pictures. It is even more mind-boggling that today, a country's government could sentence someone to whippings, beatings, and public hangings for the "crime" of writing against their faith. This sort of intolerance and medieval thinking has led to violence and has not served humanity well over the course of history, and has no place in a modern society.

Jonathan Sacks, in his 2015 book *Not in God's Name*, made the case that Judaism and Christianity underwent a process of reform and modernization over several centuries that led most of their followers to interpret the scriptures allegorically. He regards this process as a tale of people, religions, and their Gods growing up. He hopes, as do I, that a similar process will occur in Islam. Perhaps it is already underway.

The terror attacks in the United States, India, France, Nigeria, Pakistan, Afghanistan, Egypt, Israel, Sweden, and many other countries were conducted by religious fanatics who do not represent the vast majority of Muslims in the world today. Religious fundamentalism finds particular refuge and even encouragement in countries that are theocracies. Religious minorities in such states remain persecuted, brutally suppressed, and in constant danger of violence.

Belief in a BGITS God, untethered by reason, leads inexorably down the path of intolerance and violence and to a moral order where anything is justified in the name of religion. Personal, societal, and national codes of ethics are then set by the clergy, who choose to interpret religious texts to suit their narrow purposes and their ultimate goal—which is to remain in power.

Redefining God allows us to establish a clear distinction between our personal beliefs and universally accepted truths. It leads to acceptance of different beliefs that may not be justified rationally and that are not shared by everyone else on the planet. This allows us to go even further—to appreciate and enjoy the diversity of belief systems.

The success of this philosophy is evident in any of the modern secular states. America, most European countries, many countries in South America, India, and some countries in Southeast Asia are great examples. In all these secular, democratic nations, the importance of tolerance and acceptance of all religious faiths is clearly recognized. Every individual's "beliefs" are a matter of personal choice, to be respected. In laying out the American Constitution, the Founding Fathers were very careful to define a path away from preference for any one religion and to avoid persecution of minorities by providing a clear separation of church and state. Such religious plurality would have been inconceivable for most of human history. The establishment of nations based on religious tolerance has led to the peaceful coexistence of different religious faiths in these countries as never before in history.

By contrast, nations that are based on religious intolerance have been torn apart by religious conflict despite (and perhaps because of) the ruthless suppression of minorities. These regimes dominated by religious conservatives have systematically eliminated religious minorities, even different sects of the same religion, such as the Sufis and the Ahmadis within Islam. The Taliban went so far as to destroy all historical artifacts that were deemed to be un-Islamic. The destruction of the statues of Buddha at Bamiyan can only be described as faith gone mad. Afghanistan has not known peace since the rise of the Taliban, with a civil war that has driven people from their homes and made what should be a wealthy country into one that can hardly feed or clothe its own people.

Recognizing the clear distinction between subjective belief and universal reason leads us to a redefinition of God that respects both and ultimately leads to a more tolerant society. All the world's religions already have this kernel of truth within them—religious scholars and the clergy should recognize and emphasize this when addressing their faithful. We do not need to abandon our personal faith; we just need to respect the beliefs of others. This can only come from a reasoned interpretation of scripture.

Eliminating Superstition and Belief in the Supernatural

When we abandon rational thought in favor of an open-ended belief system, we open ourselves to all kinds of irrational, intolerant, and sometimes deadly possibilities. Another sad and unfortunate consequence of the open-ended belief system is that we open ourselves to superstition and belief in the supernatural. Many of these irrational beliefs are harmless, and we can brush them aside as part of popular social traditions, but not all such beliefs are innocuous.

The best-known historical example of the power of blind faith over rational thought in the Western world is the burning of innocent women at the stake after being accused of being witches. The punishment for witchcraft was almost always death—sometimes a slow, deliberate, and painful one. It is estimated that about 50,000 women were killed after being accused of being witches.

For about 500 years—well into the 1700s—any woman could be accused of being a witch by anyone. It was entirely up to the accused to prove that she was not a witch. The clergy used scripture as evidence for the presence of witches among the population. Not only that, but the scriptures were very explicit in how to identify these witches and how to make them confess to their ungodly ways. The rest of the evidence largely consisted of unsubstantiated accusations made by other citizens or clergymen. The search for physical evidence often involved the subject being stripped naked, so that the clergy and members of the inquisition could intimately examine her breasts and private parts for evidence of moles or other signs that the devil was within her.[2] There were, of course, other signs that a woman was a witch or was possessed by the devil—each one so subjective that the accused was entirely at the mercy of the clergy, who had ultimate authority to decide who would be burned alive. It was no wonder that speaking out against the clergy or persons of authority usually invited such accusations. If the contrived evidence was not sufficient, the accused were often beaten or tortured until they "confessed" to practicing witchcraft.

This practice went on unabated for over 500 years. Tens of thousands of ordinary women were burned alive while their families watched in helpless horror. As Mark Twain put it in "Bible Teaching and Religious Practice,"

> During many ages there were witches. The Bible said so. The Bible commanded that they should not be allowed to live. Therefore, the Church, after eight hundred years, gathered up its halters, thumb-screws, and firebrands, and set about its holy work in earnest. She worked hard at it night and day during nine centuries and imprisoned, tortured, hanged, and burned whole hordes and armies of witches, and washed the Christian world clean with their foul blood.
>
> Then it was discovered that there was no such thing as witches, and never had been. One does not know whether to laugh or to cry. . . . There are no witches. The witch text remains; only the practice has changed. Hell fire is gone, but the text remains. Infant damnation is gone, but the text remains. More than two hundred death penalties are gone from the law books, but the texts that authorized them remain.[3]

You might be tempted to think that these were the actions of people in the Dark Ages and that in today's enlightened scientific age, such things are unthinkable. You would be wrong. Robyn Dixon wrote in the *Los Angeles Times* about the "witch camps" of Ghana.[4] The fate of accused women is determined by whether or not a slaughtered chicken falls with its head down and its feet in the air. If it does, the woman is declared a witch and sent off to the witch camp with one unfortunate young relative to take care of her until she dies. "Even if the ritual says she is innocent," Dixon wrote, "there will be members of the community who will feel unsafe." In 2012, there were six witch camps in northern Ghana holding 800 accused witches. The camps have existed for over one hundred years, despite efforts by the government to shut them down. Such is the power of superstition derived from unquestioning belief.

Faith healers and shamans still rule the lives of many millions of people in less developed parts of the world. While the psychosomatic benefits of healers are well known, it is disturbing to see large numbers of people not seeking medical attention for ailments that clearly require serious medical treatment. Preachers and priests are often called in to "heal" or "extort the devil" from the patient.

Magicians and charlatans cheat millions of people of their money by promising to perform miracles that are often performed by sleight of hand. A "saint" in India could make ritual ashes appear beside a picture of him if a true believer would pray to him with true devotion. Many of us in the United States have seen evangelical ministers performing "miracles" on TV. A believer's wishes are granted instantly—a deaf woman can hear again, a blind woman can see again, or a lame man can walk again. For others, the individual is completely convinced that their wish will indeed be granted in due course, since it is God's will, and their donations will speed it on its way.

Investigative reporting has exposed many of these charlatans on TV and shown how they have used everything from spies in the audience to microphones and cameras to gather information on the unsuspecting believers, not to mention hiring "deaf," "blind," or "lame" accomplices. Although this exposure has helped convince many skeptical viewers that these miracles are really frauds being perpetrated on people to fill church coffers, the true believers remain unconvinced.

I met one such true believer and was told in no uncertain terms that "these sorts of miracles only occur for people that believed in the Good Lord unconditionally, with all their heart and soul." Her definition of "true belief" was, in my opinion, a suspension of any sense of reality, which I was unwilling to do. A good magician can outperform any of these miracle workers, these so-called "men of God."

The point of these examples is to show how blind faith often overcomes reason. In 2013, some clergy in Pakistan decided that vaccination against polio was against Islamic scripture. Never mind that vaccinations were beyond comprehension during the time of the Prophet—there is no conceivable way he could have had any opinion on the subject. Thousands of faithful followers refused to be vaccinated, which exposed many children to a deadly disease that was entirely preventable. Perhaps worse, since polio is a communicable disease, it set back the program that was designed to eradicate polio from the face of the earth. What an incredible missed opportunity and a tragic loss for all of humanity!

Thankfully, these beliefs have been mostly reasoned out of modern society, but remnants remain. By redefining God in a manner that is consistent with rationality and empirical evidence, we eliminate—or at least minimize—the possibility of belief in the supernatural. Superstition and magic are the domains in which charlatans flourish and the common person is victimized. With the level of understanding of the world we have today, there is no reason to accept such unverified (and often disproven) claims and supposed miracles. For many of us, the days of the shaman, of miracle cures and of spells and ghosts, are thankfully behind us. We would be foolish to allow them to return.

Viewing Faith and Clergy in the Proper Perspective

In many parts of the world, especially the theocracies, the clergy hold almost God-like authority over their flock. Religious indoctrination by the clergy starts at a very young age and the particular interpretation of the religious texts is entirely dependent on what the clergy says. The young know of no other view of the world. How could anyone, let alone a person of God, interpret any religious scripture as condoning murder? The rationale, no matter how flawed, is almost always the same: Suicide bombers kill themselves and others because they believe their faith is the only truth and that others either pose a threat or should be punished because they believe in a different God or even in a different version of the same God. This is clearly not how any reasonable person reading the scriptures would interpret them.

The extent of this youthful brainwashing is evident in the rare instances when the suicide attackers are captured and interviewed by the secular media, such as the capture of Ajmal Kasab, the young Pakistani terrorist who gunned down over fifty people in Mumbai in 2010. Well-known Indian-born journalist Fareed Zakaria documented the incident through filmed interrogations in his HBO film *Terror in Mumbai*. It is evident that this young man was a pawn in the hands of some very powerful and unscrupulous people who had identified him as a true and unquestioning believer who would do whatever he was asked to do in the name of faith.

How can we avoid such tragedies?

First and foremost, children should be educated in an environment that exposes them to a broad cross-section of ideas. They must be exposed to human history, sociology, psychology, and the arts, as well as the scientific method and the wonderful world of discovery that humanity has been living in for the past few centuries. Today, this is the case in all modern, democratic, secular countries. It is unfortunately not the case in countries where the supreme political and social authority resides in the clergy; countries that teach the supremacy of a particular interpretation of scripture over all else.

In many countries clergy are taught the scriptures but little else. If children are educated largely by the clergy, this can lead to a poorly educated population that knows very little about other cultures or about the world of science. This is why it is essential for us to separate our knowledge base from our beliefs, as I have proposed. The world of science can be taught by educators well versed in our universal knowledge base and beliefs can be taught by clergy who help establish our subjective religious beliefs and customs. Most secular countries follow this model today and it leads to well-rounded children who are accepting of all faiths.

It is important to put educators, family, friends, and clergy on an even playing field. There is nothing special about the set of people who teach us about scriptures and God. They are no more or less important and deserve no more or less respect than our educators in public schools. Do you speak to your child's elementary school teacher the same way as your pastor? Do you hold them accountable in the same way? Most people do not. If the clergy is placed on a pedestal with infallible status, we end up with children who are poorly educated and open to abuse by the clergy. The never-ending series of child abuse scandals in the Catholic Church is a classic example of how things can go terribly wrong when no one questions the actions of the clergy. By placing religious leaders on the same level as everyone else, affording them the same respect, and demanding the same level of accountability, we do them and ourselves a great service.

Ethics and Moral Order in a Secular World

One of the common justifications for God and religion is that without it, people would lose their moral compass. Do morality and ethics stem from God? Are atheists less ethical or moral than believers? What does our redefinition of God mean for ethics and morality? Will the new definition of God lead to lawlessness and moral bankruptcy? Are our ethics determined by the subjective interpretation of a religious text?

Modern scientists have examined data taken across a cross-section of populations in the United States and found no difference between the moral compasses of atheists and believers. Many of the Scandinavian and Western European countries have among the least religious populations, but they also have some of the lowest crime rates in the world and consistently appear at the bottom of the list when countries are ranked by corruption in business. On the other hand, some of the most deeply religious countries in Asia and Africa are some of the most corrupt. Data also shows that atheists are, in general, better educated, generally more law abiding than the overall population, and have much lower rates of recidivism when they do break the law.[5] From all available data, it is evident that morality, ethics, and religiosity are not correlated and may even be inversely correlated.

In fact, there is no reason to think that religion leads to ethical behavior. Certainly, a BGITS God who punishes our immorality and rewards our moral actions is a common way to view the balance between good and evil, and this may be a motivation to act morally. But it would be a very sorry reflection on the human species if we acted morally only to please a supernatural being.

Richard Dawkins, in his book *The God Delusion*,[6] pointed out that there are many evolutionary reasons why people act morally and, very often, altruistically. An evolutionary advantage is derived from establishing collaborative relationships between members of the group and the benefactor acquires a reputation for being helpful and generous in the community. He ultimately benefits from the established goodwill. Such behavior is observed not only in humans, but also in animals, where such symbiotic relationships are common.

Human beings have been blessed with a wonderful memory and intellect, and we have used these skillfully to establish complex relationships that constitute a moral code in and of themselves. Any member of the group who violates this trust loses favor with other members of the community and is at a distinct social and evolutionary disadvantage. This alone provides ample reason for humanity to adopt ethical and moral standards even in a purely non-religious world.

Louise M. Antony provides another way to look at this issue in her compelling essay, "Good Minus God," from the *New York Times*.[7] She makes the case that what we consider moral springs not from a belief in God but from a basic respect for our fellow human being. Love for our family and empathy for those around us do not require us to postulate that a supernatural being would punish us if we strayed from the path of righteousness.

Invoking God is clearly not a prerequisite to making decisions about right and wrong and good and bad. Does the redefinition of God change any of this? The simple answer is no. Since ethics and religiosity are not correlated, it is unlikely that changing our definition of God will have any impact on our morality. The disconnect between ethical behavior and belief in a BGITS god allows us to redefine God without concern for the ethical consequences. We do not have to subscribe to scripture to be ethical since our moral code does not spring from religious doctrine. We're now allowed ample choice in how we define our transcendent God and our own personal God while maintaining a universal set of ethics.

Be Intolerant to Intolerance

An open society prides itself on tolerance and protecting the rights of minorities. So should one even tolerate intolerance? Tolerating intolerance is tantamount to supporting it. Religious intolerance should be challenged at every juncture, as should racism and corruption. None of them has a place in a modern democratic, pluralistic society.

CBS News correspondent Clarissa Ward asked a well-known preacher in a London mosque if he thought a suicide bomber was justified in killing innocent people for any reason. His answer clearly implied that the murder of innocent people was justified if someone felt that their religious beliefs had been violated. He went on to say that his goal and that of every Muslim should be to establish sharia law in every country in the world. The irony was that he was able to make these statements because he lived in England—a liberal, Western democracy—a fact that was completely lost on him. The imam was not taken to task for his comments by the media or the community in which he lives.

If this sort of hate speech is left unchallenged, it will encourage violence and bloodshed. We do not let white supremacists and Nazis preach their message of intolerance and hate—religious intolerance should be treated no differently. If this interpretation of religious scripture continues being taught to our young people in the heart of a liberal, secular democratic country, there is very little hope of peace in our time.

In religion, as with racial equality, there is no room for intolerant remarks and no justification for them, even if they are supposedly based on religious scripture. Mullah Fazlullah, who scripted the Taliban point of view, is another of the many clerics who justify terrorism through quotations from the Koran. Unfortunately, there are many thousands of such clerics throughout North Africa, South Asia, and the Middle East. In Pakistan, a Christian girl was sentenced to death by the courts for sending an email that someone apparently judged to be disrespectful of the Prophet Muḥammad. In Holland, a cartoonist was stabbed to death for portraying the Prophet Muḥammad in a cartoon.

One might argue that these acts are limited to a fringe radical segment of the Muslim population. The facts unfortunately do not support this view. In the elections held in Egypt after the Arab Spring, the party that came to power was not the one made up of educated, idealistic youth who had dreamed of a modern, secular Egypt. Instead, the Muslim Brotherhood, a religious organization whose stated goal was to convert the country into an Islamic state, won the election.

In his book *The End of Faith*, Sam Harris discusses the results of a survey conducted by the Pew Research Center in 2002. This survey of 38,000 respondents asked the following question:

> Some people think that suicide bombing and other forms of violence against civilian targets are justified in order to defend Islam from its enemies. Other people believe that, no matter what the reason, this kind of violence is never justified. Do you personally feel that this kind of violence is often justified to defend Islam, sometimes justified, rarely justified, or never justified?[8]

The results are shocking and deeply disturbing. A vast majority of the respondents thought that suicide bombing was justified under some situations! And these were respondents from "moderate" Muslim countries, such as Nigeria and Jordan. It is hard to imagine what the results would have been if the survey had been taken in Saudi Arabia or Afghanistan! These results indicate that the support of religious fundamentalism runs deep in many countries that have predominantly Muslim populations and that there is very little appetite for religious tolerance in these societies.

In fact, most fundamentalists cannot even agree on what it means to be an Islamic state. Many clerics, including the ones associated with the

Taliban, have suggested that even Islamic states such as Saudi Arabia and Pakistan are not truly Islamic. In their view, these countries have not properly implemented sharia law and so should be replaced by a government that follows God's word to the letter, which we can only assume means *their* interpretation of God's word. This intolerance extends to anyone who challenges their authority, even within their own religious community.

Many examples of this sort of intolerance exist all over the world, and widespread Muslim-on-Muslim terror that seems to define Islamic fundamentalism today extends to horrific acts of violence committed by the Taliban in Afghanistan, public beheadings of innocent civilians, and the enslavement of women and children by ISIS in Syria and Iraq. Invariably, religious fanatics are not satisfied until their very narrow definition of religion is practiced by everyone. The Shia Muslims in Iran do not believe that the Sunnis in Saudi Arabia or Iraq are following the correct version of the Muslim faith. In Iraq itself, Shias and Sunnis bomb each other's mosques and commit wanton acts of terror with no apparent reason, other than the hatred of someone who believes in a different flavor of Islam.

If I appear to be singling out Islam in my examples of religious fundamentalism, it is because a remarkably disproportionate number of incidents of religious violence in the past two decades have centered around Islam. Christianity went through a violent transition from medieval beliefs to modernity, until religion was removed from the state. Christianity, Hinduism, Buddhism, and other world religions have allowed secular democracies to flourish, where religious, racial, and cultural differences are not only tolerated but celebrated. It remains to be seen whether Islam can make a similar transition.

As the youngest of the major religions, Islam stands at a critical juncture in its development. It is up to moderate Muslims to extricate their faith from the grip of fundamentalists. They should speak out against the persecution of religious minorities and stand up when millions of ordinary Muslims who have practiced their faith over hundreds of years are suddenly forced to abandon their traditional way of life, made to live under the constant threat of death, and obliged to adopt a version of sharia law that most of them find alien to their beliefs. There is no middle ground—any negotiation with or appeasement of the fundamentalists has gone nowhere.

It is downright dangerous to tolerate such intolerance. In a free society that cherishes free speech and freedom of religion, it is difficult for us to deal with groups that preach intolerance. The dilemma is evident: Are we being intolerant when we do not tolerate intolerance? This is not as much of a predicament as it may appear at first. It is an issue that has faced democratic nations for at least two centuries and much has been written about it. As a free and open society that wants to ensure the rights of every citizen to free speech, freedom of expression, and freedom of religion, it is imperative that we ensure that nothing gets in the way of delivering on these promises. On the other hand, hate speech—whether religious or racial—can have no place in our society.

Being respectful of other people's beliefs is a two-way street: In order to earn respect, we must offer it to others. Religious bigotry cannot be allowed as part of someone's religious beliefs, just as no race is afforded the right to racial bigotry. In the United States, we have, over the past three decades, become sensitive to discrimination of people on the basis of race or sexual orientation. Anyone making a racially offensive comment is quickly denounced, and there have been many instances where prominent businessmen, politicians, and leaders have lost their social and professional stature by making public statements that are racially or otherwise insensitive. No such penalty is forthcoming when it comes to religious intolerance. It is not uncommon for religious preachers to openly state their wish to impose their beliefs on the entire country. Although such claims are not taken very seriously in a secular and religiously diverse society such as the United States, they should be; the hate behind them is very real.

It is fortunate that the Founding Fathers of the United States had the wisdom, vision, and foresight to recognize that such religious intolerance was the root cause of a lot of human strife. Peace between people with different religious faiths can only be achieved by guaranteeing everyone's freedom to choose what they believe as long as they respect other people's right to do the same. This freedom is so basic to our current system of secular democracy in the West that we take it for granted. However, it is not the norm even today around the world. Relatively few countries offer the same religious freedoms the United States, Europe, and India do. When religious fervor meets secular democracy, there is an impasse that cannot be easily removed.

Redefining God as we have done here allows us to openly and unequivocally reject religious intolerance and offer an alternative. By rephrasing the moral and ethical edicts in scripture in terms of a definition of God that directs us to be more tolerant and accepting of other faiths, we can ensure that religious conflicts are reduced. This is a lofty goal that we have set for ourselves, but it's an achievable one.

Cultural, Religious, and Civil Rights of Religious Minorities

Besides the most egregious instances of religious intolerance given above, less conspicuous forms of religious differences and conflict continue in many multi-cultural societies. Here again, our redefinition of God can help better illuminate and perhaps resolve some of these differences.

Redefining God allows us to more clearly see two key points: (a) that we as human beings have a lot more in common through our universal knowledge base than we think, and (b) differences in religious belief stemming from our traditions are deeply personal and should be celebrated but not at the expense of creating conflict with others.

In most Western democracies, social conflicts involving civil and religious rights and obligations of individuals, corporations, or governments may be at times difficult to resolve, but they are in fact resolved in civil courts in accordance with secular laws. Societies respect the diversity of religious faiths because they have implicitly accepted the personal nature of faith and respect personal freedom. This acceptance leads inevitably to secular ideals, where the separation of church and state ensures the rights of religious minorities and avoids the egregious intolerance that is often practiced in the world's theocracies.

How Should We Educate Our Children?

There is growing evidence that modern-day fundamentalism and fanaticism is a product of religious indoctrination both at home and at religious schools.

Frontline reported on how children are educated in ISIS-held territory in Afghanistan and Pakistan.[9] Children are taught from a very young age that their faith is superior to others; that they must protect and spread it through violence as a way of life. After spending their most formative years with these teachings, they are completely convinced that this is the way the world is structured. The importance of religious dogma and unquestioned religion is reinforced by their relatives and neighbors. Respect and adulation from their peers comes not from accomplishments but from an expression of their faith, even if it means the wanton destruction of those around them.

This is a powerful motivator. Some suicide bombers, interviewed after deciding not to follow through, tell similar tales of brainwashing and of believing their suicide would be seen as a badge of honor by their family and regarded by society as the ultimate act of sacrifice and courage. Rewarded in heaven and revered on earth. To believe this rhetoric, children must be fed doctrine from a very young age on a consistent basis. Drilling religious fundamentalism into an impressionable child's mind is a lot easier than convincing a thinking adult to do the unthinkable.

It would be incorrect to assume that only poorly educated people can fall victim to such blatant falsehoods. Many of the young Arab men who crashed planes on 9/11 were well educated. Some had college degrees in the sciences or engineering and took the blessings of modern society for granted. For them, the religious imperative of destroying the infidel formed the foundation of their belief system, laid in their religious schools in Saudi Arabia.

This is why it is so important to fundamentally change primary education in countries where religious fundamentalism is the dominant part of early education. As long as primary education remains within the purview of the clergy, religious and social tolerance will remain a pipe dream.

The point of view that was adopted by the Founding Fathers of the United States and of most Western democracies is as clear as can be. The only things that should be taught in our schools are those facts that have been established beyond a shadow of doubt through the application of scientific principles, our knowledge base. All other opinions, religious doctrine, and cultural traditions belong elsewhere. Should members of the community choose to enjoy these traditions and share their customs, this is of course welcomed and appreciated.

My children's curriculum in public school in the United States was strictly nonreligious. However, during important religious occasions, we all celebrated each other's traditions. Christian children celebrating Christmas and Easter shared their stories with the other children. The Jewish children introduced everyone to Hanukkah, the Hindu children were proud to present Diwali, and the Muslims, Eid. This was done in the spirit of establishing better communication and understanding among the different religious groups at school. Religious conversion or proving the superiority of one religion over another was not on anyone's radar.

Teaching the biblical version of creation is a great example of a controversy stemming from a confusion of belief with fact. Fundamentalist practitioners of the Christian faith want to teach their cultural and religious heritage to their children in school, even if it violates all known scientific principles and empirical evidence. To moderate Christians, nonbelievers, and people of other faiths, this view of creation is scientifically inaccurate and therefore inappropriate for a public classroom. The simple laws laid out in the US Constitution clearly separate church and state, specifying that only nonreligious content can be taught in public schools.

Our religious beliefs have no place in our classrooms; they are personal and belong at home. The universal knowledge base we have been so careful to define is what is appropriate for every classroom in every school.

The Role of Prayer

By redefining God in the manner proposed in this book, the role of prayer is altered in a subtle way. First and foremost, abandoning the BGITS definition of God eliminates the possibility of a quid pro quo for our prayers. We can still pray to God that we may do well on a test or ask for anything that requires divine interference in our affairs, with the clear understanding that this exercise serves mainly to satisfy our emotional needs. This can be a sufficient reason for a lot of people to pray. If prayer can bring peace of mind, it has served an extremely important purpose.

If we ask God for something but don't expect him to deliver, why should we pray? What good will it do? There are a large number of people who see no need for prayer and would rather be doing something "more useful." I once saw a bumper sticker that read, "Prayer is God's junk mail." Maybe so, but it is essential for the people who believe in its power.

Prayer has an important role to play even when the BGITS definition of God is abandoned. We can pray to a universal God who is a symbol of the ultimate reality, whatever name we choose to give it. We can contemplate this ultimate reality without the need for personal gods. Prayer can be a meditation on the grandeur of creation, a search for our place in this universe, a time of deep reflection, and an opportunity to calm our mind. Prayer can be a meditation on the self.

Prayers could also be offered to a personal God. In fact, our redefinition of God provides a great deal of flexibility in the nature, purpose, and object of our prayers. Most important, people find praying to be a time of reflection that calms the mind. I myself find a few minutes of prayer and meditation to be essential to good health and to focus my attention on the present moment, rather than letting it wander in wasteful directions. For the more philosophically inclined, the jnana yogis, contemplation and prayer to a transcendent divine being may be preferred. For a deeply emotional person, the bhakti yogis, prayers to a personal God may be the most appealing. To the karma yogis, prayers may not be necessary at all; being involved with the family, being a good dad or mom, and excelling at work and play are prayer enough for them.

Therefore, although the nature of the prayer may be the same, the expectations from it are completely different under our new definition of God. There can be no expectation of miracles or divine intervention. The primary motivation may be to become more aware of the many external forces and factors in the world around us that control our success or failure and to pray that these different and varied forces work with us to help us achieve our goals. Or the goal may be to focus our mind and body completely on the task at hand. Or it may be to provide emotional and mental solace and comfort. Prayer should remain an essential component of a person's religious life and the individual is free to choose how they use this powerful tool to influence their lives.

The Importance of Ritual

The elaborate rituals associated with prayers at places of worship are clearly meant to inspire the faithful into a sense of awe and wonder. These rituals are important in their own right and serve a very important function in satisfying our unconscious emotional needs. There are, however, some unintended consequences when one loses sight of their primary function.

When my children were growing up, we had a tradition of doing a back-to-school *havan* for them and their friends. A *havan* is a formal Hindu prayer ceremony where we all sit around a small sacred fire, recite prayers, and perform basic rituals prescribed in the Vedas. One of the most common questions the children asked was why we still follow these ancient rituals. Can we not pray to God in our own minds and not have to undertake an elaborate ceremony?

There is no doubt that, from a purely rational point of view, the children were right: We could have offered our prayers to our own mental conception of a God in the privacy of our rooms. God would not have noticed the difference, and from a purely functional point of view, this would have been the same as the community prayer we were performing. Why then do all religions perform prayers in groups and with associated rituals?

The children who asked it provided the answer to this question. When I asked them whether they would rather do it by themselves or as a group, every one of them said they much preferred the group, because it was so much more fun. One of them remarked that he looked forward to this event every year, because it provided him with a sense of community support and belonging; a recognition that he was not alone. He felt reassured and refocused on the academic challenge ahead after a fun but hectic summer. Other children felt that it provided them a sense of continuity and calmness that helped them to better focus on the school year ahead. Given that the prayers mention nothing about the school year and are in a language that none of the children (and hardly any of the adults) comprehended, it was remarkable that the central message of the prayer got through loud and clear. The message was conveyed not through the words of the prayers but through the acts performed by family and friends. The needs being satisfied were not primarily rational—but the deep emotional needs we spoke about in chapter 8.

Just about every important social event has its own special set of symbolic rituals. Weddings are another great example of the importance of ritual, as I often remind my children. There is nothing illegal, immoral, or unethical about getting married in a small private ceremony, and there are a good number of people who prefer to be wed this way. However, for a vast majority of us, in all cultures around the world, weddings are a time of social and religious togetherness. It is an opportunity for family and friends to enjoy the occasion together and share in the joy of the couple. The ceremony can be elaborate, and the vows are taken aloud for everyone to hear and be a part of the event.

The ritual and the spectacle serve no logical purpose, especially given the financial dent it can put in a young couple's finances. Why then do people opt for such elaborate rituals? I think the answer is obvious: It's fun. It satisfies in us the deep emotional need to share our lives—particularly, our happiest moments—with those we love. It would be foolish for anyone to suggest that in matters of everyday life and social interaction, it is sufficient to satisfy only our logical minds!

If you need any further evidence that ritual satisfies our emotional needs, look no further than prayer altars, church services, and the pomp and ceremony associated with political events, such as the swearing in of a new president. Why should the inauguration of an American president, or the coronation of the Queen of England, be held with such pomp and ceremony? There is no logic to justify such public displays of traditional ritual. An incoming president could simply sign a piece of paper. But the elaborate ceremony, not to mention the speeches, attendees, and the visual spectacle are essential to highlight the importance of the event. They communicate to the people who participated in the electoral process that it and the president are indeed real. Besides, it wouldn't be any fun without the glitz and the razzmatazz, would it?

Rituals performed with the expectation of satisfying a BGITS God are clearly unrealistic and unreasonable. There is no evidence that performing rituals in a certain manner with a certain set of prayers on a particular day will do anything to influence the outcome of an event. The expectation is inconsistent with our universal knowledge base and must, therefore, be rejected as the most logical motivation for ritual. Many rituals, sacrifices, and gifts made to a BGITS God fall into the category of superstition, witchcraft, and folklore, and are often wasteful and sometimes downright dangerous.

Rituals primarily serve to satisfy our emotional and uniquely human unconscious desires. They help us reinforce and act out our personal beliefs and in doing so enrich our lives. Redefining God in the manner proposed in this book helps us place rituals in this proper perspective.

What Is the Purpose of My Life?

The most basic of human questions centers on the purpose of our existence. Why are we here? For many people, answers to this question are strongly associated with their definition of God. Belief in a BGITS God may provide an answer that says something like, *We are here to serve God's purpose*, which is a restatement of the question and not an answer at all.

A scientist can, with a degree of certainty, answer the question of how we came to be here. Our evolution from single-celled organisms to amphibians through the development of mammals and our particular species is well documented in the fossil record. However, this doesn't tell us *why* we are in this world for the brief period of our lifetime.

This question is much more difficult to address since it involves speculation about the specific intent of either a supernatural creator or the forces of nature. Or perhaps there is no grand design for our existence. If we are here as a result of the forces and laws of nature, then it is logical to conclude that there is no divine intent for our existence. We are here because of the unique set of circumstances that have led to the creation of intelligent life-forms. The fact that God has no specific purpose for us does not lead to the conclusion that our existence has no purpose. As intelligent human beings, we can define the purpose of our lives ourselves, without resorting to belief in a supernatural creator. We bear the responsibility and also have the freedom to define this purpose for ourselves.

I encourage you to do a quick experiment. Ask the ten people that are closest to you what they think the purpose of their life is. After the initial shock wears off and they're finished rolling their eyes and feeling your pulse to make sure you're not seriously ill, they may give you a thoughtful answer. I don't know what the results of your survey will be, but when I conducted mine, I was pleasantly surprised to find out that just about every one of the people had a very different answer. Some misinterpreted the question and told me what their immediate goals were: paying off their mortgage or ensuring they have enough money for retirement or losing fifteen pounds. The more philosophically inclined gave broader responses: to be the best physician they could be, to ensure that the elderly are properly cared for, to find ways to better educate the children in their classes, to be the best writer they could be, and so on. They were deeply personal answers that reflected what had become the most important goals in their lives—what drove them to do what they did in their lives. These were the purposes (plural!) of their lives.

Note that the purposes of their lives were usually not associated with any divine plan. Not one of them mentioned any connection between their life's purpose and divine intent. This may be the result of the company I keep and you may get entirely different results. The one theme common to all of them was that they all, in their own way, wanted to make their community a better place. If you were to compel me to state the purpose of our lives in one sentence it would be, *Our purpose is make our world a better place*. That is the purpose of our existence.

What Are My Social Obligations?

Once we define why we are here, we may be able to say something about how we should act and what our role in society is. My social obligations are defined by the goals and purposes of my life. As I noted in the previous section, in the absence of divine intent, every individual must define his or her life's purpose. If the purpose of our lives is to make this world a better place, then our social obligations are obvious: to serve humanity in the best way we know how.

The task of satisfying and pleasing a BGITS God is no longer at the top of the list. The rituals, prayers, and sacrifices are no longer intended to placate the gods. Instead, they are replaced with actions directed at people and society: helping the poor and less fortunate; educating people in new skill sets that I may be adept at and that may be helpful to them; supporting and building institutions that will allow financial, medical, and emotional support to reach all those in need. To accomplish these obligations, we must maintain good mental, emotional, and physical health so that we can help others. These social obligations spring directly from our rejection of the irrational notion that the gods must be appeased; a concept that is central to our redefinition of God.

The Question of Free Will

One question that has bothered philosophers for many centuries—particularly since the scientific revolution—is the following: If every aspect of human activity is determined by the physical laws that govern the world around us, what role does our free will play? Are we simply robots, powerless to choose and therefore change the course of our destiny?

During the Renaissance, philosophers resolved this problem by separating the physical universe from the realm of the human mind and thought. They said the laws of nature determined the physical world, whereas our free will was a product of our mind, not controlled by the same laws that determined the inanimate objects of the physical universe. This useful duality helped preserve the belief in our ability to make independent decisions about uniquely human concepts of morality and religiosity. The concept of free will, therefore, allowed us to break free from the constraints of physical laws that seemed to prescribe the behavior of all human beings. Our minds are capable of empathy, anger, love, imagination, and so much more that seems to lie beyond the purview of physical laws.

This line of thinking was brought into question with developments in psychology and neurology. As our understanding of the human brain improved, scientists realized that many aspects of our thinking—the emotions and desires created by our minds—could be explained based on the biochemical interactions in our brain. For example, sensations of pain or pleasure could be induced or suppressed simply by electrically or chemically stimulating different portions of the brain. It is now well established that our emotions can be mapped to neural activity in specific regions of our brain. By targeting these regions with specific chemicals, powerful new drugs can suppress emotional responses such as anxiety and paranoia. Although we are still a long way from understanding the complete workings of our brain, there is very little doubt among neuroscientists that over the course of the next few decades, we will have an even greater ability to regulate and control different aspects of our behavior and emotions.

Incredibly complex and intricate as we are, humans are, in our essence, built from the same elements as the universe and governed by the same laws of physics and chemistry. These laws have allowed us to conquer once-mysterious diseases that ravaged humanity and destroyed civilizations. We now understand that the causes and cures for these ailments lie not in the wrath of a supernatural being but in the bacteria and viruses that we have discovered through the scientific method.

It is no different for the human brain. The laws of nature determine human behavior. Free will is a product of the laws of nature and it is very much bound by the laws of nature, although we cannot yet describe and map this complex process in detail. Instead, we use *effective* theories to do this, which are attempts to explain a phenomenon without claiming to know all the causes. We commonly use effective theories in psychology and economics to explain phenomena that are much too complex to be modeled in detail. Free will is a natural part of our makeup; we simply don't fully understand its mechanics yet. Once we do, it will be added to our knowledge base.

Summary

Redefining God by combining the concept of a transcendent God with one or more personal gods is the only way to satisfy both our rational minds and our deepest emotional desires. This definition of god is not new.

In fact, it goes back to our most ancient religious traditions; we have come full circle and returned to our philosophical roots. It provides a way to reconcile differing religious beliefs and to ensure peace and religious tolerance. The consequences are far reaching in both religious and social terms.

The scientific method provides a way to define this transcendent god and unveil the nature of this ultimate reality. The laws that govern nature constitute a universal and dynamically evolving knowledge base—testable and verifiable by anyone. Its contents are not a matter of personal opinion or belief. This knowledge base reveals the order in the universe and forms a universal set of principles that binds us all together. This is the Rtá of the ancient Aryans, the Egyptian Maat, the Chinese Tao, Plato's forms, Spinoza's substance, and Einstein's god.

This concept of God is, however, emotionally remote and does not satisfy many of our basic emotional desires. The Aryans fully recognized that this remote God would do little to excite the imagination of the masses. More concrete and immediately accessible gods were introduced to ensure that the emotional needs of the people were met. Many hundreds of these gods and goddesses have survived the test of time and are worshipped today.

We therefore redefine God in terms of both a transcendent supreme being and much more personal gods. Such personal gods are not BGITS gods. They do not intervene in human affairs, don't need to be appeased with rituals and sacrifices, and do not perform miracles. In fact, they conform in every way to the universal laws of nature, to the Rtà.

This redefinition of God eliminates belief in the supernatural, in ghosts and fairies, miracles, soothsayers, and witches. It also provides a basis for religious tolerance and acceptance of other people's beliefs. By recognizing the clear separation between a universal knowledge base that we all accept and a set of personal religious beliefs that are not universal, we accept the fact that differences in religious beliefs can and should exist. These differences are subjective and personal and are no reason for conflict.

The concept of a secular democracy follows logically from this redefinition of God. The freedom to choose a personal god is inherently democratic. Acceptance of the diversity of faith and distinguishing such beliefs from the universality of our human knowledge base is the cornerstone of our new definition of God, and the universal knowledge base forms the fundamental rational basis upon which a secular sociopolitical system can be built.

As the Founding Fathers of the American Republic so wisely wrote into the constitution of the United States, the church and the state must remain separate. One ensures the freedom and safety of people of all faiths, and the other caters to the emotional needs of segments of society. By establishing this clear distinction, we clearly define the role of religion and keep it away from the social and political arena. This, as we have learned through difficult lessons of history, is the best and perhaps the only way to tame one of the most destructive forces in our history, religious bigotry and intolerance.

Redefining God in this manner also has an important consequence with regard to how people with widely different personalities and intellectual strengths relate to God, since it offers great deal of flexibility. The ancient Aryans clearly saw the need for people to realize God in their own way. For the philosophically inclined, the path of knowledge or jnana yoga is the appropriate path; for the deeply devoted and religious, the path of devotion and utter surrender to a personal God, or bhakti yoga is the recommended path, and for a person perfectly happy to live life to the fullest, karma yoga is best. Each one of these paths to or relationships with God can be equally effective; one is not better or worse than the other. People must discover for themselves the path that works best for them at a given point in their lives.

Ethics do not spring from religious doctrine or dogma. Our ability to recognize what is ethical stems entirely from a universal knowledge base common to all humans. In fact, that is precisely why all religions make virtually the same moral demands of their adherents. Although the words may differ, the sentiments expressed in the Ten Commandments are found in all religious traditions. Our redefinition of God does nothing at all to change our basic ethical framework.

In redefining God in the manner described in this book, we are coming full circle to a place of higher understanding. Following in the path of our ancient ancestors, respecting existing cultures and traditions, and armed with modern scientific methods, we have a unique opportunity to redefine God and thereby reduce religious conflict, eliminate superstition, and focus our efforts on making this world a better place for all of humanity.

Notes

Preface
1. Amy Sullivan, "The Rise of the Nones," *Time*, March 12, 2012, http://content.time.com/time/magazine/article/0,9171,2108027,00.html.

Chapter 1
1. Diana Blanton, "More Believe in God than Heaven," *Fox News*, http://www.foxnews.com/story/2004/06/18/more-believe-in-god-than-heaven.html.
2. Gregory Paul and Phil Zuckerman, "Why Do Americans Still Dislike Atheists?" *Washington Post*, April 29, 2011.
3. Tamara Audi, "Americans Unaffiliated With Any Religion Outrank Catholics, Study Says," *Wall Street Journal*, May 12, 2015, http://www.wsj.com/articles/americans-unaffiliated-with-any-religion-outrank-catholics-study-says-1431403261.
4. Bertrand Russell, *Autobiography of Bertrand Russell* (New York: Routledge, 2000), 36.
5. Alonso Ricardo and Jack W. Szostak, "The Origin of Life on Earth," *Scientific American*, 301, September 1, 2009, 54–61.
6. Rebecca Morelle, "Creating life in the laboratory," *BBC News*, October 19, 2007, http://news.bbc.co.uk/2/hi/science/nature/7041353.stm.

Chapter 2

1. Wendy Doniger (trans.), *The Rig Veda* (London: Penguin Classics, 1981), verse 10.129.
2. Adapted from Gurudev, "List of English Words derived from Sanskrit via Latin Greek Persian," *HitXP* (2014), http://www.hitxp.com/articles/culture/sanskrit-greek-english-latin-roman-words-derived-pie-proto-indo-european-language.
3. Maurice Bloomfield, *The Religion of the Veda: The Ancient Religion of India* (New York: Putnam, 1908), 109.
4. Friedrich Max Müller (1859). *A History of Ancient Sanskrit Literature So Far as it Illustrates the Primitive Religion of the Brahmans* (Williams and Norgate, 1890).
5. Bloomfield, *The Religion of the Veda*.
6. David W. Anthony, *The Horse, the Wheel, and Language: How Bronze-Age Riders from the Eurasian Steppes Shaped the Modern World* (Princeton, NJ: Princeton University Press, 2007), 49.
7. Bloomfield, *The Religion of the Veda*.
8. Bal Gangadhar Tilak, *The Arctic Home of the Vedas* (Poona, India: Tilak Bros., 1903).
9. Bloomfield, *The Religion of the Veda*, 79.
10. Ibid., 177.
11. Tilak, *The Arctic Home of the Vedas*.
12. Doniger, *The Rig Veda*, verse 1.92.6.
13. Bloomfield, *The Religion of the Veda*, 126–127.
14. sreenivasraos blog, "Varuna and his Decline: Part Two," 2012, https://screenvisarao.com/2012/1064/varvna-and-his-decline-part-two.
15. *Rig Veda* verse 7.86, www.ancientvedas.com/Chapter/7/book86/
16. Friedrich Wilhelm Nietzsche and Walter Arnold Kaufmann (trans.), *Thus Spoke Zarathustra: A Book for All and None* (New York: Modern Library, 1995).
17. Karen Armstrong, *The Great Transformation: The Beginning of our Religious Traditions* (New York: First Anchor Books, 2007), 8–12.
18. Piloo Nanavutty (trans. and commentary), *The Gathas of Zarathustra: Hymns in Praise of Wisdom* (Ahmedabad: Mapin, 1999).

19. Anthony, *The Horse, the Wheel, and Language*, 49–50.
20. sreenivasrao blog, "Varuna and his Decline: Part Two," 2012.
21. Bloomfield, *The Religion of the Veda*, 228.
22. A. Parathasarthy, *Bhagavad Gita* (Triplicane, India: Parthasarthy, 2008), verse 22.22.
23. Swami Chinmayananda, *The Holy Geeta* (Mumbai: Central Chinmaya Mission Trust, 1996).
24. Swami Nikhilananda, *The Upanishads: A New Translation* (New York: Harper and Brothers, 1949).
25. Rohit Mehta, *The Call of the Upanishads* (Delhi: Motilal Banarsidas, 1970).
26. Patrick Olivelle, *Upanishads, A New Translation*, Oxford's World Classics (Oxford University Press, 1996).
27. Bloomfield, *The Religion of the Veda*, 281.

Chapter 3

1. Karen Armstrong, *The Great Transformation: The Beginning of Our Religious Traditions* (New York: First Anchor Books, 2007), 30.
2. Ibid., 90.
3. Wayne W. Dyer, *Living the Wisdom of the Tao: The Complete Tao Te Ching and Affirmations* (Carlsbad, CA: Hay House, 2008), verse 1.
4. Ibid., verse 32.
5. Ibid., verse 37.
6. Ibid., verse 43.
7. Armstrong, *The Great Transformation*, 223.

Chapter 4

1. King James Bible, Judges 2:17.
2. Armstrong, *The Great Transformation*, 54.
3. Joe Brusherd a.k.a. Yosef, *Hebraic Insights: Messages Exploring the Hebrew Roots of Christian Faith* (Bloomington, IN: iUniverse, 2011).
4. Martin Sicker, *Pondering the Imponderable: Jewish Reflections on God, Revelation, and the Afterlife*, (Bloomington, IN: iUniverse, 2010), 79.

5. J. Slater, "Jesus's Direct Experiences of God the Father: A Paradox Within Jewish Theology and Gateway to Human Experience of God," *Koers: Bulletin for Christian Scholarship* 76 (2011): 479–504.
6. Ibid.
7. Sicker, *Pondering the Imponderable*.
8. Miroslav Volf, *Do We Worship the Same God? Jews, Christians, and Muslims in Dialogue*, (Grand Rapids, MI: Eerdmans, 2012), 62.
9. Mat. 2:2–12 (New International Version).
10. Luke 6:20–26 (NIV).
11. Mat. 6:10 (NIV).
12. 1 Cor. 15:50–58 (NIV).
13. Rom. 10:9 (NIV).
14. Louis Pojman and Michael Rea, *Philosophy of Religion: An Anthology*, (New York: Wadsworth, 2011), 227–230.
15. John M. Robertson, *A Short History of Christianity*, 2nd ed., (London: Watts, 1913).
16. Wikipedia, https://en.wikipedia.org/wiki/Shia_view_of_Ali
17. Reza Aslan, *No God but God: The Origins, Evolution, and Future of Islam*, (New York: Random House, 2012).
18. Zulfiqar Ali Shah, *Anthropomorphic Depictions of God: The Concept of God in Judaic, Christian, and Islamic Traditions*, (Richmond, VA: International Institute of Islamic Thought, 2012), 487.
19. Ibid. 401.
20. Ibid. xxi.
21. J. Slater, "Jesus's Direct Experiences of God the Father."

Chapter 5

1. Will Durant, *The Story of Philosophy*, (New York: Simon and Schuster, 1967), 104.
2. Ibid., 132–134.
3. Francis Bacon, *Novum Organon*, 1620. Quoted by Carl Sagan in *The Demon Haunted World, Science as a Candle in the Dark* (New York: Ballantine Books, 1996), 202.

4. Francis Bacon, *Francis Bacon: The Complete Works* (New York: Centaur Classics, 2015), 82.
5. Galileo Galilei, Letter to the Grand Duchess Christina of Tuscany, 1615, Text from the Internet Modern History Sourcebook.
6. Ibid.
7. Ibid.
8. Ibid.
9. Ibid.
10. Will Durant, *The Story of Philosophy* (New York: Simon and Schuster, 1967), 209.
11. Ibid., 203.
12. Steven Nadler, "Baruch Spinoza," *The Stanford Encyclopedia of Philosophy*, Edward N. Zalta, Editor (Palo Alto: The Metaphysics Research Lab, Stanford University, 2008).
13. Ibid.
14. Albert Einstein, *The Expanded Quotable Einstein*, ed. Alice Calaprice (Princeton, NJ: Princeton University Press, 2000).
15. Thomas Jefferson in a letter to John Trumbull, February 15, 1789, http://www.loc.gov/exhibits/jefferson/18.html.
16. John Locke, *A Letter Concerning Toleration*, (New York: Routledge, 1991).
17. Voltaire, quoted in Will Durant, *The Story of Philosophy*, 209.
18. Ignatius Viyagappa, *G.W.F. Hegel's Concept of Indian Philosophy*, (Rome: Gregorian University Press, 1980).

Chapter 6

1. Peter R. Henriques, *Realistic Visionary: A Portrait of George Washington* (Charlottesville: University of Virginia Press, 2006).
2. Frank E. Grizzard Jr., *The Ways of Providence: Religion and George Washington*, (New York: Mariner Publishing, 2005), 5.
3. Walter Isaacson, *Benjamin Franklin: An American Life*, (New York: Simon and Schuster, 2004), 492.

4. Edmund Clarence Stedman, Ellen Mackay (Hutchinson) Cortissoz, *A Library of American Literature: An Anthology in Eleven Volumes*, vol. 3: *Literature of the revolutionary period, 1765–1787* (New York: Webster, 1891), 284.
5. Charles Darwin, Letter 8837 to N. D. Doedes, 2 April 1873, Cambridge: Darwin Correspondence Project, 2016. https://www.darwinproject.ac.uk/letter/DCP-LETT-8837.xml.
6. Charles Darwin, Letter 12041 to John Fordyce, 7 May 1879, Cambridge: Darwin Correspondence Project, 2016. https://www.darwinproject.ac.uk/letter/?docId=letters/DCP-LETT-12041.xml.
7. Emma Wedgewood, Letter 441 from Emma Wedgewood, 2 November 1838, Cambridge: Darwin Correspondence Project, https://www.darwinproject.ac.uk/letter/?docId=letters/DCP-LETT-441.xml.
8. Charles Darwin, *The Autobiography of Charles Darwin* (New York: Barnes & Noble, 2005/1887), 67, 69–70.
9. Albert Paine, ed., *Mark Twain's Notebook* (New York: Read Books, 2006).
10. Mark Twain, *No. 44, the Mysterious Stranger* (Berkeley: University of California Press, 1982), 186–187.
11. Paine, *Mark Twain's Notebook*.
12. Mark Twain, *The Bible According to Mark Twain: Writings on Heaven, Eden, and the Flood*, ed. Howard Baetzhold and Joseph B. McCullough (Athens, GA: University of Georgia Press, 1995), 319.
13. Albert Einstein, Telegram to Rabbi Herbert S. Goldstein, April 24, 1929.
14. Helen Dukas and Banesh Hoffman, eds., *Albert Einstein: The Human Side* (Princeton: Princeton University Press, 2013), 66.
15. Albert Einstein, "Religion and Science," *New York Times Magazine*, November 9, 1930, http://www/sacred-texts.com/aor/einstein/einsci.htm=TIMES.
16. Walter Isaacson, *Einstein: His Life and Universe* (New York: Simon and Schuster, 2007).

17. Steven Hawking, *Curiosity*, season 1, episode 1: "Did God Create the Universe?" (Discovery Channel, 2011).
18. Steven Hawking quoted in "Archimedes to Hawking" by Clifford A. Pickover, *Der Spiegel*, October 17, 1988.
19. Steven Weinberg, *Dreams of a Final Theory* (New York: Pantheon, 1993).
20. Steven Weinberg, *A Designer Universe?* Reply to a talk given in April 1999 at the Conference on Cosmic Design of the American Association for the Advancement of Science, Washington, DC.

Chapter 7

1. Maurice Bloomfield, in *The Religion of the Veda: The Ancient Religion of India* (New York: Putnam, 1908), 30.
2. Bertrand Russell, *History of Western Philosophy* (New York: Simon and Schuster, 1945), 463.
3. Thomas Aquinas, *Summa Theologiæ*, article III, objection 3.
4. Albert Einstein, Telegram to Rabbi Herbert S. Goldstein, April 24, 1929.
5. Will Durant, *The Story of Philosophy* (New York: Simon and Schuster, 1967), 221–222.
6. Maurice Bloomfield, *The Religion of the Veda: The Ancient Religion of India* (New York: Putnam, 1908), 126–127.
7. Durant, *The Story of Philosophy*, 222–223.
8. Srinivasa Rao, "Rta in nature," accessed at http://creative.sulekha.com/varuna-and-his-decline-part-two-2-of-7_480736_blog.
9. Baruch Spinoza, "Ethics," in Steven Nadler, "Baruch Spinoza," *The Stanford Encyclopedia of Philosophy*, Fall 2016 ed., Edward N. Zalta (ed.), http://plato.stanford.edu/archives/fall2016/entries/spinoza.
10. Kena Upanishad, from Rohit Mehta, *The Call of the Upanishads*, (Delhi: Motilal Banarsidass, 1990), 33.
11. Durant, *The Story of Philosophy*, 39–40.
12. Rohit Mehta, *The Call of the Upanishads*, 141.
13. Mundaka Upanishad, from Ibid., 118.

14. Ibid., 134.
15. Albert Einstein, *Einstein on Cosmic Religion and Other Opinions and Aphorisms* (New York: Dover), 2009.
16. Albert Einstein, *The World As I See It* (1949; repr., New York: Citadel, 2006).
17. Lao Tzu, *Tao Te Ching*, trans. Stephen Mitchell (London: Frances Lincoln, 2009).
18. Ibid.

Chapter 8

1. Mark Stevens, *God Is a Salesman: Learn from the Master* (New York: Hachette, 2008), 14–15.
2. Leonard Mlodinow, *Subliminal: How Your Unconscious Mind Rules Your Behavior* (New York: Vintage, 2013), 22.
3. Ibid. 23.
4. Ibid. 35.
5. Michael Shermer, *The Believing Brain: From Ghosts and Gods to Politics and Conspiracies: How We Construct Beliefs and Reinforce Them as Truths*, (New York: St. Martin's Griffin, 2012), 87.
6. Ibid. 87.
7. Ibid. 165.
8. B. M. D'Onofrio, L. J. Eaves, L. Murrelle, H. H. Maes, and B. Spilka, "Understanding Biological and Social Influences on Religious Affiliation, Attitudes, and Behaviors: A Behavior Genetic Perspective," *Journal of Personality* 67 (1999):953–984.
9. Niels G. Waller, Brian A. Kojetin, Thomas J. Bouchard Jr., David T. Lykken, and Auke Tellegen, "Genetic and Environmental Influences on Religious Interests, Attitudes, and Values: A Study of Twins Reared Apart and Together," *Psychological Science* 1 (1999): 138–142.
10. Bernard Spilka, Ralph W. Hood Jr., and Richard Gorsuch, *The Psychology of Religion: An Empirical Approach* (Englewood Cliffs, NJ: Prentice-Hall, 1985).
11. Steven Reiss, *Who Am I? The 16 Basic Desires That Motivate Our Actions and Define Our Personalities* (New York: Berkley Books, 2000).

12. Adapted from Steven Reiss, *Who Am I?*
13. C. Sue Carter, "Neuroendocrine Perspectives on Social Attachment and Love," *Psychoneuroendocrinology*, 23 (1998): 779–818.
14. C. Loring Brace and Ashley Montagu, *Man's Evolution: An Introduction to Physical Anthropology* (New York: Macmillan, 1965).
15. Spilka et al., *The Psychology of Religion*.
16. Bertrand Russell, *Why I Am Not a Christian: And Other Essays on Religion and Related Subjects*, (New York: Touchstone, 1967), 22–23.
17. Reiss, *Who Am I?* 223–245.

Chapter 9

1. Albert Einstein, "Science and Religion," from Science, Philosophy and Religion, A Symposium: The Conference on Science, Philosophy and Religion in Their Relation to the Democratic Way of Life, Inc., New York, 1941.
2. Sarvepalli Radhakrishnan, *The Principal Upanishads*, (New York: HarperCollins, 1953), 35–36.
3. Ibid. 37.
4. Gregory Paul and Phil Zuckerman, "Why Do Americans Still Dislike Atheists?" *Washington Post*, April 29, 2011.
5. Amy Sullivan, "The Rise of the Nones," *Time*, March 12, 2012, http://content.time.com/time/magazine/article/0,9171,2108027,00.html.

Chapter 10

1. Mark Twain, "The Lowest Animal" (1896).
2. Carl Sagan, *The Demon Haunted World: Science as a Candle in the Dark* (New York: Ballantine Books, 1996), 120.
3. Mark Twain, "Bible Teaching and Religious Practice," ed. Charles Neider, *The Complete Essays of Mark Twain* (1923; Boston: Da Capo Press, 1991).
4. Robyn Dixon, "In Ghana's Witch Camps, the Accused Are Never Safe," *Los Angeles Times*, September 16, 2012.

5. Richard Dawkins, *A Devil's Chaplain* (Boston: Houghton Mifflin, 2003).
6. Richard Dawkins, *The God Delusion* (New York: Bantam Books, 2006), 190–239.
7. Louise M. Antony, "Good minus God," *New York Times,* December 18, 2011.
8. Sam Harris, *The End of Faith: Religion, Terror, and the Future of Reason* (New York: Norton, 2005).
9. *Frontline*, "ISIS in Afghanistan," November 17, 2015, http://www.pbs.org/wgbh/frontline/film/isis-in-afghanistan/.